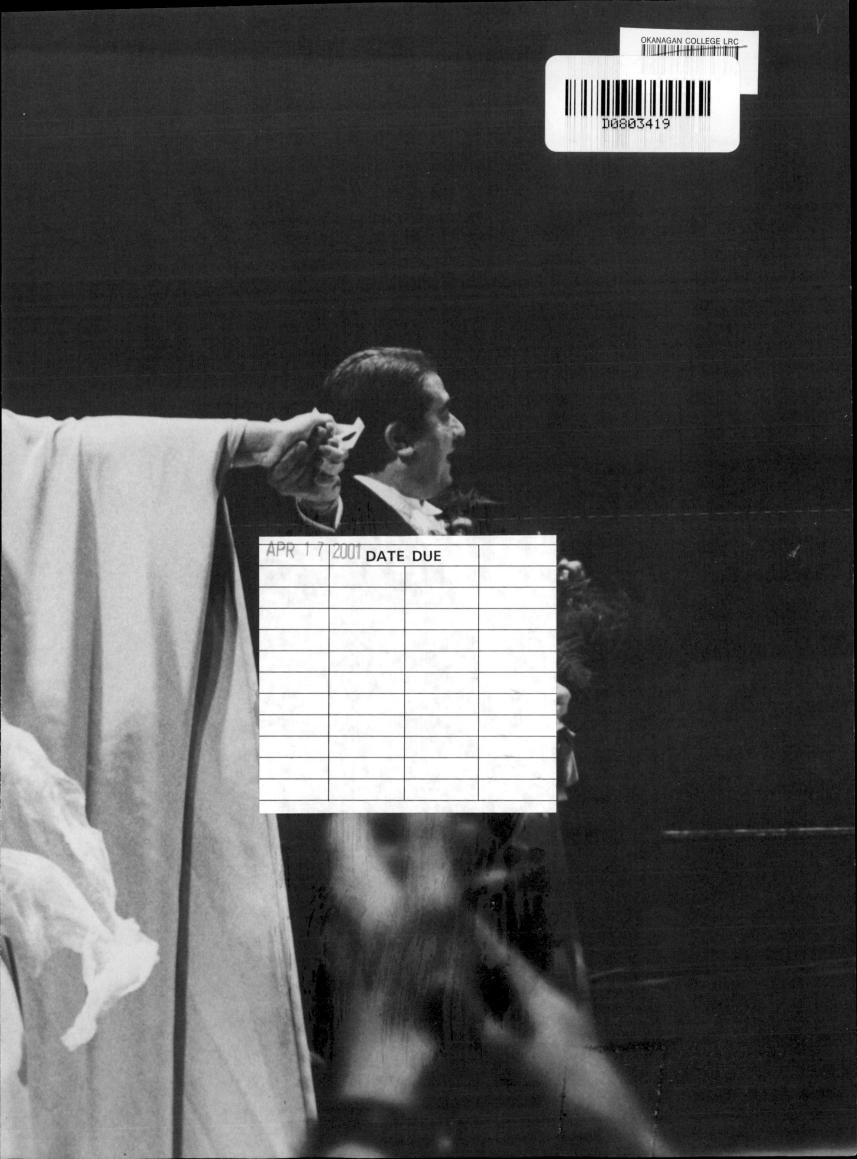

CALLAS

CALLAS

THE ART AND THE LIFE

BY JOHN ARDOIN

THE GREAT YEARS

BY GERALD FITZGERALD

DESIGNED BY
HOWARD SPERBER

HOLT, RINEHART AND WINSTON
NEW YORK / CHICAGO / SAN FRANCISCO

Published simultaneously in Canada by Holt, Rinehart
and Winston of Canada, Limited.

ISBN: 0-03-011486-1
Library of Congress Catalog Card Number: 74-4410
First Edition

Printed in the United States of America

Grateful acknowledgment is made to
Claudia Cassidy and the Chicago Tribune
for permission to reprint from a review.

Page 282 constitutes a continuation of this copyright page.

ACKNOWLEDGMENTS

For fifteen years, as long as I have been a professional writer, I have known I must deal fully with Maria Callas. It was only a question of time and of a viewpoint toward this multifaceted artist. Callas has exerted a primary influence on my musical thinking, and it has become a passion to understand, to attempt to measure the breadth and depth of this influence not merely on myself but on music. Three years ago I thought I knew what must be said and how. Yet, the final form of this book comes as a surprise to me (though a pleasant one), for it was not what I had planned. My initial idea was to trace Callas through the legacy in sound which she has given us today and which remains for those who come under her influence tomorrow. This study occupied me for two years. But as I listened to each note and wrote a mass of detail, a larger view developed. In effect, I was writing two books—a careful dissection of the musician and, on a broader scale, a portrait of a creative figure who had made an enormous impact on her age. Myopically, I could not discern what had happened; I was too immersed in Callas the musician. It was my editor, Marian Wood, who saw clearly what had taken place and made me see it many words later. She wisely urged me to separate the two books, and the first is this essay which attempts to capture in large terms the artist and the woman, hopefully offering an explanation and understanding of both. The second book, Callas's work and development as a musician as reflected in her recorded legacy, will follow. Neither can say everything there is to be said. There are as many books possible about Callas as there are viewpoints. The fact that a study of Callas has such open horizons, where the possibilities with other singers would be considerably more confining, is an indication of the scope of her art.

Many have helped me during the making of this book—lending materials, reading proof, questioning conclusions—but I must single out the heavy debt owed Lawrence Kelly, general manager of the Dallas Civic Opera. His encouragement and his special understanding of Callas through a long artistic and personal association helped me with many a difficult section.

Also, Catherine Fallin was an indispensable liaison, coordinating the maze of proofs and corrections, working countless extra hours, keeping calm under intense pressure. Karen Gillis kept an expert eye on the production standards and a firm hand on the schedule. Natalie Chapman was unfailingly helpful and considerate. And finally, Howard Sperber's infinite patience, attention to detail, and great skill as a designer contributed inestimably to the book.

Much more than gratitude is due the two people most closely connected with this project from the beginning. My agent, Helen Merrill, was the first to urge me to begin this book. It was a pipe dream until she insisted on its becoming a reality. Her enthusiasm and support went beyond what an author has a right to expect of an agent, much less a friend. Finally, without Gerald Fitzgerald's collaboration, this book would lack the strong dimension now present thanks to his knowledge of Callas's art and career and his graphic sensibilities. I am particularly grateful to him because he followed the progress of the manuscript closely, making many welcome and pertinent suggestions, and because he made available to me the wealth of interview material he gathered to accompany the picture section. Particularly valuable were tapes with Franco Zeffirelli and Sandro Sequi.   JOHN ARDOIN, DALLAS

Trying to recapture the career of Maria Callas on the printed page has been a frustrating experience. No matter how vivid the incidents, how dramatic the photographs, they can only intimate what Callas was like onstage. One is inevitably left with a partial view. What I present here, then, is but a vestige of how she was. What made her that way, we'll never really know.

I saw Callas many times in many roles, beginning with the night of her U.S. debut as Norma in 1954. Despite long personal experience, for my text I depended largely on the words of colleagues who went through rehearsals and performances with Callas during the high tide of her career. They, I felt, were better qualified to discuss her work than any outside observer. Since most of these artists were interviewed in Europe, my journeys there permitted discovery of many photographs never before published. The courtesy encountered during my quest for memories and pictures was a reflection of the genuine respect Callas engendered in her associates. Opera being a field rife with selfishness and petty ego, this in itself proved a revelation.

On three separate occasions, and with a generosity that beggars description, Franco Zeffirelli gave of his knowledge, insight, and encouragement. A beautiful man. In addition to Zeffirelli, I extend deep gratitude to stage directors Luchino Visconti, Margherita Wallmann, and Sandro Sequi; set and costume designers Nicola Benois and Piero Tosi; conductors Gianandrea Gavazzeni, Carlo Maria Giulini, Thomas Schippers, and Antonino Votto; impresarios Carol Fox, Antonio Ghiringhelli, and Francesco Siciliani; singers Luigi Alva, Franco Corelli, Elvira de Hidalgo, Tito Gobbi, Nicola Rossi-Lemeni, Giulietta Simionato, and Richard Tucker. Special thanks are due stage director Alberto Fassini, who arranged my reunion with Visconti. Through the intercession of Erika Davidson, comments about Callas were obtained from Jon Vickers.

Unstinting cooperation from Erio Piccagliani, official photographer of La Scala, Milan, in large part makes possible the picture documentation of Callas's repertory. He saw theatrical history unfolding before his lens and captured it. I am indebted to him and to his right hand, Nino Costa, surely Callas's most devoted admirer in Europe. In the United States, this title is held by a beloved friend of many years, Frances Moore, who lent rare photos from her extensive private collection. Others who helped: Mr. and Mrs. Dario Soria, John Coveney of Angel Records, Countess Wally Toscanini Castelbarco, Vittoria Serafin, Giovanna Lomazzi, Lorenzo Siliotto, Georgette Rostand of the Paris Opéra, Kensington Davison of the Friends of Covent Garden, Harold Rosenthal of *Opera*, and Frank Merkling of *Opera News*.

No designer could have contributed more time, talent, energy, and conscience to a book than Howard Sperber has to this one. He toiled with me over a ten-month stretch to reach the final format of each page. In addition, with Helen Merrill, he spent countless other hours retouching damaged photos to pristine condition. Nor for my editor, Marian Wood, am I at a loss for words, though they are perforce brief: she has an increasingly rare commodity—unremitting integrity.

A final thought about Maria Callas. What she herself did through music inspired, sustained, and, in the end, made this book a reality. How are thanks expressed to a Callas? Here is one heartfelt attempt.   GERALD FITZGERALD, NEW YORK

THE ART
AND THE LIFE
BY JOHN ARDOIN

"Happy are the fiery natures which burn themselves out, and glory in the sword which wears away the scabbard."

CAMILLE SAINT-SAËNS
Writing of Pauline Viardot

THE ART

I first heard the voice of Maria Callas on records. It was a disturbing and alien experience. The recording was *Lucia di Lammermoor*, the year was 1953. Her singing was dark and moody in music which to me had always been bright and dazzling. I gave the set away after a single hearing. Yet, in the months that followed, the sound of her voice reverberated in my mind's ear; I could not escape its pull. Finally, I bought the recording a second time and began to listen beyond the sound to what was happening musically through it.

It was much later that I met Callas. Midway in our conversation she asked with her Sagittarian directness: "Did you like my voice when you first heard it?" A penetrating sixth sense knew without knowing my initial dilemma. Returning the force of her glance, I answered, "No." "I thought not," she said matter-of-factly. "Generally, I upset people the first time they hear me, but I am usually able to convince them of what I am doing."

"Upset" seems a mild word to describe the effect Callas has had upon listeners. It is more accurate to say she has perplexed and infuriated as many as she has excited and inspired. One thing is certain—no one is indifferent to her. Her innate ability to generate vivid emotions is one of the major forces behind her career, but it has also clouded the real issue: What use did she make of her artistic resources?

Complicating matters, Callas, like all mythic personalities, has reflected a variety of images to the public. To the world, she is the essential prima donna, capricious and embroiled in scandal and feuds. Here is a singer who "walked out" on the President of Italy on opening night of the Rome Opera in 1958; who, later the same year, was fired by Rudolf Bing from the Metropolitan Opera; a stout soprano who lost more than seventy-five pounds to become trim and elegant; and the much publicized companion of one of the world's wealthiest men. All of this, blown out of proportion into a maze of truths, half-truths, and fiction, sold newspapers and magazines but obscured the real woman and artist.

Of course, distortions are often the residue of enormous fame, but in the case of Callas, these distortions made many falsely assume her career was primarily a product of extramusical matter, more smoke than fire. Yet, the Callas myths were born long after solid successes in major opera houses—only following her dramatic loss of weight did the tabloids take notice. While they were introducing the general public to a sensational Callas, the broad world of the arts was being aroused by a singer as never before in the twentieth century. Indeed, to find another point in time when singers exerted the same fascination and appeal throughout the artistic community, one would have to go back to the nineteenth century and such legendary figures as Maria Malibran, Giuditta Pasta, and Pauline Viardot. For the last century was an era not only of great singing but of great appreciation of singing as a forum for expression. The letters of Chopin, Liszt, and Berlioz prove this as richly as do the writings of Stendhal, Alfred de Musset, Gautier, Heine, and Turgenev. With a gradual decline in the art of singing, this broad interest began to wane. Callas alone in our time has had sufficient dimension to make the influence of a singer again felt beyond the boundaries of the music world.

"The extraordinary success of Maria Callas appears, at first glance, one of the strangest phenomenons in the world of performance of our time," observed conductor-writer René Leibowitz in a full-dress article on Callas which appeared in Jean-Paul Sartre's respected journal *Les temps modernes*. "Unique among sopranos, the reputation of this prodigious singer has crossed the limits normally set for even the most prestigious and great operatic artists. Other singers, of course, have succeeded in provoking enthusiastic reactions and even in unleashing passion, but this has always been within the relatively limited confines of opera lovers. The case of Callas is completely different. Her name today is familiar even to those who have no real contact with opera nor with the art of singing in general."

Within the world of music, Callas's most vehement opponents have admitted her enormous influence on repertory and styles of performance. Two decades ago in America, the bel canto repertory was limited primarily to *Lucia di Lammermoor* and *Il barbiere di Siviglia*. *L'elisir d'amore* was a novelty, *Norma* a rarity. Callas's impact on the repertory had not yet made itself felt in American opera houses, and her nineteenth-century vocal manner, which was to influence many singers who followed her, was still unknown. At the time of Callas's American debut in Chicago in 1954, Joan Sutherland's Lucia was five years in the future, the names of Renata Scotto and Leyla Gencer meant little even in Italy, Beverly Sills was Micaëla not Maria Stuarda, and Montserrat Caballé was a conservatory student, Elena Souliotis a schoolgirl. Today, for these spiritual children and grandchildren of Callas, opera houses have revived dozens of forgotten bel canto works, so that it now seems a natural course of events for Dallas, Santa Fe, and New York to mount individual new productions of Donizetti's *Anna Bolena*. "She opened a door for us," Caballé has said, "for all the singers in the world, a door that had been closed. Behind it was sleeping not only great music but great ideas of interpretation. She has given us the chance, those who follow her, to do things that were hardly possible before her. That I am compared with Callas is something I never dared to dream. It is not right. I am much smaller than Callas."

Even those unable to grasp the individuality of Callas's art have conceded her importance on a more superficial level, recognizing the luster she restored to the term "prima donna," a title she bears as though by birthright. Surely, she must appreciate the stony retort of nineteenth-century soprano Adelina Patti. Criticized for making more money in one month than the President of the United States in one year, Patti asked: "Then, why doesn't he sing?"

Yet, to think of Callas only as a prima donna is to miss her ultimate importance. Gibraltar is not just a rock. In an era of faceless music making and prepackaged art, Callas has stood apart with a clear-cut vision of herself, her responsibilities to music, and her worth. She was a revolutionary who turned the traditional operatic scene inside out, resetting its course; she was history repeating itself, a throwback whose singing has been characterized as "a song from another century." But her "song" was one not easily understood or appreciated, for it was sung with a type of voice that had long been extinct— the *soprano sfogato*.

To understand the particulars of this sound and the consternation caused by its rebirth in our time, it is necessary to reach back first to the eighteenth century when castrati, with few exceptions, reigned supreme in Italian opera and the finished performance of complex vocal patterns was considered the summit of vocal art. Castrati were purveyors of the *stile fiorito*, a flowered style which favored heavily embellished melodies. The composer was a carpenter who constructed the platforms on which castrati performed their vocal tricks. Eventually, *stile fiorito* became more popularly known as *bel canto,* or "beautiful singing," and a singer in this period was thought to be deficient as an artist unless possessed of a full command of roulades, trills, arpeggios, appoggiature, and other ornaments.

Gradually, the influence of castrati declined even as their number did—the castration of young boys, to preserve their girlish timbres, was proscribed by the Church. By the nineteenth century, the female soprano voice had begun to exert a primal pull. This was partly based on trapeze aspects—high notes and virtuosic floridity—held over from castrati. But its appeal was also due to a demand for physiological differences of character and for credibility onstage. Correspondingly, there was a growing emphasis on grace and femininity, two tenets of romanticism afforded a particularly expressive outlet by the soprano voice. With the upsurge in romantic sentiment, expressed in Rossini's *opere serie* and the great tragedies of Donizetti and Bellini, the purely vocal bravura of the eighteenth century gave way to a more considered balance of voice, drama, and expression.

Rossini (1792–1868)
Donizetti (1797–1848)
Bellini (1801–1835)

Simultaneously, a phenomenon arose in the art of singing: A select number of contraltos—most extraordinarily Malibran and Pasta—succeeded in extending their range into soprano territory with no loss of quality or notes in the lower register. This hybrid voice, with its airy and open horizons, was the *soprano sfogato,* or "unlimited soprano." In time, minus its extension above high C, it became known as a *soprano drammàtica d'agilità,* and Verdi adopted this genre for his early heroines, Abigaille in *Nabucco* and Lucrezia in *I due Foscari.* From accounts of the day, it is clear the *soprano sfogato* brought a previously undreamed-of excitement, power, and fullness to high-lying phrases and to passages which called for great agility and scintillation. Writers of the day note time and again the "pathetic" expressive colors of these voices, the "melancholy" in their art, and how these summoned from a listener the deepest emotions. It was for such a voice—Pasta's—that Bellini wrote *Norma* and *La sonnambula* and Donizetti conceived *Anna Bolena,* operas which would later be the pinnacle of Callas's art.

This vocal extension, however, was markedly abnormal and not acquired without sacrifice. The voices of Malibran and Pasta, and of those who attempted to imitate their successes (Cornélie Falcon and Malibran's younger sister, Pauline Viardot), lacked the homogeneous color and evenness of scale once so prized in singing. There were unruly sections of their voices never fully under control. Many who heard Pasta, for example, remarked that her uppermost notes seemed produced by ventriloquism, a charge which would later be made against Callas.

Recalling Pasta in his memoirs in 1862, English critic Henry Chorley not only brought to life this compelling singer, but virtually defined the *soprano sfogato:*

"She subjected herself to a course of severe and incessant vocal study to subdue and to utilize her voice. To equalize it was impossible. There was a portion of the scale which differed from the rest in quality and remained to the last 'under a veil.'...There were notes always more or less out of tune, especially at the commencement of her performances. Out of these uncouth materials she had to compose her instrument and then to give it flexibility. Her studies to acquire execution must have been tremendous; but the volubility and brilliancy, when acquired, gained a character of their own....There were a breadth, an expressiveness in her roulades, an evenness and solidity in her shake, which imparted to every passage a significance totally beyond the reach of lighter and more spontaneous singers.

"Madame Pasta was understood to be a poor musician—a slow reader; but she had one of the most essential musical qualities in perfection—a sense for the measurement and proportion of time. This is more rare than it should be, and its absence strangely often passes unperceived even by artists and amateurs, who are sensitively cultivated in other respects. It is not such mere correctness as is ensured by the metronome; not such artful licence in giving and taking as is apt to become artifice and affectation; but that instinctive feeling for propriety, which no lessons can teach—that due recognition of accent and phrase—it is that absence of flurry and exaggeration, such as make the discourse and behavior of certain persons memorable in themselves...that intelligent composure without coolness, which at once impresses and reassures those who see and hear it. . . .

Giuditta Pasta
(1798–1865)
as Anna Bolena

"But the greatest grace of all—depth and reality of expression—was possessed by this remarkable artist as few before her—as none whom I have since admired—have possessed it. The best of her audience were held in thrall, without being able to analyse what made up the spell, what produced the effect—as soon as she opened her lips.

"Her recitative, from the moment when she entered, was riveting by its truth. People accustomed to object to the conventionalities of Opera—just as loudly as if all Drama was not conventional, too—forgave the singing, and the strange language, for the sake of the direct and dignified appeal made by her declaration. Madame Pasta never changed her readings, her effects, her ornaments. To arrive at what stood with her for truth, she labored, made experiments, rejected, with an elaborate care, the result of which, in one meaner or more meagre, must have been monotony. But the impression made on me was that of my being always subdued and surprised, for the first time. Though I knew what was coming—when the passion broke out, or when the phrase was sung, it seemed as if they were something new, electric, immediate. The effect is as present to me at the moment of writing, as the impression made by the first sight of the sea—by the first snow-mountain—by the first hearing of the organ—by any of those first emotions which never utterly pass away. These things are totally distinct from the fanaticism of a *laudator temporis acti*. With honest people, I dare to believe and hope, Death only takes away the power of honest admiration."

By the time these words were written, Pasta's career was at an end, the day of the *soprano sfogato* was in its twilight, and the theater and principles of bel canto were being readapted to vocal display rather than employed for dramatic truth. Eventually, the bel canto style and repertory would be eclipsed by the music dramas of Wagner and Verdi and obscured by the dawn of verismo, when opera reached out for a slice of life. By the twentieth century, the agility once so essential to a singer's training and appeal had become minimized, then localized in bantamweight soprano voices. During this same period of transition and evolution, female voices, which from the eighteenth century well into the age of Wagner had been designated merely as "soprano" or "contralto," began to be separated by type and by repertory. The soprano who once sang everything began to specialize and was labeled a "coloratura," "lyric," "dramatic," or "mezzo." Adelina Patti, for example, would be considered a dramatic-coloratura, for she was both Aida and Lucia. She was also a singer with an enormous penchant for bravura and, to a great extent, was instrumental in making *Lucia*, *Sonnambula*, and *Barbiere di Siviglia* vocal rather than dramatic vehicles. Given Chorley's rich veneration for Pasta, it is easy to understand his objections to Patti, and his declaration—together with Rossini—of a decay in the art of song.

Chorley's unwillingness to accept a new mood in singing was not unlike that of writer-publisher Victor Gollancz nearly a century later. A Callas partisan, Gollancz was observed stamping from a Sutherland performance at Covent Garden booming: "God, she's as dull as Melba!" Sutherland, like Patti and Nellie Melba before her, is an offshoot from another branch of the bel canto tree—the natural soprano as opposed to the unnatural, extended contralto voice. Comparisons have been made between Sutherland and Giulia Grisi, who created Elvira in *I Puritani*, and they are as apt as those drawn between Callas and Pasta. For with only certain qualifications, Chorley's words on Pasta can be applied directly to Callas, a true *soprano sfogato*.

Callas was, as Italian critic Teodoro Celli has so eloquently stated, "a star wandering into a planetary system not its own." Few if any understood her special nature at first, for her vocal type had been all but forgotten by 1949. I wonder, as does Celli, if in the beginning Callas herself realized she was so exotic a musical creature. She was certainly aware of her unusual facility as a singer; it had been inbred premeditatively by her principal teacher, Elvira de Hidalgo, a notable "coloratura" of the World War I period. Callas first thought of her bel canto schooling as a utilitarian necessity; it gave her voice "*souplesse,*" as she has termed it. In the beginning Callas considered herself a dramatic soprano, and this is how she began her career. Her first professional roles in Italy were Gioconda, Isolde, Turandot, and Tosca, repertory today sung by Birgit Nilsson (with the exception of Gioconda, which Nilsson could sing if she wished). To be sure, in 1948, Callas had scaled the summit of bel canto roles, Norma. But at the time, this did not indicate the direction in which she would eventually travel, for many dramatic sopranos have grappled with Norma.

Far more significant was another Bellini role Callas added to her growing repertory the following year: Elvira in *I Puritani*. Unlike Norma, Elvira had never tempted bigger voices, remaining instead the property of lyric and coloratura sopranos. Thus, Callas's assumption of the role lacked a contemporary parallel. It also brought the first public awareness of the extraordinary extension in her voice above high C.

Callas came to this lighter part in a curious but dramatic way. In January 1949, she was engaged by Teatro la Fenice in Venice to sing Brünnhilde in *Die Walküre*. During the same period, *Puritani* was to go into rehearsal with Margherita Carosio as Elvira. Tullio Serafin, who two years earlier had led Callas's Italian debut in Verona as Gioconda, was hired to conduct both operas. Long a mentor of singers—he had artistically befriended Rosa Ponselle at the Metropolitan Opera during the 1920s—Serafin took Callas under his wing. It was he who coached and conducted her first Norma and who recommended her for Brünnhilde to the management of Fenice.

Five days before the first *Puritani*, Carosio fell ill and no replacement could be found. Remembering Callas as Norma, Serafin had her sight-read Elvira's music (she knew only "Qui la voce," learned during student days with de Hidalgo). Serafin decided on the spot Callas must sing *Puritani*. She protested. Her voice was all wrong for the part, "too heavy." But Serafin insisted: "You are young. I know you will make it. I gamble on you."

Callas sang her last two Brünnhildes while learning Elvira. Three days after her final *Walküre*, she sang her first *Puritani*. This marked the turning point in her career and made clear that a unique apparition had arisen on the operatic scene. She invested the Bellini role with the fullness of a dramatic soprano and the ease and felicity of a lyric. In retrospect, it seems impossible Serafin was merely taking a gamble. He was well aware of Callas's vocal prowess and certainly knew, as he later told Callas, of the nineteenth-century precedents for her singing both Norma and Elvira. Surely he was the first to sense history as Callas began to remake it.

In the years following the Venice *Puritani*, as Callas understood her true nature and added such roles as Lucia, Amina in *Sonnambula*, and Anna Bolena, battle lines began to be drawn; conflict was inevitable. For the public, unaware of the historical properties of Callas's art, but aware of her alien qualities as a singer, the controversy settled into one of beauty of sound versus an expressive use of sound. This contention is as old as opera itself. In 1723, Pier Francesco Tosi, in a still viable treatise on singing, wrote: "I do not know if a perfect singer can at the same time be a perfect actor; for if the mind is at once divided by two different purposes, he will incline, no doubt, more to one than the other. What a joy it would be to possess both to a perfect degree."

This tug-of-war is a question of taste: On one side are those who value above all a beautiful vocal quality, regardless of a loss of expression; on the other are those who require a sense of words and drama at the price of unevenly matched tones. Reduced to its most simplistic level, this underlay the Callas-Tebaldi fracas of the 1950s. Here were two singers who should never have been compared, for Renata Tebaldi is a modern soprano whose training was as based in verismo as Callas's was rooted in bel canto.

Tebaldi had been a pupil of Carmen Melis, herself a singer well known for such later Tebaldi roles as Tosca, Minnie in *La fanciulla del West*, Fedora, and Madama Butterfly. Melis's schooling and musical outlook became Tebaldi's as surely as de Hidalgo's became Callas's. Without the guidance of a more complete singer, technically speaking, Tebaldi never developed her fullest potential. The simplest ornamentations were foreign to her; trills were either omitted or approximated, while scales and ornaments were cumbersomely sung. Her stylistic command remained limited to the turn of the century. She was most secure in certain Verdi works (*La forza del destino, Aida, Otello*) which demanded little or no agility, and completely at home in the operas of Puccini and Giordano, which, in their seeking for reality, asked for none.

Tebaldi's sound was a ravishing one, however, and her nature sympathetic. A public unable to cope with the peculiarities of Callas, especially her timbre, found recourse in meaningless comparisons between the two. The voice of Callas was dismissed as "ugly" and her repertory as "unrealistic." Both verdicts demand investigation. Callas's voice, spanning nearly three octaves, was never beautiful in a classic sense; there was too much metal in it. Like Pasta's, it turned acidulous without warning, the lower and middle ranges were often so heavily covered they sounded bottled, and the top at times went out of control and wavered violently. It was also a voice that, in attempting to embrace the full drama of a text, expressed, in no uncertain terms and for the first time in this century, unvarnished hatred. Other voices have moved audiences by conveying love, poignancy, fear, rage, and ecstasy. To these sensations, Callas added the disquieting element of loathing. It was not a comfortable emotion to encounter and required an adjustment on the part of a listener. Many for whom opera was a release or escape refused to accept it.

Yet it was her unique color (Chicago critic Claudia Cassidy once described it as "part-oboe, part-clarinet") and her capacity (as Norma or Medea) for hatred which helped set Callas's sound and mode of singing so apart from others. Even her deficiencies, the unstable top and the bottled lower register, contributed to making her voice forever recognizable —individual—a factor of vital importance in holding an audience's attention and establishing a bond between a singer and the public.

The words of Camille Saint-Saëns on Pauline Viardot always come to mind when attempting to describe Callas: "Her voice was tremendously powerful, prodigious in its range, and it overcame all the difficulties in the art of singing. But this marvellous voice did not please everyone, for it was by no means smooth and velvety. Indeed, it was a little harsh and was likened to the taste of a bitter orange. But it was just the voice for a tragedy or an epic, for it was superhuman rather than human. It lent an incomparable grandeur to tragic parts; light things...were completely transformed by that voice and became the playthings of an Amazon or giantess."

Maria Malibran
(1808–1836)
and her sister,
Pauline Viardot
(1821–1910)

Beyond the timbre of Callas's voice, and certain physiological flaws no amount of discipline could alter, she possessed, like Pasta and Viardot, complete technical equipment. Embellishments, trills, scales, and legati were hers to command, seemingly at will. She made the most astonishing application of her gifts in recitative. Conductor Nicola Rescigno, a longtime Callas associate, has remarked, "It is a deep mystery why a girl from the Bronx, born into a nonmusical family and raised in an atmosphere devoid of operatic tradition, should have been blessed with the ability to sing the perfect recitative. She had an architectural sense which told her just which word in a musical sentence to emphasize and just what syllable within that word to bring out." Callas has said Serafin told her to speak the words of a recitative aloud to find their proper dramatic proportions, and this is all she did. The naïveté of her statement recalls Vladimir Horowitz telling a young pianist he achieved his fiery octaves by practicing them slowly and staccato, with high wrists, a method known to every piano teacher. If either aspect of technique were so simple, the world would abound in Callases and Horowitzes. It doesn't, because to the obvious, both brought something so much their own, something so natural they were ignorant of what constituted their art.

Callas's technical command, however, would have meant little, even with the weight of history and a distinctive sound, had she not shaped music to expressive ends. This she did with consummate skill and poetry. If technique alone had been her sum, Callas would have been an interesting, provocative singer rather than a moving, influential one. A writer dealing with Mary Garden (and those with long memories frequently draw parallels between Garden and Callas) once wrote: "None of the arts expresses human emotions—they express the source of human emotion. To express the emotion of life is to live; to express the life of emotion is to make art." This was Garden's gift. It was no less Callas's.

To critic Eugenio Gara, "Her secret is in her ability to transfer to the musical plane the suffering of the character she plays, the nostalgic longing for lost happiness, the anxious fluctuation between hope and despair, between pride and supplication, between irony and generosity, which in the end dissolves into a superhuman inner pain. The most diverse and opposite of sentiments, cruel deceptions, ambitious desires, burning tenderness, grievous sacrifices, all the torments of the heart, acquire in her singing that mysterious truth, I would like to say, that psychological sonority, which is the primary attraction of opera."

Teodoro Celli has taken this idea a step further: "Perhaps, listening to all there is of sadness and terrible nostalgia, of aggression and desperation in Callas's voice, we should be able to conclude not only that it is admirably apt for realizing drama in music, but also that it contains a drama within itself, that it is an indication of an unquiet, troubled spiritual state expressing and purifying itself in sounds."

Thus, one always reaches the point at which it becomes impossible to separate Callas's voice from what she did with it. At her best, tone and intent were wondrously interlocked. Within this wedding lies her ultimate stature as an artist. In performance, Callas never offered a series of high points strung together with indifferent or unfinished patches. A recitative was as integrated and thoughtful as an aria. She forced an audience to accept or reject the whole of her performance and the character which emerged from it. To arrive at how she achieved this is to reach the point, as Gara emphasized, "at which research ends and poetry takes wing."

Naturally, she had greater affinity for some roles than others. This is true of all artists and crucial with Callas, given the immense range and variety of her repertory, which ran from Mozart's *Die Entführung aus dem Serail* to Giordano's *Fedora*. In between these extremes lay Beethoven's *Fidelio*, nearly a dozen bel canto parts (both comic and tragic), a wide spectrum of Verdi from all periods of his writing, and three Wagner heroines. A good deal has been made not only of Callas's standard repertory but also of the unusual works revived for her, as though she were a musical archaeologist. Yet, the wonder of her singing lay not so much in what she sang as how she sang. Thus, her Norma, Lucia, and Amina were true revivals, even though these roles had not gone out of currency. There are a handful of operas, however, which she restored in a historical sense: Rossini's *Il Turco in Italia* and *Armida*, Haydn's *Orfeo ed Euridice*, Cherubini's *Medea*, Donizetti's *Anna Bolena*, and Bellini's *Il pirata*. Of these, only *Medea* and *Bolena* persist onstage without Callas.

Norma,
Paris,
1964

Out of a repertory of forty-seven roles, it is as Bellini's Norma that Callas is most likely to be remembered. She sang this part more often than any other; it was also the role in which she made her American and Metropolitan Opera debuts. Norma is to a soprano what King Lear is to an actor, the final challenge of heart and mind. It is not merely the most demanding role created by Bellini; it is also one of the most complex in all opera. Norma is many women in one—mother, warrior, lover, priestess, leader; she is possessed by a full range of human emotions—hatred, vengeance, passion, and tenderness. "Norma resembles me in a certain way," Callas once said in a moment of self-analysis. "She seems very strong, very ferocious at times. Actually, she is not, even though she roars like a lion."

The difficulty of realizing Norma's drama to its fullest is compounded by Bellini's musical requirements. Needed is total mastery of recitative and fioriture plus the ability to sustain. Norma is onstage 75 percent of the opera, with flights of lyricism one moment, requiring enormous resources of breath, followed by dramatic outbursts the next. As with *Sonnambula* and *Puritani*, the late nineteenth century imposed upon Norma a posture quite different from the one Bellini had in mind when he molded the part for Pasta. Even during Bellini's lifetime the role had been misappropriated. Grisi, who created Adalgisa, was determined to take on Norma as well, despite the composer's objections. She sang the role in London in 1835, and it was, as Bellini himself noted in a letter, "a solemn fiasco.... I heard Grisi sing the cavatina badly, and that was enough for me to judge her incapable of the rest, as I had seen her in *Anna Bolena*, which, if you take away the tender part, was unbearable in the rest, especially in the tragic. Give her *La sonnambula*, *I Puritani*, *La gazza ladra*, and a thousand operas of simple and innocent style, and I can swear to you that she would be second to none; but as for noble characters, she does not understand them or feel them because she does not have that instinct or the training to bear herself with the nobility and lofty style that they require. Thus, it would be my feeling that in *Norma* she would be nothing, and that the role of Adalgisa is the only one suited to her character."

Whatever we think of the libretto and music of *Norma* in our time, Bellini believed in them as drama and wrote every line, each embellishment for an expressive purpose. By 1890, when Lilli Lehmann sang the first Norma at the Metropolitan Opera, the work had become misconstrued as staid and classic. Bellini's Norma had become Gluck's Norma in many minds. In the early decades of the twentieth century, singers would further transform it to Verdi's Norma and even to Mascagni's Norma. Callas restored Bellini's original. Her Norma was also a reminder, in her words, that "bel canto does not mean beautiful singing alone. It is, rather, the technique demanded by the composers of this style—Donizetti, Rossini, and Bellini. It is the same attitudes and demands of Mozart and Beethoven, for example, the same approach and the same technical difficulties faced by instrumentalists. You see, a musician is a musician. A singer is no different from an instrumentalist except that we have words. You don't excuse things in a singer you would not dream of excusing in a violinist or pianist. There is no excuse for not having a trill, in not doing the acciaccatura, in not having good scales. Look at your scores! There are technical things written there to be performed, and they must be performed whether you like it or not. How will you get out of a trill? How will you get out of scales when they are written there, staring you in the face? It is not enough to have a beautiful voice. What does that mean? When you interpret a role, you have to have a thousand colors to portray happiness, joy, sorrow, fear. How can you do this with only a beautiful voice? Even if you sing harshly sometimes, as I have frequently done, it is a necessity of expression. You have to do it, even if people will not understand. But in the long run they will, because you must persuade them of what you are doing."

Nowhere was Callas more persuasive than as Norma. Her performances were towering reaffirmations of the opera's lost values, a complete range of dramatic emotions joined to a mastery of vocal technique. Like Pasta before her, and unlike any singer of this century, she understood the role's musico-dramatic requirements and made them a living reality. Her lesson was not lightly learned or taught, nor should it be lightly forgotten. Rather, embodying as it did the spirit and breath of Bellini, it has formed a touchstone for the future. Her Norma stands ready in memory to remind us the end result must be, as Stendhal wrote of Pasta, "an instantaneous and hypnotic effect upon the soul of the spectator."

Though Callas sang three other Bellini heroines, only Amina in *Sonnambula* offered a proper outlet for her gifts. Despite poignant music, Elvira in *Puritani* and Imogene in *Pirata* remain cardboard figures, lacking those contrasts in mood and emotion on which Callas's art fed. *Sonnambula* is a different matter. It stands in perspective to *Norma* much as a watercolor does to an oil. An understanding of the two hinges on the realization that both were written for Pasta and both were commonly sung by the same soprano through the middle of the nineteenth century (Malibran, Jenny Lind, and Viardot come quickest to mind). When the two roles were split asunder, Norma went to heavy-voiced singers such as Celestina Boninsegna, Rosa Raisa, and Rosa Ponselle. The gentler Amina became the property of lighter voices: Amelita Galli-Curci, Elvira de Hidalgo, and Lily Pons. Yet, Bellini no more composed *Norma* for a dramatic soprano than he wrote *Sonnambula* for a *soprano leggiero*. Pasta was his choice for both because she best illuminated his text and endowed the emotions of his music with living substance.

It is little wonder, then, that Bellini's stock on the operatic market dropped to that of a pretty melodist once Norma was relegated to a stiff demeanor and *Sonnambula* to a shiny superficiality. But, as Callas restored the strength and humanity embedded in Norma, she reinstated the quiet hues and passions of Amina. Hearing Amina in a voice which endows Norma with proper human dimensions makes one aware in turn of the depth in *Sonnambula*. Taken purely on the theatrical terms of Felice Romani's libretto, Amina is a pastoral figure, a trusting innocent in a sylvan village who comes perilously close to losing her sanity and her lover. In other words, she is a composite of many of the ingredients of nineteenth-century romanticism. By the same token, if Bellini's score is considered apart from Romani's story, Amina is a first cousin to Adolphe Adam's Giselle. Yet the remarkable fusion of effort by Bellini and Romani provoked more than a stereotype. Their joining of word and tone resulted in a poetic and elegiac creature—a distillation of the feminine side of the arts in the romantic era. She finds her counterpart in Chopin's nocturnes; she is more Keats than Byron. But as Bellini designed the part, and Callas reminded us, Amina was also a figure of flesh, meant to move and not merely to delight. In place of the role's plasma, which is all that is offered by most singers, she gave us Amina's blood as well.

Nothing could have been further from the big, fiery sound of her Norma than the dreamlike, vulnerable voice of her Amina. A revealing parallel also can be drawn between her performances as Amina and Rosina. Oddly enough, Callas sang the comic Rossini–Rosina in *Il barbiere* and Fiorilla in *Il Turco in Italia*–more than the tragic; yet, while the voice which so expressively limned Amina's music was the same which so trippingly dealt with Rosina, how unalike the two were. It was not just Callas's recognition that Rosina and Amina are musical sisters, classic masks of comedy and tragedy; it was her manner of implementing so obvious a distinction. She deployed a similar lightness and elegance in both roles, but used a slight edge and greater point for Rosina, a more hollow, disembodied sound for Amina. Beyond this, there was something more intangible, something more than a sense of banter with Rosina and shyness with Amina. There was a perceptible alteration of her voice. Too frequently, opposing feelings are conveyed on the operatic stage by a mere shifting of weight. But Callas could actually reshape the focus and emphasis of her tone. While actors on the legitimate stage change their voices as they do their dress, singers tend to remain more dependent on the exterior mood of a score than their own sound to set character. An expression of sadness, for example, with most singers remains the same from opera to opera and style to style. Callas, however, made happiness one thing to Rosina and quite another to Amina.

If Callas is best remembered for Norma, it was her Lucia that caused a revolution in operatic theater, making the public rethink the work and its dramatic values. In this century, prior to her assumption of the role in 1952, Lucia had become a favorite plaything for the coloratura soprano. With the shift in emphasis from dramatic content to vocal style, Donizetti's brooding score had disintegrated to a trifling level. Callas, by her penetrating treatment of the words and music, returned tragic stature to the heroine.

In Callas's voice, Lucia became the overly protected young woman whose first emotional involvement has been traumatic, unhinging her mind and leading her to murder. The multicolored, evocative voice of Callas filled the role with urgency, passion, and sadness, and Lucia's nature materialized as credible. She brought a nobility of profile which removed layers of encrusted misuse and opened up expressive reaches only hinted at previously. Of all the roles in Callas's repertory, it was with Lucia that she herself had the strongest initial identification. The intricacies of Norma and Violetta were solved only after painstaking years of trial and search. But the character of Lucia was virtually set from her first performance. At the root of her portrayal was a single-minded pursuit of the drama.

Performance practices of this century, which cut a good deal of the score's redundancies, worked to her advantage. Callas's views toward cuts varied from score to score. She advocated, for example, keeping purely bravura sections such as "Ah! non giunge" from *Sonnambula* intact because at this moment there is a greater emphasis on voice than on drama. But she also felt that "not all music of every composer is really delicious. There are certain points in opera, even in Verdi, that are tiresome. A hundred years ago the public was different; it used to dress differently, think differently. Now the public dresses and thinks another way and we must act accordingly. We make changes to make opera a success, though always keeping the atmosphere, the poetry, the mysticism that makes theater work."

Coupled with this tightening of bel canto music was Callas's own chaste outlook in regard to ornamentation. Her taste kept embellishments to a minimum, organic and harmonically suitable. She and conductor Gianandrea Gavazzeni once seriously considered giving *Lucia* exactly as written with no embellishments, even to cutting the famous cadenza of the Mad Scene. Though both were excited by the cleanness and force of the idea, it was abandoned out of fear that audience and critics would not understand their reasons.

Second to Lucia in her trio of Donizetti heroines was Anna Bolena. Though Callas performed the role only a dozen times, and at La Scala alone, it stands as one of her most exacting characterizations. The opera deals only with the final weeks of Henry VIII's second wife; thus, Donizetti's Anna reflects none of the bright figure of her happier days. Felice Romani, the librettist, made this Anne an innocent who loves deeply, is victimized by Henry, and has been unjustly pronounced guilty. Similarly, Jane (Giovanna) Seymour is drawn as an equally hapless figure caught in Henry's intriguing and torn by two loyalties—to her queen and to her sovereign. It is on the emotions of these two women that the opera pivots.

Callas's identity with Anne's tragedy came as a culmination of all the wronged, wounded, melancholy characters she had previously portrayed, demonstrating how accumulative her art was. The emotions of one role provided a basis for another. In *Bolena* these qualities of conflict and sacrifice were transfigured by Callas's awareness that she was dealing not with the personal drama of a Violetta or Lucia, but with the tragedy of a woman who bore the weight of history. It is Anne's regal position and her dignity in the face of death which contained Callas's performance in terms of color and emphasis and so strengthened it.

Ironically, Callas achieved her ends with little regard for history. Historic study never involved her. Her response to character was often triggered by a naïve or obvious fact. Rescigno once asked her, after their performance of the final scene from *Bolena* in concert, why she had shaped a certain phrase in a certain manner. "Because she is a queen," Callas replied with little elaboration. This bare idea was enough in itself to set her imagination coursing in a new and different direction than it had with Lucia or Norma. Callas never intellectualized a role—not only because she is not an intellectual, but because to do so would have involved working apart from the score with facts that could not be translated into musical terms. The whole Callas mechanism was sparked by music. Once she understood the nature of a character in simple terms—"queen" or "gypsy," "priestess" or "peasant"—she grafted this kernel of thought to what she found within the music. That a prismatic characterization evolved in the process is beyond explanation.

Callas's approach to a role such as Bolena was also a practical one. First, the show-woman in her, as much as the musician, helped to decide matters of repertory. She was quick to remember: "De Hidalgo and Serafin taught me that the last act of an opera is the most important. For no matter how much or how well you have sung in the first or second acts, if the last act is not superior to all the rest, you might as well not sing the part. I have frequently sung operas which do not have the best last act, but I essentially chose an opera where at the end the last impression is best.

"Once you have read through a score and decided, 'Yes, I would like to do it,' you take it act by act and say, 'Does the character agree with the music?' Take Anna Bolena. Now history has its Anna Bolena, which is quite different from Donizetti's. Donizetti made her a sublime woman, a victim of circumstance, nearly a heroine. I couldn't bother with history's story; it really ruined my insight. I had to go by the music, by the libretto. The music itself justifies it, so the main thing is not the libretto, though I give enormous attention to the words. I try to find truth in the music. You take this music and you learn it as if you were in the conservatory; in other words, exactly as it is written, nothing more and nothing less. It is what I call 'straitjacketing.' The conductor gives you his cuts, his possibilities, ideas about what his cadenzas might be–and his cadenzas are never his if he is a conscientious conductor; he always builds his cadenzas according to the taste and particular nature of the composer–Bellini is quite different from Donizetti, and Donizetti is different from Rossini. We must use these embellishments to the service of expression. If you care for the composer and not for your own personal success, you will always find an embellishment, trill, or scale that justifies an expression, a feeling of happiness or unhappiness, anxiety.

"Having broken a score down, you then need the company of a pianist to remind you exactly of the value of notes and not to let one slip by you. I also used to see when the Maestro would have his readings with the orchestra so I could attend, for I am shortsighted and cannot depend on the cues given me either by the conductor or the prompter. Also, I would attend to live into the music. So, when I came to the first rehearsal with the conductor I was quite prepared.

"Finally you build the whole thing together–stage, colleagues, orchestra, chorus–and eventually you reach the point of performing the opera straight through, which you must do three or four times to measure your strength and learn where you can rest. There is one thing you must do at the orchestral rehearsals: sing in full voice for your sake, for your colleagues' sake, and above all to test your own possibilities. Also, if they could prepare my costumes for me, especially difficult ones, sooner than the first dress rehearsal, I wore them a bit to get used to them.

"At this point, it is about eighteen to twenty days by now, you have your dress rehearsal; there's no stopping, it is just like a performance and with critics. Then you must have no less than three days before the first performance. One day you are practically sick, you are so tired; the second day you unwind, and the third day you are ready to go. After the first performance good, solid work starts because then you fill in the blank spots. Before you had made a rough sketch; there is nothing like stage performances in front of an audience to fill in the details."

Medea,
Dallas, 1958

If there is a proper parallel to what Callas achieved as Norma, it is not to be found in another bel canto opera, but earlier, in Cherubini's *Medea*. The parallel is not a question of musical or dramatic similarities in the two parts, for the former are slender at best–an Italianate cantabile in lyrical passages–and the latter are on the surface. The link lies in historic attitudes toward these roles and how Callas once again shifted the dramatic emphasis. In her performances of both, benign classicism became vibrant emotionalism; friezes of sound evolved into human portraits. However, whereas *Norma* came from a single creative source, *Medea* is a hybrid. In its original form, *Medea* (or *Medée*, for Cherubini, like Meyerbeer, was a Frenchman by choice and the majority of his finest works were written for Parisian theaters) was an opéra-comique. This was the manner in which it was premiered and heard for more than fifty years, and this could well be why so theatrical a singer as Pasta chose Simone Mayr's lesser setting of the story. The recitatives performed today were added by Franz Lachner twelve years after Cherubini's death. Since Callas sang an Italian translation with recitatives, we are obliged to speak of a Cherubini-Lachner *Medea*. Even this corruption must be extended because conductors have traditionally edited the sprawling score to make their own versions. Cherubini himself recognized the necessity of this; prior to the Viennese premiere in 1802, he cut some 500 bars of music. Yet the result has not been a process of attrition but of might, for *Medea* has emerged a vivid piece of theatrical wizardry. This is particularly true of the Cherubini-Lachner-Rescigno version, which Callas sang most often.

Like Norma, Medea is possessed by primal emotions–jealousy, supreme pride, maternal love–but there is less nobility to her. Her single-mindedness is directed toward a flaming vengeance. Norma contemplated the murder of her children and turned from it; Medea not only went through with the deed, she exulted in it. Her primitivism makes Norma seem of cultured civility in comparison.

The contrast in the two characters is the basis of the contrast in Callas's performances of each. With Callas, Norma was only a woman–proud, vain, vulnerable, loving. Her Medea, however, was a duality–demigoddess and demiwoman, with the two halves at war for supremacy. It was, of course, the goddess who triumphed in the end. Callas even made a sharp difference in the woman in each, for Medea's tenderest moments (and Callas convinced us that love alone brought her to Corinth) lacked the softness and femininity of her Norma. By the same token, no outburst of Norma at Pollione ever quite reached the white heat heard in Medea's wrath against Jason. Callas's Medea could be said to have worn a mask of tenderness and supplication as it suited her needs; this was especially true in her scenes with Creon. The mask, firmly in place in the first act, was lowered little by little during the second. It was finally torn off in the last, as Callas's voice became a cauldron of evil, revealing an unretouched view of the goddess's blackest side. The look was not an easy or pleasant thing to experience, but it made brutally clear the inexorable path of revenge and death which Medea had chosen. In Callas's portent-filled, heated voice, the sorceress came to life as in no other's; it remains a characterization of never ending fascination.

If one considers Callas's repertory as tripart–tragic, romantic, and verismatic–her two forays into the world of Gluck, together with Spontini's *La vestale*, should be considered with *Medea*. Yet how unappositive they are. The static theater of Gluck's *Alceste* and *Iphigénie en Tauride* (both of which she sang in Italian as she did *Medea*) and the lesser *Vestale* confounded even Callas's arcing expressive powers and provided little more than footnotes to her career. As with *Medea*, however, Callas entertained no false concepts of "classicism" in the Gluck and Spontini works, but sang each in an ample and indispensable declamatory style. For all that, her Alceste, Iphigénie, and Giulia left more a sense of superior vocal skill than a feeling of penetrating involvement. The texts of the Gluck works, in particular, do not provide room for deep involvement, and Callas responded with a single color throughout, all but negating her vocal individuality.

These three roles came as a parenthesis between the bel canto repertory, in which she was supreme, and the Verdi parts, for which she was ideal. Of her Verdi operas, she sang *La traviata* most often. If any singer and part were fated to come together, it was Callas and Violetta. Artistically, the role was tailor-made for her voice, her perceptions as an actress, and her sensibilities as a woman. Yet, Violetta involved a long period of probing for Callas, as she lived into the intricacies of the role. It was largely a question of adjustment, of finding the colors and weights with which to mirror the text and emotions of the part. From the beginning, she was able to implant an unmistakable sense of Violetta's illness, but her chief problem lay in an overgenerosity of voice, particularly in act two, the heart of the role. Here, Violetta is confronted by the choice of her immediate happiness and Alfredo's future well-being. It is not merely her decision to sacrifice love which is so moving (after all, Leonora in *Trovatore* goes a step further and takes poison without touching our finer feelings); rather it is the nobility with which the act is done. Violetta overcomes the human defenses first of selfishness and then of self-pity. This manifestation of her frailty set aside by force of will is what so moves and convinces a listener. Coupled with Verdi's humanistic music, a remarkable union is forged. More than a century after her creation, Violetta remains a figure of universality (rather than a character caught in a web of theatrical circumstance) which still affects audiences deeply.

Callas did not close the dramatic ring of the second and final acts until the 1955 production of *Traviata* at La Scala. In this production, directed by Luchino Visconti, Callas was to realize that so personal a body of emotions required a finer discrimination in sound. She was also to resolve her previous inability to bring as consistent a veracity to spoken lines as to sung passages. In the reading of Alfredo's letter before "Addio del passato," and again in the final moments when Violetta believes she is recovering, Callas had too often sounded stilted, with certain words receiving odd stresses (the same was true of her letter-reading in *Macbeth*). There is no easy answer as to why Callas's speaking held less music than her singing. Perhaps, lacking the support lent by song and a prescribed pacing for words, she had felt exposed and ill at ease.

Giuseppe Verdi
(1813–1901);
Violetta in *La traviata*,
Dallas, 1958

There was never any reservation about her vocal suitability for the part, however. She was superbly equipped to deal with the tremendous demands Verdi makes on a Violetta. In actuality he asks for three sopranos: a coloratura for act one, a lyric for acts two and three, and a dramatic for act four. These demands stress the transitional character of *Traviata* and of Verdi as he moved from the conventions of bel canto to a more personalized, more dramatically integrated musical style. Violetta is composed of both elements, and the enormous range of her music has led many to speak of sopranos as first-act, or second- or fourth-act Violettas. For it is true that a singer comfortable in act one will often lack the body of sound needed for the later acts. The converse is just as certain.

With Callas, no such qualifications were needed. Nowhere did her bel canto upbringing pay off so well, for her "Sempre libera" in act one was as secure as her outburst "Ah! gran Dio! Morir sì giovine" in act four. One has to reach back to the *Traviata* of Ponselle to find as complete a performance. But not even Ponselle made the tragedy of Violetta so immediate and moving as did Callas by her final performances in 1958. By then, the part had been scaled to essentials and her singing, while less secure vocally, portrayed unerringly the spirit and fatality of Verdi's most touching heroine.

That the intensely human portrait of Violetta was written side by side with the conventional character of Leonora in *Il trovatore*–a figure trapped in amber–demonstrates how completely Verdi immersed himself in the characters and atmosphere of his subjects, however opposing. The one aspect shared by *Traviata* and *Trovatore* is their mixing of the old and what was to become the new style of Italian opera. *Traviata* transcends the transition by a sympathetic heroine illuminated by music, while *Trovatore* makes its way on sheer invention and vitality. Callas did more for Leonora in one sense than she did for Norma, for the Bellini heroine, however misused, was recognized as a role for a singer with a specific training and technique. But Verdi's Leonora is no less a bel canto figure, a fact decades of imprecise singing and a simplification of the music have hidden. Leonora's stylistic stance became obscured when a new Italian style of opera produced a new breed of vocal artist who sang the bel canto aspects of the role from a modern viewpoint. As *Trovatore*'s early nineteenth-century aspects were glossed over, musically vagrant Leonoras became the norm. But Callas never concerned herself with the norm, and so she learned Leonora in the only way she knew how–"like a sponge," absorbing every note and expression mark written by Verdi. Again, Callas's bel canto schooling uncovered a wealth of detail in Leonora's music. It was as if an old, romantic painting, beloved but dim, had been cleaned to its original tints.

Of Verdi's ladies, Leonora is among the most melancholy, and this made her particularly ripe for Callas's personal mode of expression. Callas had a special empathy for wronged, unhappy women, and though Leonora's character is of limited dimensions, it is a part filled with the sort of contrasts which lent Callas dramatic impetus. In *Trovatore* she ranged through a variety of attitudes and emotions from the dreamlike (as a not too distant cousin of Bellini's sleepwalker) to the impassioned. Callas not only gave life to these qualities but wrapped them in a unique aura of mystery.

Her Aida was another matter altogether. Understandably, it had to be less fascinating because the part contains lesser contrasts. In *Aida*, Verdi painted in big strokes and, to achieve his broad, epic canvas, he sacrificed niceties of character delineation. The figures which people *Aida* are one-dimensional. They undergo no development and lack the intimate detail found in the characters who people *Don Carlo* and *Otello*. Indeed, one could substitute for each role in *Aida* an emotion: jealousy for Amneris, hatred for Amonasro, passion for Radames, torment for Aida. While Callas lavished a wealth of emotion on Aida's music—using to strong advantage that concentrated legato so much a feature of her singing and which so drenched a line with feeling—it was a role which failed to engage her full sympathy. Only Amneris's drama would have offered Callas a proper challenge.

Aida presented Callas with another problem—that of performing a "vocal" as opposed to a "dramatic" aria. Aida's "O patria mia," unlike "Ritorna vincitor!" deals with a single thought and there is little outlet for emotional contrasts, though an excellent chance to make beautiful phrases for their own sake. Such a bent was never a part of Callas's makeup, though it came naturally to a famous Aida like Zinka Milanov, whose primary response to music was vocal. Milanov could produce an exquisite "O patria mia" and, usually, an uneven "Ritorna vincitor!"; with Callas the opposite was true. Where Aida's first aria brimmed with the sense of a besieged heart, the second seemed aloof once past the recitative with its "Io tremo," a sentiment Callas was never at a loss to know how to voice. But a four- or five-minute lamentation for "the green hills, the perfumed shores of home," could never appeal to the theatrical instincts of a Callas.

"O patria mia" also lay bare another problem evident even when Callas was at her most vocally secure: the question of dealing with high C, a special note for the soprano. This primal sound often lay out of balance with the rest of Callas's vocal scale. With no difficulty she could handle C-sharp or B, but C itself was a fearsome hurdle. It could always be touched, but sustaining it (especially given the sort of ascending approach found in "O patria mia") was physically and mentally more a matter of willpower than technique. In 1971, when working on her voice and talking of a return to her career, Callas described this struggle as her *"battaglia del do"*—"battle of the high C."

Violetta, the *Trovatore* Leonora, and Aida were the Verdi parts Callas performed most often. Beyond these were a handful of roles sung much less frequently. Ironically, of these Elena in *I vespri siciliani* was sung by Callas more often than any of the other Verdian parts with which she is more readily identified, such as Lady Macbeth, Abigaille in *Nabucco*, and Amelia in *Ballo in maschera*. In fact, Callas sang Elena (as well as Isolde) nearly as often as Elvira in *I Puritani*. But, while Callas made Elena a strong-willed woman, especially gripping in the first act, it was a fragmented characterization, for *Vespri* is a diffused, sprawling score, and it is little wonder Callas is associated more closely with the direct, forceful figure of Lady Macbeth. This fully formed theatrical role is as special to Callas's career as it was to Verdi's, even though she sang the role only a few times.

Verdi espoused the psychology of Lady Macbeth's drama with such thoroughness that he permits us—no, invites us—to encircle and know her from all sides. Four solo pieces comprise the backbone of the role. The first, "Vieni! t'affretta!" is a traditionally cast bel canto aria and finds a parallel in Abigaille's "Anch'io dischiuso" in the second act of *Nabucco*. The second, "La luce langue," is freer and mixes arioso stretches with punctuating recitative-like moments. The Brindisi, while as square a bit of writing as its counterpart in *Traviata*, is made to function with anything but squareness; the dramatic quality of the aria stems from its juxtaposition within the drama of the banquet scene. Finally, there is the unearthly Sleepwalking Scene. If Verdi used conventional means in "Vieni! t'affretta!" as an exposition of Lady Macbeth's strength, the Sleepwalking Scene is unconventional to show the disintegration of that strength.

Callas recognized, consciously or unconsciously, the function each set piece plays in deepening the character and adjusted her voice accordingly. Her pacing of what is expressed within and without the character in an aria (and on a broader scale from aria to aria) realized the potential for character Verdi lavishly provided, and her voice created scenery and action for the mind's theater through a luminous range of inflections and tints. A key to her thinking here came in 1968 in a discussion of her recording of the Sleepwalking Scene:

"I was in quite good voice that day, for you know we have our ups and downs. I was proud when I stepped down to listen to the playback, and I told our then artistic director Walter Legge, 'That was, I think, some good singing.' 'Oh, extraordinary,' he said, 'but now you will hear it and you will understand that you have to redo it.' I was a bit shocked and said, 'What do you mean by that?' He said, 'You'll listen to it and you'll see.' In fact, I did listen to it, and it was astonishing, perfect vocally. But the main idea of this Sleepwalking Scene was not underlined. In other words, she is in a nightmare-sleepwalking stage. She has to convey all these odd thoughts which go through her head–evil, fearsome, terrifying. So I had made a masterpiece of vocal singing, but I had not done my job as an interpreter. Immediately, as soon as I heard it, I said, 'Well, you are right; now I understand,' and I went and performed it.

"You see, I think she must have at least six mental thoughts that come to her here, one completely different from the other. For she has reached a state of mind that is, shall we say, conscience. She is a very ambitious lady, and for the sake of her vanity, she has persuaded her husband to kill the king so that he could become king. Disaster has come because she could not stand her guilt and went mad. She finally copes with her madness in this Sleepwalking Scene. A mad person, of course, has one thought into another without continuity. One minute she is talking about the bloodstains on her hands, terrified that she can never get them clean, and right away she says, 'Come now, we must get ready to receive these people; everything is fine.' All of a sudden, she comes back to another mental attitude. So you cannot perform it with only one line from beginning to end. You have to break it into every one of her thoughts.

"The first section begins by saying, 'There are stains on my hands. Go away! Damn them. One, two....This is the time. Why are you trembling? Are you not going in?' Already we have two changes: 'One stain with the other. Why don't they go away?' All of a sudden she comes out saying, 'This is the hour, let's get ready.' Then, 'Why are you afraid to go in? You, a *great* warrior....How could you be such a coward. Oh, shame on you. Come quickly.' Changing again she says, 'Who could have imagined in that old man there could be so much blood.' This is being stark mad. How could you convey this all in one beautiful quality? Even speaking the lines you could not convey 'God, so much blood' as you would 'How could you be such a coward?' Her mind is wandering one minute, terrified the other, commanding the next. And Verdi helps you convey this, for instance, at 'tanto sangue immaginar,' by marking the notes *sforzando*, which means 'touching.' They are rhythmically accented to convey terror: 'Could-not-i-ma-gine.'

"Though she is interrupted by the doctor, she cannot hear him. She is completely sleepwalking, cannot understand anything, and does not look at anything. She hears only the thoughts going on in her mind. These thoughts come back to the same obsessiveness, 'I cannot clean the blood on my hands. No one can ever clean it.' Verdi has marked this section 'Di sangue umano' triple piano, and it should be nearly husky in quality, nearly eerie. It is terror. Hasn't it ever happened that you are so terrified that you only whisper because you are afraid people will hear? Then on 'Arabia intera' there is an outburst followed by a pianissimo. Again she becomes quiet because of fear. When you have these outbursts, incidentally, you have to rebuild within the musical phrase, because it is always an outburst that must not be so loud that it erases the pianos.

"The next section, when she urges Macbeth to bed, is suddenly very lyrical, because she is a very persuasive woman. She has such strength over her husband that she must not have been a terribly ugly woman. She must have really been very fascinating to have been able to do with him as she pleased. When she says, 'Come, let's go, don't be afraid, let's go to bed,' this is a woman who is absolutely one with her husband. This next idea, 'Batte alcuno,' comes from her stark-raving mind, however. In the first act she has heard a knocking at the door and people coming and saying, 'God, we have found the king dead.' This and all the Sleepwalking Scene is a recollection of the past, of the very beginning of the opera and throughout the opera. So you see, this is actually a mad scene in sleepwalking form. How can a mad woman with crazy thoughts jumping from one to the other be conveyed in a straight, lovely kind of evenly placed vocal piece? It cannot. Therefore I had to break it into all these pieces, and Verdi helps a singer so with all his diminuendos, crescendos, and allargandos. But you cannot do this all alone. It is so important to have a great conductor with you who will help you with his orchestra. You need also a great stage director and good colleagues. It is a teamwork of seriousness, great science, great faith, great sacrifice. We depend one on the other for the success of the performance."

Another Verdian heroine Callas performed even less frequently than Lady Macbeth but with as significant results was Gilda in *Rigoletto*. Had Gilda remained an active part of her repertory, she might well have made the public revalue this role as it did Lucia. Again she uncovered an unsuspected dramatic dimension by making Gilda an innocent whom circumstance transforms into a woman. She fashioned the part at the outset as an ingénue, not a soubrette, using what has been termed her "little girl voice," a sound frequently heard in her *Sonnambula*, *Lucia*, and even in parts of *Traviata*.

This unmistakable sound was created by a brightening of her dark timbre with a very forward placement of vowels and with little of the covered mixture of vowels and consonants she used in weightier parts.

Act three was the turning point in Callas's portrayal; here her Gilda was changed by tragedy into a heroine. The opportunity for such dramatic expansion was always in the score, but Callas was the first to seize the possibility. Without a full dramatic sound in the part, a sense of the tragedy of Gilda is lost. Another entrée into Callas's thinking has been supplied by Teodoro Celli. Having listened to Callas's recording of *Rigoletto* several times, he was "struck by–among much else–one very brief 'accent,' four notes that Gilda sings in the second scene. The dramatic situation is familiar to everyone: The Duke having furtively entered the garden of Gilda's house, lingers in the girl's presence and ardently declares his love. And Gilda, disturbed, replies at first to the Duke's 'Io t'amo' with an invitation to that audacious gentleman to leave. The libretto's word is 'Uscitene.' That word from the already enamored girl resounds in Callas's voice with a strange coloration, between timid and ardent, a *mezza voce* of private innocence. It certainly expresses her infatuation, but I could not explain its effect to myself. So I asked Callas why she had given so very special an accent to a word of apparently small importance. Callas replied: 'Because Gilda says "Get out," but wants to say "Stay!"' Take note of what acute psychological justice there is in this intuition, how appropriate it is to the simultaneously ingenuous and passionate character of Verdi's heroine and to the motion of the drama, and how revealingly it is realized by means of that chaste vocal color. Such 'accents' tell much about the labor, the minute study Callas gives to the musical text before attempting to sing it."

Though Leonora in *La forza del destino* and Aida were the first Verdian roles sung by Callas, her development was best served by another, Abigaille. It was a role she sang only a very few times, but one for which again her voice and her training were particularly suitable. Only a personality geared to great emotional responses can bring this role fully to life, only an Isolde voice which commands *Puritani* can make complete sense of Abigaille's musical lines. Callas not only did both in her only contact with the role in Naples, 1949, but she compounded its difficulties by the inclusion of a full-throated high E-flat in the third-act confrontation with Nabucco.

It was in the period before *Nabucco* that Callas invaded Wagnerian territory. Though evidence of her time there is sparse, she has stated "Wagner is much easier than Verdi. He is clean-cut. From the beginning there is no doubt where the music and the drama will go. Take Brünnhilde; she is a heroine from the start. She never changes, there is really no delineation of character, her music poses no technical problems, there are no embellishments. She is one solid rock, never uncovered vocally. The orchestra is always so powerful under her that a singer feels secure. Isolde–I found her easy as well. She too is fortified by a tremendous orchestra, the notes are not extremely difficult, and the high notes are not all that many, not nearly as many as Norma, who sings far more music. Again there are few technical challenges, no fioriture. There is very little to it actually." In effect, Callas is echoing the sentiments of Lilli Lehmann, who once confessed she would rather sing all three Brünnhildes in an evening than one Norma.

Callas created no lasting association with Wagner, but her influence was strongly felt in the arena of verismo. As surely as the works of the bel canto mirrored the mood of romanticism, the operas of Puccini and Giordano reflected the turn-of-the-century theater as it attempted to portray life as it exists rather than life as it had earlier been idealized. There was no room in verismo for the conventions which had served opera through the middle of the nineteenth century–the structure of aria and cabaletta, trills, arpeggios, scales, and other decorations. The truth of verismo, by necessity, was of a different, more aggressive, and explicit sort, and in reducing plot and circumstance to essentials, the movement created a new type of singer, one who thought in eighth and quarter notes rather than in sixteenths and thirty-seconds.

There is a certain irony in that Callas was introduced to Italy not in a bel canto role but in Ponchielli's *La Gioconda*, an opera often cited as the gateway to verismo. Like *Aida*, *Gioconda*'s figures are straightforward and without complexity. What depth of conflict exists is to be found in Gioconda herself, but it is of the most obvious sort; even her death is anti-climactic. The opera is, however, a sturdy platform for full-bodied singing from a quintet of principals. The springboard of Callas's performance was the enormous emotions of the title role, emotions she colored with almost neon vividness. The sharpness of attack in phrases and the inevitability of their direction gave her Gioconda a stark quality. It seems inconceivable that the breadth of sound and the dark, menacing colors of Callas's Gioconda came from the same throat which so well conveyed the rapture and innocence of Gilda.

Despite the satisfaction Gioconda gave Callas, it did not play that great a part in her career. More significant were her appearances as Tosca. Callas has expressed her disdain for Tosca as well as for the music of Puccini. Yet, the role remains closely identified with her. It was her first major part with the Athens Opera at the age of eighteen, and it was as Tosca that she made her last operatic appearance before a self-imposed exile of eight years. Callas's reservations about the role must center in part on its lack of opportunity for the sort of cantabile singing found in bel canto operas. Also Tosca's one aria, "Vissi d'arte," is a meditation which holds up the stream of drama. Tosca's redeeming virtue is that she is the opera's protagonist. The drama swirls about her as though she were the eye of a hurricane, except there is no calm within Tosca herself. She is in a constant state of flux, her inner crisis matching the larger storm without. Callas's Tosca was at its best a total theatrical experience. Though she captured the role's full-bodied emotion, it was the small brushstrokes of detail which made her portrait so finished. Where as Gilda she unfolded the woman in the child, as Tosca she highlighted childish aspects within the woman. The possibilities of contrast again fired Callas's imagination, for this Tosca was fearful of her love with Cavaradossi and fiercely protective of that same love in conflict with Scarpia. It was the interplay and mixture of these two aspects of character which made the woman rather than the prima donna emerge and turned Callas's Tosca into so intimate an experience.

The same contrast distinguished her Turandot, a role which accounted for a good measure of Callas's early reputation in Italy. As Turandot, she offered not only the ice of the character but the fire which burns underneath, vouchsafing in turn more a sense of the woman within the princess than others have chosen to reveal. Her Turandot also demonstrated how exactingly Callas sang on the word and found the necessary tint or accent to portray a dramatic thought. Her voice often seemed like a vessel which could be filled or drained to various levels of intensity at will. The tap which controlled this flow was the text; this was as true of her Butterfly as of her Turandot.

Many singers have understood in varying degrees the potential of Madama Butterfly. Given a basic sympathy for the role's drama, a certain success is guaranteed, for much of the character's veracity and appeal were built into its music by Puccini. Yet few have carried Butterfly to such compelling heights as Callas. Her Cio-Cio-San was a composite of previous dramatic factors: Amina's innocence and quiet devotion, Gilda's metamorphosis and betrayal, and Violetta's passion and sacrifice. Not only did these dramatic pieces form a new character mosaic, but vocal elements from each were employed as well. If there was one dominant source, it was Gilda, whose transition from maiden to woman in Callas's voice parallels the same transition in Butterfly. Yet the whole of Butterfly is strikingly different from its parts. The tragedy of Puccini's geisha is a private one; even the maid Suzuki is kept on its perimeter. Callas defined this dramatic premise in inward, concentrated terms, reaffirming her gift of acclimatizing herself to a specific theatrical terrain.

While Callas sang three performances of Butterfly onstage, she performed Mimì in *La Bohème* only in the recording studio. Medeas will always be in short supply, but there has never been a scarcity of Mimìs, and this is doubtless why Callas was never asked to sing this loveliest of Puccini heroines onstage. Yet, her portrayal is affecting, and a comparison between her singing of Violetta's intimate moments and virtually every moment of her Mimì is inescapable. It seems certain her experience in *Traviata* supplied the truth for *Bohème*. The facts that Violetta and Mimì are young, French, of a certain morality, and consumed by the same disease probably linked them less in Callas's mind and throat than did the fate they shared in common. Mimì, of course, contains none of the musical complexities of Violetta, nor is she so fully drawn a character. Looking at her story and music dispassionately, if such is possible, she is forthright and of a single color. Yet, within this confine, Puccini fashioned a nature so sympathetic that Mimì makes the most direct appeal possible to a listener's sensibilities. This appeal is what Callas so thoroughly exploited.

Another Puccini role sung only for records was Manon Lescaut. Though Callas's voice was not at its steadiest when the set was made, she conveys a full sense of the poignancy of Abbé Prévost's heroine. Too often, this Mediterranean Manon is sung with a gusto more suitable to Tosca. The simplicity of line and gentleness of tone in all but Callas's top notes touchingly suggest more of Manon's vulnerability than of her fickleness, and this seems to have been uppermost in Puccini's mind as well. As critic Edward Greenfield said in summing up the Callas Manon, she "injects the last degree of emotion without disturbing the rhythm or shape of the vocal line, yet there is no stiffness at all and the singing sounds entirely spontaneous."

Apart from Puccini, Callas's performances in the verismo repertory were less consistent. Her undertaking of Maddalena in *Andrea Chénier*, for example, was an oddity with not much to distinguish her well-sung performance from any other. Countering this is the surprise of her Nedda in *Pagliacci*, another role she sang only for the microphone. In recent years, the role has usually gone to a light soprano who makes the character, if any sense of personality is imparted, more giddy than not. Callas, however, created (once past an oversung "Ballatella") a willful young woman filled almost to the bursting point with life ("piena di vita," as Nedda herself puts it). Here, as in her singing of Santuzza in *Cavalleria rusticana*, the music was not slurred or slighted in building the role, yet the dramatic values remained as forceful as the musical ones. In this sense, Callas's singing was as much a model for verismo as it was for bel canto.

No consideration of Callas's repertory would be complete without mention of her single French role, Bizet's *Carmen*. Carmen was also a part she never sang onstage, and it raises a question which remains without answer. When Callas recorded *Carmen*, the operatic world was at much the same impasse with French opera as it had been with bel canto opera when she first sang *Puritani*. It is intriguing to speculate on the fate of Massenet and Meyerbeer had Callas turned her energy and gifts in their direction. She possessed an uncommon affinity for French music, and her trademarks of legato and expression stayed intact when singing in French. Instinct must have told her singing on vowels was no less a consideration here than in Italian. Many singers have tried to make the public believe French music should be crooned, spoken, or even whispered, when it is music to be sung with a full and legitimate tone. Baritone Pierre Bernac, so expert in this area, has said that, without a command of bel canto, without the ability to sing Handel and Mozart, a singer cannot deal properly with French music.

Carmen was a role which had long been urged on Callas, and she no doubt responded as much to its challenge as she did to its rewards. Apart from Norma, no role has so intrigued singers. Sopranos (lyric and dramatic), mezzo-sopranos, and contraltos have sung the part with varying success, and Callas was not the first singer whose repertory embraced both Norma and Carmen. The prime example of this duality was Lilli Lehmann, who sang the two roles at the Metropolitan Opera. In this century one can point to Ponselle, Dusolina Giannini, and, more recently, Beverly Sills. It is not difficult to understand the obsession with Carmen which has attracted such diverse singers as Ernestine Schumann-Heink, Geraldine Farrar, and Maria Jeritza to attempt to conquer the role. The part is extremely popular with the public and it allows a singer to run a gamut of dramatic impulses and moods with unprecedented individuality.

Callas would be the first, however, to proclaim that singing Carmen was a lark after Norma, for Bizet's elusory gypsy has none of Norma's lofty musical challenges and technical requirements. Indeed, Carmen's music has been abused with enormous success. It is the drama of Carmen and her mercurial nature which exert so strong a pull. In Callas's voice, Carmen became a bright, defiant, healthy creature. She was also very French in attitude, given Callas's fastidiousness of voice and language. More than any other, Callas made one feel Don José was (in Carmen's mind) an interlude in which her vanity was wounded rather than a culminating affair in which her destiny was sealed. Of course, singing Carmen on records is a different matter from acting her onstage—in a very real sense, it avoids the part's ultimate challenge. Yet so luminous is Callas's recorded Carmen that it remains compelling on its own.

Given so wide a repertory and her complete involvement with her roles, there is no doubt Callas demanded more from her voice than it could comfortably deliver. Even de Hidalgo felt "Maria abused her God-given gifts." But this was a fate she shared with Viardot, who late in life remarked to a student, "Don't do as I did; I wanted to sing everything and I ruined my voice." Callas and Viardot, however, shared in common an intense commitment to music. Indifference or compromise was not a part of their makeup. One might prefer Callas in one role to another and she may seem entirely wrong for a certain opera or style of opera, but she could not be accused of being half-hearted or careless in performance. Director Franco Zeffirelli feels, "Maria is a stupid woman, so professional that if she cannot cope with all the notes written or expected, she will not do a piece. This is a crime. She could have done so many more *Norma*s if she had cheated a bit; but she couldn't accept the principle. Dancers do, even great dancers. Look at Margot Fonteyn. Why deprive the audience, a new generation, of certain things because you cannot cope with a few notes?" Rescigno also recalls her uncompromising nature. At a rehearsal for Bellini's *Il pirata* in Carnegie Hall in 1959, he took the stretta of the first-act finale at an unusually brisk tempo. It was a tempo which "required a machine gun rather than a singer. Maria looked at me a bit frightened when her solo passage was coming up, and she didn't make it. I told her next time around I would put on the brakes just before her entry. 'No, don't do that,' she countered. 'I like the tempo very much; it is very valid, and I don't want you to help me.' 'Well,' I said, 'what if you don't make it in the performance?' 'That's my business, not yours,' she answered. However, out of that fantastic willpower of hers came this superb, exciting thing at the performance, all in order. This woman was uncompromising when it came to music. I have seen her undergo the anguish of not singing good notes, but, however the note, she had to do what the music demanded. She had thought it out in a certain way and was not going to give in. This takes guts and a tremendous amount of artistic integrity." Of course, had Callas put herself in less peril, had she taken fewer chances or greater care, she would not have been Callas. You do not achieve as she achieved by halfway measures. Beverly Sills understands this very well: "I would rather have ten sensational years like Callas than twenty years like another," she has remarked.

For one full decade—the 1950s—Callas's voice and expressive powers were in their finest balance. Her apprentice years (and an understandable amount of rough and even wild singing) were behind her, and the eventual decay of her voice was yet to come. It was during this same period that she also undertook a prodigious loss of weight, becoming as convincing to the eye as to the ear. Callas had long sensed her bulk posed a deterrent to what she wished to achieve as a singing actress. This concern became insistent as she entered the bel canto, bella donna repertory, leaving behind Aida, Turandot, and her Wagner roles where the emphasis was more on voice than appearance. The final determination to correct this physical flaw came with her first Medea, in Florence, in 1953.

To Callas, her jawline was too soft and rounded for the sharp look she felt Medea needed. She tried expedients of makeup—darkening the area under the chin and cheeks—but realized that this only minimized the problem without solving it and was, to her mind, dishonest. At the same time, she was hungry for acceptance offstage as a woman. The two needs fused, forcing her to embark on a strict diet. In the next year and a half, she shed some seventy pounds (and brought into being the glamorous figure of today). The transformation was completed by the time of her American debut and her first Scala collaboration with Visconti.

Many have ascribed the tenuousness in Callas's upper register as the price she paid for her great loss of weight. But this is too facile a conclusion. At times her top was as precarious when she was heavy as it was rock-solid when she was slim. Much more than weight was involved in whether her upper voice responded to her wishes. The inherent characteristics of her voice, her juxtaposition of repertory, the approach to a particular note, her health (for Callas has been plagued with draining physical problems throughout her career), and her state of mind all combined to contribute to the problem.

More was gained than was lost, however, by her physical transformation. With it came new confidence in her appearance and new expressiveness and security in her acting. Callas seen, to be sure, is not as precisely explained as Callas heard, for her legacy in sound through recordings is as steady as memory is unstable. Yet, there are dramatic qualities which persist, because in every instance they are linked indelibly to musical values. Callas as an actress made one listen more directly than ever before and drew one into closer contact with the score. Like her singing, her acting was of a single piece and remarkable in its concentration. She used her body and face as much as her voice to convey what she found within the text and music, for as she searched to justify a vocal color or capsule a dramatic sentiment, so she labored for a gesture to achieve the same end. The results were neither choreographic nor balletic, but there was no mistaking that sight and sound had been fused into a single expressive unit.

Three things come to mind when I summon a mental image of Callas: her eyes, her hands, her walk. Callas's face was not beautiful in the conventional sense, but it was better than beautiful for the needs of the theater. Offstage, her eyes, mouth, and nose have a quality of exaggeration. But these very proportions were what made it possible for her face to speak so eloquently from the stage of even the largest opera house. People who saw her from the upper reaches of La Scala or the Metropolitan Opera are still able to describe details—a spark or tear in her eyes—with the accuracy of one sitting downstairs. This facial projection had all the immediacy of a cinematic close-up. Callas knew the power of her eyes so well she was able to build the climax of the murder scene in *Tosca* around a single look. As Scarpia prepared the safe-conduct pass for Cavaradossi, Callas, breathing heavily, stood by the supper table, poured a glass of wine, and drank it desperately. She stopped for an instant to catch her breath and then froze, her eyes riveted on the table. In that moment, the power of her glance made it clear she had seen the knife and was deliberating the murder of Scarpia. As her eyes remained locked on the knife, only her hand with the glass moved. Though only a matter of seconds, it seemed an eternity as her hand traveled the distance from her lips to the table. Callas then turned calmly and slowly, her back to the audience as Scarpia approached. From seemingly nowhere an arm shot upward, the knife flashed for a second and plunged. As Scarpia fell, she stood above him stabbing the air, her eyes wide and wild, fiercely willing him dead.

Oddly enough, one noticed Callas's mouth most when she was not singing. Then, it so often shaped itself into a peculiar half-smile, a bemused look as though she sensed an irony which had escaped the rest of us. This look had about it all the enigmatic beauty writers have long ascribed to Leonardo's Gioconda. It was easier to digest those snarled, black looks that accompanied the rages of Medea or Norma than this simpler, infinitely more mysterious glance.

When one wasn't mesmerized by her face, one was held by her arms and hands. They too sang with a range of mood and accent comparable to those in her voice. When she spread her arms full, and usually with a slight arch in her wrists, her long, slim fingers seemed to extend from stage left to stage right, so powerful was the gesture. She usually kept the fingers of her open hand tightly together, so that the line of her arm came to a single, fine point rather than a diffused or blunted one. Yet she could also contract her arms and hands to the most intimate of gestures and frequently wrapped herself in them, cradling her body as she sang. Except in moments of extreme urgency, Callas moved almost as in slow motion. When she moved more forcefully, it was not so much a walk as a lanky stride of strong, decisive steps (a "Gary Cooper lope," one writer termed it). But more often she stood still, knowing full well the effectiveness of making the drama, Mohammed-like, come to her.

Though director Sandro Sequi did not work with Callas in a production, he watched her performances with the trained eye of a man who thinks music in terms of movement. To him, "she was never in a hurry. Everything was very paced, proportioned, classical, precise. Probably this was her Greek origin, I mean the history behind her which came out. When one has seen Callas only in photographs and not onstage, you might think she was like a crazy woman in *Medea*, for example, running around the stage and shouting. Not at all. She was extremely powerful but extremely stylized. Her gestures were not many, if you consider the whole interpretation of a role. I don't think she did more than twenty gestures in a performance. But she was capable of standing ten minutes without moving a hand or finger, compelling everyone to look at her."

This gift of acting without movement, of commanding a stage while immobile, belonged to George London as well,

Callas's Scarpia in *Tosca* at the Metropolitan in 1956. He has explained the force as "an inner spiritual and artistic motor, something which is always running and is part of an internal identification with character. That kind of energy, which is an energy of the mind and spirit, has an irresistible thrust into an audience. But to work, it requires an innate dramatic personality. You can't teach it to someone. It's like talent. How do you teach that? You can teach the superficial aspects of what must be enacted, but you cannot create a Callas out of Miss X, even if she were to do in every detail what Callas did in a given situation onstage, because it came from Callas's inner strength and that cannot be fabricated."

Lucia,
La Scala, 1954, with
Herbert von Karajan

Franco Zeffirelli, who directed Callas in five productions, felt Herbert von Karajan (stage director and conductor for her Scala Lucias) most successfully capitalized on this quality. "Karajan didn't even try to direct," Zeffirelli remembers. "He just arranged everything around her. She did the Mad Scene with a follow-spot like a ballerina against black. Nothing else. He let her be music, absolute music. It was the best you could do with Callas. I think he was the only one who really got it. With someone like Sutherland, I had to do the opposite in *Lucia*, make a tremendous scene, have her chase the image of Edgardo, run diagonally up and down steps, head up, head down—she did it all. She was sensational because she could also cope vocally; there were no limits. But you could not stop for more than thirty seconds on the still image of Sutherland. Her head is very large, very ugly. But Callas—you could spend years looking at her. It was tremendous, that half-smile of hers, the mouth, the eyes. She was enchanting, living music, the perfect illumination of the music. No director taught her this, she was born with it, she found this way of trusting herself, the right gesture, the right moment, not one motion more or less than was necessary. She somehow knew the incredible trick of achieving the maximum with a minimum of effort.

"You know, when you work with people you adore, you worship, like Maria, Elizabeth Taylor, or Anna Magnani, you want to see the things you love in them come out. So I, at least, don't have that perverse instinct of destroying like, unfortunately, Pasolini did in his film of *Medea*. He destroyed Maria, tried to make her look different from what she is. I adored her, and I wanted her to be at her best. So everything I did was to emphasize her qualities. I never dreamt of showing her a gesture or anything like that. I always fed her imagination with visual images. When we did *Traviata* in Dallas, I was very young at the time, rather immature and innocent. I went to her full of beautiful conceptions and words. She would listen to me but didn't react to anything. I could tell she wanted something more. So, I had a picture of a girl of the 1840s blown up, and I gave it to her in a silver frame. She looked at it, and she understood. You know, the less you speak to artists, actors, or actresses, the less you fill their minds with 'concepts,' the less you look for trouble. You must give them very precise and very clear, simple essential indications—love, hate, happiness, resentment—whatever you like, but it must be as for children. Beyond that, they are their own personalities. How much can you change a Callas in a production? Ninety percent of what goes onstage is what she has accumulated through the years. It's what has been given by God. A director can build something around her, make her go in one direction or another, but she will remain herself.

"The magic of a Callas is a quality few artists have, something special, something different. There are many very good artists but very few who have that sixth sense, the additional, the plus quality. It is something which lifts them from the ground; they become like semigods. She had it, Nureyev has it, Olivier. But Olivier is also a case of an extremely rich knowledge of everything. He is completely coherent in life, onstage. Whatever he does is part of a complete personality. Maria is a common girl behind the wings, but when she goes onstage, or even when she talks about her work or begins to hum a tune, she immediately assumes this additional quality. For me, Maria is always a miracle. You cannot understand or explain her. You can explain everything Olivier does because it is all part of a professional genius. But Maria can switch from nothing to everything, from earth to heaven. What is it this woman has? I don't know, but when that miracle happens, she is a new soul, a new entity."

It is disheartening that the one existing film of Callas in performance is the second act of Zeffirelli's 1964 *Tosca* production at Covent Garden. While its uniqueness gives the document importance, the camera work is poor; it tends to stay on whoever is singing at a given moment, and Callas was often at her most exciting and involved when reacting to another. This was particularly true of her scenes with Tito Gobbi as Scarpia, one of her few colleagues who was also her peer. The powerful interplay which existed between this mighty pair is only suggested by the film.

There had been earlier efforts to capture Callas on film–the operatic Callas, not the Callas of Pier Paolo Pasolini's *Medea*, a different and lesser matter. The idea of a film dates to 1958 with the Zeffirelli *Traviata* which was cinematic in style, based on the principle of flashback. Beginning with that production, Zeffirelli tried to persuade Callas to make a film with him, but she was hesitant to enter so foreign a medium. Then, in 1961, when she once again sang Medea at La Scala, a proposal was made to film the production. This too failed. Finally, in 1964 after the London *Tosca*, Callas agreed to do a film version of the Puccini work, to be made on location in Rome with Gobbi as Scarpia and Edmund Purdom (plus the voice of Carlo Bergonzi) as Cavaradossi. The sound track was recorded, and Callas began to prepare herself dramatically with film experts.

Meanwhile, Zeffirelli arranged wide distribution to assure there would be no undue worries over production costs. But what Zeffirelli had not arranged for, Karajan had: the rights to film *Tosca* from Puccini's publisher, Ricordi. The German firm of Beta, of which Karajan was artistic director, suggested a joint collaboration between itself and the Zeffirelli-Callas team, but Callas rejected the partnership. Aristotle Onassis is said to have offered to buy Beta's rights to *Tosca*, but the company was not interested unless Karajan was retained as conductor. This Callas would not countenance; the soundtrack had already been completed, with Georges Prêtre conducting. Thus, the entire project foundered, and all that remains is the soundtrack which E.M.I.–Angel Records later issued commercially. In Zeffirelli's mind, the "real loser was the audience, because what remains? When we see something such as the Mona Lisa of Leonardo, we don't ask what was the agony, or what happened behind the making of the painting. We just look at it. What matters is that we have it. We don't have such a painting of Maria. We missed the historical opportunity of preserving this woman's art."

Tosca,
London, 1964, with
Franco Zeffirelli

THE LIFE

Maria Callas has a reputation as a fighter, but those who know her well have found that she is surprisingly shy and, in many unsuspected ways, insecure. To this day, she often masks her insecurities with the cover of aloofness.

Much of her uncertainty can be traced to childhood, when she was overweight and felt herself in competition with an older sister for their mother's affection. The third child of Evangelia and George Kalogeropoulos, Callas was born Cecilia Sophia Anna Maria at Fifth Avenue Hospital in New York City only a few months after the family's emigration from Greece. Shortly before the family left Athens, a three-year-old son had died. Evangelia desperately hoped for another boy for the life just beginning in America. The birth of Callas on December 3, 1923, was a profound disappointment, and at first the mother refused to see the baby. Though she eventually accepted the new daughter, it must have been dismaying to see the child grow up at first in a shapeless and clumsy manner.

By the age of eight, Maria had begun piano lessons and showed herself to be unusually gifted musically. Even before formal study began, she would pick melodies out on the piano; by the age of ten she sang arias from *Carmen* and a few ballads, including "La paloma" and a song called "The Heart Is Free." Evangelia started to promote her younger daughter's talent with the classic zeal of a stage mother; this led to the first of many arguments with her husband concerning the child. George Callas–for he had shortened the family name after arriving in America–felt Maria was being pushed too quickly. The mother's ambition, however, overrode her husband's objections, and this ambition soon became as necessary to Maria's identity as to Evangelia's. Not only did singing provide an outlet for gaining her mother's approval and attention, but it was a means of combating a shy, introverted nature–partly brought on by the quarrelsome nature of her parents–and the embarrassment of thick-lensed glasses. (Callas, unable to tolerate contact lenses, still wears heavy glasses in private.) Singing also took Maria's mind off her weight. "My sister Jackie was a beautiful girl," she has said, "but I was very fat and full of pimples. I was also much too mature for my age and not very happy. I certainly was the ugly duckling."

In 1934, in Chicago, Callas took part in a nationwide amateur contest hosted by Jack Benny. She lost to an accordion player but was given a wristwatch as a consolation prize. During this time, Mary Ann, as she was then called, attended public school in New York's Washington Heights and there won a role in the school's production of *H.M.S. Pinafore.* Other contests followed, including the Major Bowes Amateur Hour. In 1937, Evangelia, still the central force behind Callas's growing ambitions as a singer, decided to return to Greece with her two daughters. In Athens, Maria's voice could be properly trained and her life directed without George Callas's objections.

Evangelia,
Maria,
Jackie, and
George Callas,
New York,
1924

Maria was thirteen and had just finished eighth grade when she and her mother arrived in Greece. (Jackie preceded them by a few months.) Evangelia attempted to have Maria admitted to the prestigious Athens Conservatory, but she was too young. By falsifying Maria's age as sixteen, admission was obtained to the city's lesser National Conservatory. Callas's teacher there, Maria Trivella, was a singer of no great importance, but she was quick to recognize the exceptional abilities of her new student. After a year of daily one-hour lessons, Trivella presented Callas in the school's annual showcase recital and entered her in the proficiency exams of the National Conservatory. Callas won a prize and made her first operatic appearance, singing Santuzza in a student performance of *Cavalleria*. She was fifteen years old.

After two years with Trivella, Callas again auditioned for the Athens Conservatory. This time she was accepted, at the insistence of de Hidalgo, but on a probationary arrangement because of her age. Elvira de Hidalgo became her teacher and the major influence—apart from Evangelia—on Callas during the years in Greece. De Hidalgo, a specialist in the bel canto repertory and a former member of the Metropolitan Opera, had arrived in Athens as prima donna of a touring opera company. Like Callas, she had been trapped in Athens by the war. Unable to leave Greece, she accepted a post at the Athens Conservatory.

De Hidalgo keenly remembers her first encounter with Callas: "The very idea of that girl wanting to be a singer was laughable! She was tall, very fat, and wore heavy glasses. When she removed them, she would look at you with huge but vague, almost unseeing, eyes. Her whole being was awkward and her dress was too large, buttoned in front and quite formless. Not knowing what to do with her hands, she sat there quietly biting her nails while waiting her turn to sing."

However, when Callas sang—"Ocean, thou mighty monster" from *Oberon*—de Hidalgo heard "violent cascades of sound, not yet fully controlled but full of drama and emotion. I listened with my eyes closed and imagined what a pleasure it would be to work with such material, to mold it to perfection." This meeting marked the beginning of a five-year association during which Callas threw herself into her studies with insatiable curiosity and trenchant, possessed determination. There was no room in her life for anything but music. She arrived early at the Conservatory each day, heard the other lessons de Hidalgo taught, took her own and was among the last to leave, often walking home with her teacher. De Hidalgo quickly sensed the burning need for acceptance in her protégée and gradually became as much a friend as a teacher, spending extra time with Callas, answering her torrent of questions about music and the world of opera.

During the years with de Hidalgo, Callas first came into intimate contact with the bel canto repertory, as well as with an enormous range of literature not associated with her—songs of Schubert and Brahms, the *St. Matthew Passion* of Bach and the *Stabat Mater* of Pergolesi, Purcell's *Dido and Aeneas*. De Hidalgo had Callas appear in a student performance of act three of *Un ballo in maschera*, and in 1940 gave her the title role in the Conservatory production of Puccini's *Suor Angelica*, which de Hidalgo staged herself. The same year (she was seventeen), with de Hidalgo's help, Callas secured her first professional engagement and made her formal debut in a production by the Royal Opera of Franz von Suppé's *Boccaccio*, taking the small role of Beatrice. Her mother recalls that she "sang and danced in a barrel!" Two years later, her first major chance came when a soprano of the Royal Opera, who was scheduled to sing Tosca, fell ill. Callas took the part on short notice and sang some twenty *Tosca*s altogether in a makeshift outdoor theater.

Elvira
de Hidalgo
as Rosina
in *Il barbiere
di Siviglia*,
La Scala, 1916

Leonore
in *Fidelio*,
Athens,
1944

Life grew increasingly difficult during the German and Italian occupation, with food in short supply. Callas gave recitals in Athens and Salonika for opera-loving soldiers in exchange for spaghetti and vegetables. "I knew real privation then," she later recalled. "We were poor and miserable, we lacked clothing and food which became more scarce daily. It was then that I suffered." During this trying period and later, as civil war followed the withdrawal of enemy troops, the Royal Opera managed to continue, off and on. Callas added the roles of Marta in d'Albert's *Tiefland* and Leonore in *Fidelio* and sang in the world premiere of *Ho Protomastoras*, by Manolis Kalomiris, then head of the Athens Conservatory.

In 1945, Callas decided to return to the United States. (Her mother has written that the American Embassy in Athens urged her to return because they felt she was in danger of losing her citizenship; yet Callas was a natural-born American.) When she arrived in New York in July, she severed for all practical purposes her mother's dominant influence. Eventually there would be a total and violent break between mother and daughter which would be headlined in the press, creating a rancor toward Callas that still persists. De Hidalgo, however, was to continue to influence Callas and to be a force during her La Scala period and, later, during her vocal difficulties in the 1960s.

Before a year had passed in New York, Callas had auditioned for Edward Johnson, then general manager of the Metropolitan Opera, who found her voice "impressive" and offered her a contract to sing Madama Butterfly and Leonore in

Fidelio, which Callas refused. She believed herself physically too large for *Butterfly* and would not sing *Fidelio* in English as Johnson required (that assignment eventually went to Regina Resnik). Later Johnson admitted Callas "was right in turning it down; it was frankly a beginner's contract. But she was without experience, without repertory. She was also quite overweight, but that didn't come into our thinking at all—the young ones are usually too fat."

There were other auditions (with Gaetano Merola of the San Francisco Opera) and a good deal of advice (from Giovanni Martinelli, among others), but no concrete engagements. Meanwhile, Callas met an opera-loving lawyer, Edward Bagarozy, whose wife, Louise Caselotti, was a professional singer and vocal coach. The couple sensed the potential of Callas's voice, though both felt it rough on top and in need of equalizing. Caselotti offered to work with the young artist to help eliminate the faults she heard; Callas accepted and an intense period of study followed. Listening to his wife and Maria at work rekindled a long-held dream of Bagarozy's, an opera company of his own. He now had a dual reason for turning his dream into a reality. Moreover, with the war over, there was also a wealth of talent to be tapped abroad.

Bagarozy began in earnest to formulate repertory and to engage singers for his United States Opera Company. In a short while he had assembled an impressive lineup—including Nicola Rossi-Lemeni, Cloe Elmo, Max Lorenz, and Mafalda Favero—and had settled on *Turandot* as the company's opening production. Chicago, then without resident opera, was chosen as the site for the debut of the United States Opera and of "Marie Calas" (as she was announced in the newspapers). But at the last moment, hoped-for backing failed to materialize and Bagarozy's dream toppled while *Turandot* was still in rehearsal. From the disaster, however, came a meeting between Callas and retired tenor Giovanni Zenatello, the original Pinkerton in *Madama Butterfly*. He had come to New York seeking singers for the second postwar season at the Verona Arena. Though he intended to engage Milanov for the title role in *Gioconda*, an audition with Callas settled the matter. So excited was Zenatello by Callas's voice, the veteran artist leaped up and joined her in an impromptu performance of the fourth-act duet "Enzo!...sei tu!" For her Enzo in Verona, Zenatello engaged another American at the outset of his career, Richard Tucker.

Opera is a keenly competitive business and however strong Callas's performances were in Verona, she lacked a reputation and was considered a beginner. Serafin, who conducted the Verona *Gioconda*, would eventually provide a breakthrough. Meanwhile, Callas met an aging industrialist who began to woo her in gallant fashion. Giovanni Battista Meneghini, a native of Verona, was thirty years Callas's senior, a stocky, unromantic figure, distinguished by a ruthlessness in business, tremendous vitality, and machine-gun speech. During their courtship and following their marriage in 1949, he supplied the funds and insulation with which Callas could bide her time as her reputation grew and her career took shape. Meneghini continued in this role until 1959, as the demand for Callas's voice spiraled skyward. He gave up his business to devote full time to her career. Callas soon became more than his wife. She was a mission, the same source of self-importance and purpose she had been for her mother.

Balancing the emotional and financial security offered by Meneghini was the unflinching belief of Serafin in Callas's gifts. The close relationship which existed between the two has been given many shadings, even to the unlikely suggestion of a Svengali-Trilby association. There is little doubt that, after de Hidalgo, Serafin was the greatest influence in molding Callas's musical outlook. Though she was aware of the bel canto repertory from de Hidalgo, it was Serafin who led her to it, and his power in the Italian theaters provided most of her early engagements. The first of these was *Tristan und Isolde* at Teatro la Fenice in the fall of 1947. Though Callas did not know Isolde, when Serafin (remembering his impressive *Gioconda* of the preceding summer) offered the role, she quickly agreed to sing it. She had spent the months following Verona unsuccessfully making the rounds of agents in Milan. She was eager to sing again and if Serafin wanted her for Isolde, why not? An appointment was set to go over the role. Only after Callas had sight-read the second act did she admit she did not know Isolde. "So what?" snorted Serafin. "One month of study and hard work is all you need." *Tristan* was followed by a host of new roles sung for the first time under Serafin's baton and learned under his tutelage: Aida, Norma, Brünnhilde, Bellini's Elvira, Kundry, Violetta, and Rossini's Armida. Much later there would be Nedda and Manon Lescaut in the recording studio. Their artistic relationship lasted through Callas's 1960 recording of *Norma*, though it was principally restricted to recordings after 1953. At odds with Scala's management, Serafin did not share the triumphs of Callas there or elsewhere during the high-water period of her career.

Callas described Serafin at his death in 1968 as "an extraordinary coach, sharp as a *vecchio lupo* [sly fox]. He opened a world to me, showed me there was a reason for everything, that even fioriture and trills...have a reason in the composer's mind, that they are the expression of the *stato d'animo* [state of mind] of the character–that is, the way he feels at that moment, the passing emotions that take hold of him. He would coach us for every little detail, every movement, every word, every breath. One of the things he told me–and this is the basis of bel canto–is never to attack a note from underneath or from above, but always to prepare it in the face. He taught me that pauses are often more important than the music. He explained that there was a rhythm–these are the things you get only from that man!–a measure for the human ear, and that if a note was too long, it was no good after a while. A fermata always must be measured, and if there are two fermate close to one another in the score, you ignore one of them. He taught me the proportions of recitative–how it is elastic, the proportions altering so slightly that only you can understand it....But in performance he left you on your own. 'When I am in the pit, I am there to serve you because I have to save my performance,' he would say. We would look down and feel we had a friend there. He was helping you all the way. He would mouth all the words. If you were not well, he would speed up the tempo, and if you were in top form he would slow it down to let you breathe, to give you room. He was breathing with you, living the music with you, loving it with you. It was elastic, growing, living."

As revealing as her words are, the question remains: How many singers received Serafin's advice and how often had it produced results that transfigured performances? The answer, of course, is that such advice was often given and seldom were the results so deep as when Callas sang. Closer to the truth, Serafin brought out, reaffirmed, and reinforced what Callas felt intuitively. Had she been deprived of his musical counsel, she might not have made her way as quickly as she did, and certainly not as quickly to the bel canto repertory. But, she would not have been any less a musician left on her own. For at the mainspring of Callas's art has been an instinct about the shape and logic of music which she followed unerringly, more by her nose and heart than her mind.

The turning point of her career, however, was that week in Venice when she sang both Brünnhilde and Elvira, and the mastermind of that was Serafin. In the century before, such a feat would have seemed less sensational, given singers like Lilli Lehmann (an Isolde as well as a Queen of the Night) and Lillian Nordica (a Brünnhilde and a Lucia). In 1949, however, Callas's achievement seemed authentic and unprecedented, and she quickly became the talk of Italy. Radio Italiana invited her to demonstrate her versatility in a broadcast with arias by Wagner, Bellini, and Verdi. On the basis of that program, Callas cut three 78-rpm records for the firm of Cetra. These first commercial discs, issued in Italy in May, 1950, are the earliest known documentation of her voice, and on these are built the Callas legacy. She remained with Cetra only a short while, however, for Walter Legge (the husband of Elisabeth Schwarzkopf and an official of the enormous British combine that is Electrical and Musical Industries) heard Callas as Norma in Rome and spirited her to the E.M.I. labels.

Legge found Callas at a crucial moment. The record industry, just entering the LP era, was in its infancy in terms of packaging and promotion. Callas not only rode the crest of this new phonographic wave (as did Tebaldi on the Decca/London label), but she greatly contributed to its fortunes and its emergence as a mature artistic medium. Thanks to Legge's commitment and faith, she made between two and four complete opera recordings a year during her prime, and virtually all with Legge as producer. Too often even stereo recordings suggest rather than mirror the actuality of a voice. Fortunately, the recordings of Callas for E.M.I. in the 1950s capture with remarkable fidelity the tone and intent of her singing. Although performing in a studio for a microphone is quite a different matter from performing in an opera house before an audience, Callas projected more sense of the theater in her records than do most singers.

She felt in recording: "It takes a little more time to get into the role, but not very much more. In making a record you don't have the sense of projection over a distance as in an opera house. We have this microphone and this magnifies all details of a performance, all exaggerations. In the theater you can get away with a very large, very grand phrase. For the microphone you have to tone it down. It's the same as making a film; your gestures will be seen in close-up, so they cannot be exaggerated as they would be in a theater."

The month before the Cetra discs were issued, Callas made an unscheduled debut at Italy's foremost theater, La Scala in Milan. Her two performances as Aida, however, were as a last-minute substitute for Tebaldi rather than as a member of the company. Callas and Meneghini expected that a permanent contract would be offered after the final *Aida*, but press response had been indifferent and general manager Antonio Ghiringhelli remained silent. By this time, however, Callas did not need the cachet of La Scala to secure good engagements. Indeed, it soon became obvious that Scala needed Callas. Twenty months after the guest *Aidas*, and after she had refused a second guest appearance, Ghiringhelli capitulated, and Callas officially joined the company. Her formal debut inaugurated the 1951 season. The opera was Verdi's *I vespri siciliani*, and in the decade to come there would be five more opening nights: *Macbeth* (1952), *La vestale* (1954), *Norma* (1955), *Un ballo in maschera* (1957), and *Poliuto* (1960). Though she made her Covent Garden, Chicago, and Metropolitan debuts during the same period and continued to appear throughout Italy, Scala became her artistic home and the scene of her most significant achievements. Unlike other houses in which Callas sang at this time (with the notable exception of two short seasons in Dallas), Scala consistently mounted new, artistically conceived, carefully prepared productions for her. Paramount among these were those uniting Callas with stage director Luchino Visconti, a theatrical giant who exerted as great an influence on her art as did Serafin. Visconti had known of Callas for a long while and had been one of the sponsors behind the production of Rossini's *Il Turco in Italia*, which she sang in Rome in 1950. Though he did not work with Callas or in opera until the *Vestale* production, behind him were a knowledgeable and passionate love of music and a growing reputation as one of Italy's foremost film directors. As his fame increased, so did Scala's overtures, and Callas was the catalyst which finally brought him to the house for the first of their five collaborations. *Vestale* was followed by *Sonnambula*, *Traviata*, *Anna Bolena*, and *Iphigénie en Tauride*.

Like Serafin, Visconti sensed from the first the strength of Callas's instincts and quickly learned her spongelike ability to absorb a suggestion and flesh it out to a reality. Visconti has said that in working with Callas, his was "a freedom to operate within a general framework, but nevertheless a considerable freedom. I don't believe anyone can 'maneuver' someone like Callas without allowing her particular engine a greater number of revolutions than could be foreseen at rehearsals. I've always given her certain guidelines within which to work, certain objectives; but within those lines I've always allowed her to do what she wanted. A simple example is *La traviata*, act one, the moment when Violetta hears Alfredo's voice. I would tell her: Run downstage to the window, but *how* you run is up to you. And she would find her own way of doing it. Not only that, but once found, she would always execute the action in exactly the same way. Callas, you see, is one of those artists who, having once worked out and perfected a detail, doesn't keep changing it; they have no need to search for something different every time.

"Another example is the opening of Gluck's *Iphigénie en Tauride*. Callas would enter, walk up a very high staircase, suspended almost in midair; then she'd come tearing down again, during the famous storm, get to the footlights and begin to sing. All I had told her was to go to the top of the steps, stand there in the wind and come down again to the downstage position in time for the first note. That's all. I gave her no timings. But Maria has timing in her blood; it is absolutely instinctive. And you know how shortsighted she is! In the dark, those steps were marked only with white lines, but that was enough for her. Standing there in the wings I'd die a thousand deaths seeing her run like that, trailing twenty-five yards of cloak, with a wind-machine on her back, up the staircase and down again with split-second timing, *and* with enough breath left to start fortissimo dead on cue. You can only allow such things when you've got someone you know you can absolutely trust, because you know her sense of timing, her musical instinct, and her ability as a dramatic and tragic actress. I'm certainly not saying that you should use this method with every artist; but we are talking of Callas, and I would defy anyone to direct her differently. There are some directors, especially German ones—and great ones, too—who I believe would have some difficulty in keeping control over a Callas."

The public sees a prima donna, especially a great one, as arrogant, selfish, and uninterested in anything not directly connected with her own personal success. With Callas, Visconti felt "it would be difficult to imagine anything further from the truth. I have worked for years with actors in the theater and the cinema, with dancers and singers. I can only say Maria is possibly the most disciplined and professional material I have ever had the occasion to handle. Not only does she never ask for rehearsals to be cut down, she actually asks for more and works at them with the same intensity from beginning to end, giving everything she's got, singing always at top voice, even when the director himself suggests she shouldn't tire herself out and she need only indicate the vocal line. She's so involved in the total outcome of a production she gets irritated when a colleague is late. If being a prima donna means anything different from that, then Callas is no prima donna."

What Visconti has said in effect, and what those who work closely with Callas invariably learn, is that her "tempera-

Iphigénie,
La Scala, 1957,
with
Luchino Visconti

ment" is actually stubbornness rather than willfulness. She is impatient with those unwilling to give as much as she or reach as high. Her refusal to "make do" or compromise is as admirable as it can be frustrating. Of course, more is involved than standards and stubbornness. Callas literally and figuratively sees the world myopically and interprets everything—from news events to the weather—in terms of herself. Such ego is a means of insulation that every artist possesses to some degree. In Callas, it is as outsized as her talent, insecurities, and feelings. She tends to overreact, often to see things in an exaggerated manner. These instincts served her well in the theater but have often been her enemy in life. They were at the basis of many of the Callas "scandals" which rocked the world in the 1950s and which ultimately eroded the foundations of her career and her self-confidence at the very moment she was artistically at her most incandescent.

There had been Callas flare-ups from the start, as far back as her Athens days, when she was baptized in backstage jealousies and maneuverings. But most artists in the operatic or spoken theater have at one time or another locked horns with a colleague. This is taken as a matter of course in these volatile worlds, where emotions can overheat in seconds. Such sparks, when they flare out, are inevitably reported in the press; artists have always been good copy. Because Callas was Callas, with her strange and powerful chemistry, to ascribe mere "temperament" to her was not enough. To the press, and in turn the public, she became the "tigress," and this image found a face after her last performance in the 1955 Chicago Lyric Opera season. Having completed the final act of *Madama Butterfly*, an emotionally draining experience, she walked into the wings to be faced by a process-server who hit her on the arm with a summons on behalf of Bagarozy. Prior to the abortive United States Opera episode, Bagarozy had Callas sign an agreement giving him a percentage of future engagements he obtained. Callas maintained Bagarozy secured no engagements for her, therefore she owed him nothing. He thought otherwise. When rudely stuck by the summons, Callas exploded and flashbulbs popped. This picture, with her eyes blazing and the mouth flared, went around the world overnight. To the public, it summed up better than words the tempestuous, willful prima donna, the "tigress." Those who knew better took the matter as a momentary explosion. Midway between, Claudia Cassidy inquired: "Suppose she is capricious, formidable, self-centered? Does anyone think the average woman has what it takes to make a Callas?"

Perhaps the tag of "tigress" would have been dropped there had Chicago been an isolated case. But the next few years brought incidents which fanned the sparks of notoriety into a conflagration. On the eve of her Metropolitan Opera debut in 1956, Callas was featured on the cover of *Time* magazine, and the accompanying story chose to overplay the temperamental prima donna and underplay the musician. Two statements in the story—one anti-Tebaldi and the other anti-Evangelia—particularly contributed to a hostile audience the night of her debut. On Tebaldi, Callas was quoted as saying: "When I am angry, I can do no wrong. . . . I sing and act like someone possessed. But Tebaldi wilts. She's got no backbone. She's not like Callas." Evangelia was hit harder: "I'll never forgive her," Callas is quoted as saying, "for taking my childhood away. During all the years I should have been playing and growing up, I was singing or making money. Everything I did for them was mostly good and everything they did to me was mostly bad." *Time* went on to tell how, in 1951, Evangelia—living in Athens with Jackie on very little money—wrote Maria asking for $100, "for my daily bread." According to the magazine, Maria answered: "Don't come to us with your troubles. I had to work for my money, and you are young enough to work too. If you can't make enough money to live on, you can jump out of the window or drown yourself." Callas has steadfastly denied making this statement. In fact, for a long while Callas has contributed to the support of her mother and sister in Greece, as she did for her father until his death.

The following August, Callas, under strong pressure from the Scala management and against her doctor's wishes, agreed to participate in the company's visit to the Edinburgh Festival. Her doctor had certified her as exhausted, on the verge of collapse. Indeed, Callas had just returned from Athens, where heat and dryness had forced her to cancel one concert and had left her physically drained. But because the Edinburgh engagement was a prestigious one for Scala, it needed Callas's name, and at length, she consented to four performances of *Sonnambula*. So successful were these that, despite Callas's obvious vocal fatigue, Scala's management announced a fifth. It had no contract with Callas for the extra performance and, in fact, had Renata Scotto on hand as a cover. When Callas refused the additional Amina, the management pleaded, "You must save La Scala." Callas, however, knew she was too exhausted to save anyone. Recalling that moment, she has said: "When a singer pours as much energy and determination into a performance as I do, it is exhausting both physically and emotionally. Before a performance I am tense from the effort of preparing to give everything I can. During it, I am under the most severe self-control trying to deliver every note, every gesture exactly as it should be. It is an immensely difficult, an immensely tiring ordeal, and I cannot go through it when I have no strength left. I refused the request to 'save La Scala.' I did agree, for Scala's sake, that it could be said I was unable to sing the fifth performance because of indisposition certified to by a doctor."

When Callas left Edinburgh, the mayor of the city and his wife came to see her on her plane. Callas flew to Milan to rest and then attended a party given by her friend Elsa Maxwell in Venice. It was a tactical mistake, and matters were not helped when Maxwell touted Callas's appearance at the party in her column. Newspaper headlines proclaimed Callas had broken her contract and was "fleeing the country." In Italy the press condemned her for having "damaged" Scala's name. Scala's management should have come forward with a statement of the facts but said nothing.

Had it not been for Edinburgh, the next Callas crisis might never have taken place. Following Edinburgh, she was to make her debut in San Francisco as Lucia, and then to sing Lady Macbeth. Because she had unwisely undertaken Edinburgh and then a recording of *Medea*, she was now in no condition to sing in San Francisco. She cabled impresario Kurt Herbert Adler word of her indisposition and offered to come for the second month of his season. Adler, perhaps believing the adverse world press, not only canceled her contract but brought charges against her through the American Guild of Musical Artists for failing to appear as contracted.

It is ironic that Callas should have come under fire for cancellation, for she had a remarkable record for honoring contracts. Out of the prior 157 performances for which she had been engaged at La Scala, she had missed only two in six years, none in Chicago, and only one at the Metropolitan. Few singers have so clean a slate. In fact, in 1959, when scheduled for *Medea* in Dallas during a period of separation proceedings in Milan with her husband, she commuted between Italy and Texas (in the days before jet travel) in order not to miss a performance.

Eventually, AGMA released its ruling which stated Callas "would have been justified in not performing because of her physical and mental condition at the time. But the board further finds that...Callas did not rely entirely upon medical advice, and, in fact, indicated to the San Francisco Opera Association her willingness to perform during a portion of the period covered by the contract. In view of these circumstances...the board concludes that she was under an obligation to come to the United States at the time called for by her contract." In other words, AGMA felt all or nothing at all was in order, that Callas should have arrived in San Francisco whether she sang or not. Its verdict was in effect a draw.

Edinburgh and San Francisco, however, were only warm-up rounds before the main bout. This took place on the second day of January 1958. The new year broke with the blackest storm in Callas's career, an event which dogs her steps to this day. The setting was Rome's Teatro dell'Opera, and the occasion was *Norma* to inaugurate the new season. Before the evening was over, Callas might well have paraphrased Norma's final lines, saying, "Deh! Non volermi vittima del suo fatale errore."

Two days before the opening, Callas was in bed with a cold caught during rehearsals in the unheated theater. "The manager came to me," she recalls, "and said, 'Maria, you have to get better. You have to sing.' I did get better—well enough. I had medicine, and I phoned a nurse to say that I would probably need her help. I knew I could not be in my best possible voice, but it was an important opening in front of the president of Italy; if I had postponed, I would have been severely criticized anyway. I thought I could manage somehow. But I could not. The human voice is not like a piano. One can never be certain that it will do what it is meant to do. That night in Rome I sang the first act, but I could feel my voice slipping. I always have enemies in any audience, and I could hear them calling rude things: 'Go back to Milan!' 'You cost us a million lire.' Afterward some people said I left the performance because of this rudeness. Anyone who knows me knows this is ridiculous. Hisses and yells do not frighten me, for I am not a stranger to the enmity of claques. When my enemies stop hissing, I'll know I've failed. They only make me furious, make me want to sing better than ever to drive the rudeness down their throats. I do not leave a performance so long as I can sing. But that night in Rome I was unable to sing. My colleagues knew I could not continue, but after the first act the stage director and everyone else came to my dressing room and said, 'You must not stop.' They even tried to convince me that I had never sung better. This was absurd, but it was Rome's opening night and the opera house had no substitute ready.... Many singers have had colds during operas, and many of them have been substituted for during the performance. It happens all the time. The opera house must either have a substitute ready, or else it must take the responsibility. Rome did not do either one. At the end of the first intermission, instead of accepting responsibility and canceling the performance, they actually brought the president back to his box, thinking they could convince me that I should continue. When they finally realized that I would not sing with a lost voice, they said, 'All right, don't sing. But you are an actress. At least go out and act!' In some operas this might be possible, but *Norma* with a soprano who does not sing would be a travesty. I went home to bed.

Madama Butterfly,
Chicago, 1955,
with process-server;
Norma "walkout,"
Rome, 1958,
with Franco Corelli

"In the morning a doctor sent by the opera house examined me and reported that I had bronchitis and tracheitis but could possibly sing again in five or six days. The president's wife telephoned and said, 'Tell Maria we know she was sick and could not continue.' Unfortunately, she did not tell the newspapers. The newspapers demanded pictures of me sick in bed, but I am a serious artist, not a soubrette, and I do not pose for pictures in bed. I refused, and the newspapers decided that it would be more interesting to imply that I was perfectly healthy but had lost my nerve because of the insults. . . . My name was seriously damaged by this incident, and I still find it unjust that an artist who had great triumphs in Italy for eleven years should have to explain one cold and be condemned for it.

"It should not take much imagination or humanity to understand what I went through during that period. I was desperate and terribly hurt by the unkindness and the unfairness. It seemed impossible to clear my name, and in the papers I read nothing but insults and criticism. But two things happened after Rome which stirred me deeply. I returned to America to sing, first in Chicago, then at the Metropolitan. At both places, the first time I walked out on the stage wondering how I would be received after the destructive publicity, the public gave me an ovation before I sang a single note. Both times the ovations went on and on until I asked myself, how can I ever sing well enough to thank them? I will never forget those tributes for the rest of my life."

Like La Scala in Edinburgh, the Rome Opera remained silent, but this time Callas took action with a lawsuit against the house. After nearly a decade, she was awarded damages by an Italian court in 1965. Still the myth of the Rome "walkout" persists and is still cited in articles as proof of Callas's "capriciousness." People write and read what they wish to believe. This was certainly the case in 1956, when Callas appeared with George London in a scene from the second act of *Tosca* on the Ed Sullivan television show. "When I learned that I would sing Scarpia to Callas's Tosca," London has said, "I must admit I had a few forebodings. So much had been printed about this 'stormy' star that I was prepared for almost anything. 'Look, she can't do more than actually kill you in the second act,' my wife Nora said to me calmly. . . . 'What are you worried about?' My first rehearsal reassured me. Here was a trouper, a fanatic worker, a stickler for detail. . . . At one point during the dress rehearsal, after she had 'murdered' me, I fell too close to the desk and she couldn't pass to cross the stage and pick up the two candelabra which Tosca places next to the dead Scarpia. Callas stopped and announced to the director, 'There are just too many legs around here.' We had a good laugh; I fell thereafter so that she and her long train could pass, and that was that. Yet, the day after the telecast many newspapers reported that Callas and I had had a tiff during our rehearsals. I tried to tell my friends that this was just not so. But I finally gave up. For I realized that Callas, the prima donna reincarnate, fires not only the imagination of her audiences but also of the press. They want her to be 'tempestuous' and 'fiery' and that is the way it is going to be."

Director José Quintero, a man more of the legitimate than the operatic theater, has shed further light on the Callas "temperament." While making plans for new productions of *Cavalleria* and *Pagliacci* that he was to direct at the Metropolitan, he happened to be in "the back of the house when Callas arrived for a rehearsal of *Tosca*. She was in a state. She thought Bing would give her a piano rehearsal with the principals and then an orchestral rehearsal. But nothing of the sort. What she got was only a pianist and substitute singers. Of course, she blew her stack. But Bing was what Bing was. Once he made up his mind, there was no changing it, and he would give her no more. So they were at war. But their fight was much bigger than the actual one which took place between them. I don't think she got angry for Callas alone. She was fighting for every artist who sets foot onstage. She was condemning piecemeal work, the idea it was enough for people to buy tickets on the strength of her name and to hell with the production. She fought for a complete and integrated show that made dramatic sense, something she never got at the Metropolitan. She was right. This woman deserved more. Any director of consequence would be staggered by her singing and devastated by her dramatic presence. There was no movement that woman made that was not the essence of drama. Just her standing onstage before she sang a note was drama. And, of course, when a director is challenged by a presence like hers, he goes and wrestles with dramatic questions in a more fascinating way than he would with an ordinary artist. And this is how she wanted to work, for she didn't just sing her roles, she lived them. She and Martha Graham are two of the greatest actresses I have ever seen; both were of profound influence on me."

The Roman fiasco in 1958 was the beginning of the end of Callas's career in Italy. Returning to Scala after her second Metropolitan season, Callas sang five performances of *Anna Bolena* and five of a new role for her, Imogene in Bellini's *Il pirata*. During this period, from the beginning of April until the end of May, the difficulties which had been simmering between Callas and Scala came to the boil. Ghiringhelli had not spoken out on Callas's behalf in the matter of Edinburgh, and during her second season of *Bolena* made a point of not speaking to her at all. When the time arrived for the May *Piratas*, Callas was again not well and had to undergo an operation before her final week of performances. "Only my doctor and a few intimate friends knew about it," she remembers, "for by then I had learned that Callas is not allowed to postpone a performance or even to have a cold. For six days after the operation I was in pain, for I am allergic to narcotics and cannot have them. I had no sleep and almost nothing to eat. On the day after the operation I sang *Il pirata*." A week later was the final performance. "When the opera was over and the long ovations and curtain calls finished, while I was still onstage with my friends and the audience still in the house, the great iron fire curtain was suddenly rung down. I know of no single act in the entire repertoire of operatic insults as brutal as this one. It is a blunt, iron signal that says, 'Show's over! Get out!' But in case I and my friends had missed the point, a La Scala fireman appeared on stage to say, 'By order of the theater, the stage must be cleared.'"

To Callas, this was a period of such harassment and rudeness that the making of art became "physically and morally impossible. For my self-defense and dignity, I had no choice but to leave La Scala. La Scala did not 'dispense with my services,' I resigned." In resigning, she vowed to stay away as long as Scala was under Ghiringhelli's direction. Two years later, however, Callas patched up her difficulties with Ghiringhelli and returned in a new role, Paolina in Donizetti's *Poliuto*. Together with her final performances as Medea it provided a coda to her Scala career. These Scala performances—ten in all—were her last in Italy.

Between the Rome scandal and the Scala break there was a further and damaging eruption in Callas's career. It came in November 1958 in Texas where she was performing her first American Medea and the Zeffirelli *Traviata* with the fledgling Dallas Civic Opera. Callas, who had inaugurated the company with a concert the year before, had been brought to Dallas by Lawrence Kelly, a visionary impresario and a cofounder of the Chicago Lyric Opera (which Callas also launched). The Bagarozy incident in Chicago had been the tip of an iceberg of trouble within that company. Behind the scenes, the Lyric's cofounders were locked in struggle, with Kelly and Rescigno on one side and Carol Fox on the other. That story is part of Callas's story in that she cast her loyalty with Kelly. When he went to Dallas following the schism, Callas had chosen to sing there rather than Chicago.

In November 1958, just hours before her first Dallas *Medea*, a telegram arrived from Bing dismissing her from the Metropolitan. Her contract for its 1958–59 season had called for, among other things, the first Met production ever of

Macbeth, in which Callas was to appear with baritone Leonard Warren. This contention between Bing and Callas centered on her remaining repertory. Her contract called for *Tosca* and *Traviata*. She had already appeared with the Metropolitan in both productions and disliked them intensely. But her principal concern was not so much the Met's "shabby" *Tosca* or Oliver Smith's "lousy" *Traviata*, as she termed it, as it was alternating so heavy and dark a role as Lady Macbeth with Violetta which demanded lightness and flexibility. In his memoirs, Bing claimed Callas alternated repertory just as extreme in Dallas in 1958—Medea and Lucia—and with less time between performances than the Met offered. Bing is in error. During the period in question, the autumn of 1958, Callas was singing a Violetta-Medea pairing in Dallas, not Lucia and Medea. Nor were the two extremes mixed as Bing would have required, for Callas finished her Medea performances before going on to Violetta in 1958 or on to Lucia in 1959.

In the fall of 1958, after the Dallas season opened, Bing wired Callas, offering to switch *Traviata* for *Lucia* and demanding immediate confirmation. The telegram arrived during the *Medea* dress rehearsal and was not given to Callas until afterward. The next day she answered Bing, refusing the *Lucia*s; but before her telegram reached him, he dispatched a wire revoking her contract and, to the delight of the press, provoking a new scandal. To replace Callas in *Macbeth* Bing engaged Leonie Rysanek, paying a claquer to shout "Brava Callas" at Rysanek's first entry in hopes of arousing sympathy for the newcomer. This trick created further ill will for Callas at a time when she had a surfeit of it. It took far longer for Callas and Bing to mend their differences than it had for Callas and Ghiringhelli. Seven years later, when Callas finally returned to the Met, it was ironically enough in the same weary production of *Tosca* she had protested in 1958.

Il trovatore, Chicago, 1955, with husband Meneghini; with the Met's Rudolf Bing; with La Scala's Ghiringhelli

Though Callas had ridden out the worst storms of her career, other headlines were gathering. In 1959 she met Aristotle Onassis. Both were celebrated figures in their own worlds, and each held an immediate fascination for the other. Callas's fame and magnetism attracted Onassis, while Onassis offered a side of life previously unknown to Callas. She and Meneghini were invited for a summer cruise on Onassis's yacht; among the other guests were Sir Winston and Lady Churchill. In the beginning it was Sir Winston on whom the newspapers concentrated. But before the trip ended, the triangle of Callas-Meneghini-Onassis was the news. Less than two months after meeting Onassis, Callas left Meneghini and her life took a dramatic turn. She was caught up in the excitement she found with Onassis and his glamorous circle. "She had this stupid ambition of becoming a great lady of café society," Zeffirelli has reflected. "You have to go back to the difficult childhood this woman had to understand why she was always dreaming to reach certain positions. First there was that terrible husband of hers; they lived a very suburban, middle-class life. Onassis was a step higher."

"The world has condemned me for leaving my husband," Callas stated in *Life* magazine in 1965, "but I didn't leave him—he left me because I would not let him take care of my business affairs anymore. Battista himself said it was pointless if he had not complete power over me—that's all he wanted, I believe. I didn't want to marry an impresario, and if I had, I would have at least married a good one....I was kept in a cage so long that when I met Aristo and his friends, so full of life and glamour, I became a different woman. Living with a man so much older than myself, I had become prematurely dull and old. I got heavy like Battista thinking of nothing but money and position."

For the first time in her life there was no single strong person behind her career, urging her on, supplying artistic confidence (which, after Rome, she needed more than ever) and sustaining her. Though Onassis was entranced by the woman and impressed with her celebrity, Callas the artist and musician meant little to him. From 1960 to 1965, the year she began an eight-year break in her career, a gradual disintegration took place in the remarkable artistic machinery she had so carefully built and so scrupulously maintained over twenty-five years. There was a shrinking of both her range and her volume and what had been flaws of the moment became permanent faults. As her personal life altered and eventually took the upper hand, she curtailed her professional activity. The performances she gave (and there were more concerts than opera appearances) were traumatic as she attempted to cope with her own legend with increasingly limited means. At the time of the Paris *Normas* of 1964, Claudia Cassidy reflected that "this extraordinary woman is almost entirely self-made, as a great beauty and as the supreme exponent of a great and all but forgotten art whose Norma, Violetta, and Lucia a decade ago blazed a trail unique in our time. She can still sing magnificently when not challenging the stratosphere. Even there, sometimes when you have come least to expect it, the rocket booster works. Her voice still has that curiously poignant color...that to the devotee makes so many other voices pallid and wan. It can spin a pianissimo of the most ravishing texture and stab the heart in mezza voce.... It can also dry up, turn harsh and out of tune, and sound desperately forced in the merciless tessitura of Bellini bel canto, painfully pinched in the acrobatics of fioriture....Must we settle for this, who have such dazzling memories? Is her voice irreparably ravaged, or can she recover the stellar ground lost in the very years of idleness that should have established her in supreme security? With most people I should say that she and we are out of luck. With Callas I am not so reckless."

Of these same *Normas* Andrew Porter wrote, "Callas has a superlative technique to draw subtle, flexible lines, exquisitely controlled and ravishing in timbres ranging between soft compassion and fierceness. Only at climaxes above the staff is the line drawn with a slate pencil. The voice will not take pressure today; it could not ring out as once it did to dominate the great twin climaxes of the finale and an attempt to throw out a bold, ferocious high C brought momentary disaster. Yet, I feel sorry for anyone who, after ninety-nine perfect notes forming one sublime paragraph, then finds all spoilt by the single, horrid, or fairly horrid sound.

"True the ugly notes were uglier than before. But there was also a new sort of vocal ease and happiness in the performance, as if Callas had accepted the fact that some parts would never come right and that we and she should make the most of what was memorably sung–by far the greater part of the role. She gave a noble, dedicated interpretation, a performance so rapt and serious that it created its own atmosphere and made one oblivious of the extramusical tensions which inevitably build up around anything she does. She is the greatest musician on the stage today. The performance was acted much as the London *Normas* were, with that curious, almost loping dignity of gait, with decisiveness in the large public gestures and detail in the private ones. She looked superb, with a Pasta-like regularity of feature and great luminous eyes brimming with emotion or flashing with fire. The matching of gesture, glance, and tone as she commented wistfully on Adaglisa's narrative, or delivered the simple, terrible phrase 'Si, Norma' at Pollione...were as memorable as ever. Of Pasta, too, it used to be said that with three notes she could stir an audience to the depths of their being."

Rescigno, who worked closely with her during this time in concerts and recordings, offers a penetrating description of the period: "When Maria was living the life of a vestal virgin, so to speak, it was home–theater–home. A dinner out was a big treat and an exception. When she broke that discipline, it was not the voice, I think, which suffered. It was the whole mechanism, for her voice had become a highly oiled machine which produced inhuman feats. Her repertory included everything, and she perfected a psychological and physical means to achieve the demands of this repertory. When there was an interruption, when these gears were slowed, a change took place. This began to be evident about the time of her separation from her husband in 1959. I don't think Maria herself realized exactly what went into her singing; it had been so ingrained for so long by her way of living, of thinking. It had become a completely natural thing. When this naturalness was no longer there, it shocked her, and she couldn't fully understand it or cope with it."

"My biggest mistake," Callas admitted, "was trying to intellectualize my voice. It set me back years. Everyone thought I was finished. I tried to control an animal instinct instead of leaving it as it was–just a God-given gift....On top of that, the press was writing so frequently that I had lost my voice, I got to the point of believing it myself. I began to think,

'Well, they all say it, so it must be true.'...I got complexes for the first time and lost my audacity. My vocal cords have always been and are perfect, thank God. But I got so many complexes from the continual negative criticism which contributed to what I admit was a vocal crisis....I had a big wobble in my voice...and I pushed and opened my mouth too much. The sound just poured out without control."

As her voice failed, so did her courage, and at the point when her need for support was the greatest, she met the person who next fulfilled the dominating role that earlier had been taken by her mother and by Meneghini. Michel Glotz was a producer for E.M.I. in Paris, where Onassis lived and where Callas moved following her separation from Meneghini. Glotz was an ambitious person to whom Callas was a means rather than an end, but he bolstered her waning courage, and under his influence came a new spate of recordings (all made in Paris), a return to the operatic stage (*Tosca* in London, 1964), her formal debut at the Paris Opéra (*Norma*, 1964), and a two-performance return to the Met (*Tosca*, 1965).

It is no coincidence that in the summer of 1965 when Callas broke with Glotz for reasons she is still reticent to discuss, she gave her final public appearance for more than eight years. She was once again without an external guiding personality. The next three years of her liaison with Onassis were artistically empty as the woman dominated the artist. When the relationship ended in 1968, Callas found herself without a career, without (in her words) "even a good friendship."

With Aristotle Onassis, 1967

There is little doubt of the depth of her feeling for Onassis and her hope of becoming his wife. In 1966, she renounced her United States citizenship not only for tax purposes and to end financial difficulties with Meneghini, but also to pave the way for marriage to Onassis. By reverting to her Greek citizenship alone, Callas nullified her former marriage, for, not having the sanction of the Greek Orthodox church, it was recognized only in Italy. Once the Italian laws were changed, Callas applied for and obtained a divorce.

Onassis's chief steward, Christian Cafarakis, has written that in 1968, following a row between the couple, Callas insisted Onassis marry her. "Among other things," Cafarakis wrote, "she told him that it would soon be too late for her to have children, a long-cherished dream she didn't intend to sacrifice.

"Onassis replied without hesitation: 'All right, let's get married.' Maria had won....The wedding was scheduled to be held in London during the first week in March. Onassis left Paris with his maid Hélène and settled in the Savoy Hotel. To avoid publicity, Maria took a suite at Claridge's. The wedding was set for a few days after their arrival. The witnesses were to be two directors of Olympic Maritime, and a Greek Orthodox priest was ready to fly in from Athens to officiate. Unfortunately, Maria lacked one important document–her birth certificate–and I believe she had to wait two weeks for it....Finally, it was only a few hours before the ceremony, the plane had left for Athens to pick up the priest and all was in readiness. Then, suddenly, the bride and bridegroom had a violent argument that caused them to break up forever. Onassis immediately left the hotel and took a plane to Athens. Maria returned sadly to Paris."

Her one recourse to this wrenching personal crisis was to return to singing, but to do so presented a new and strange set of problems. Her life as an artist had previously been built not only on her will but also that of her mother, of Meneghini, of Glotz. She now faced the necessity of singing for herself and her own needs, but with the realization that she must sing in competition with the ever widening specter of her own legend. She knew full well her voice was not that of her prime, of her recordings (which were all a new generation knew), or even that of her last public appearances.

Though she had worked with de Hidalgo during the Onassis period and she herself had expressed confidence in her voice, what she lacked was the corresponding confidence of someone beyond a teacher whom she trusted. Had he not had commitments of his own, had he been more self-ambitious and less devoted to Callas the human being, Lawrence Kelly might well have filled such a role. When Onassis broke with Callas in 1968 and remarried, Kelly helped her to formulate a full-scale return to her career. First, she would open the 1969 San Francisco Opera season (both *Norma* and *Traviata* were discussed with Adler), proceed to Kelly's company in Dallas for either *Traviata* or a new bel canto role, and cap all with her first Metropolitan Opera *Medea*, the role she longed to perform in New York. Little by little the grand design shrank. Repertory and rehearsal period were the snag in San Francisco, Bing and Callas could not agree on dates, and finally only Dallas was left. *Traviata* was announced for the company's 1969 season, then in April the Verdi Requiem was substituted. Hopes for Callas even in concert dissolved when she let it be known the Requiem was no longer to her liking and that Kelly's announcement of it had been "premature." A more plausible explanation was that, without the day-by-day urging of someone who could rebuild her confidence, the courage to make a return evaporated.

As she backed away from the edge of performance, it became essential and obsessive for Callas to keep herself alive artistically in her own mind, and in the eyes of others, by holding out the hope that a comeback was just around the corner. A tantalizing cat-and-mouse game ensued. Yet the questions of "Will she?" or "Won't she?" were hardly necessary to keep Callas's name and presence alive. The mystique which made her newsworthy during her singing days did not abandon her in exile. Nor could the press's attention be put down as simply interest in "the other woman."

When she at last signed a contract, it was not with San Francisco, Dallas, or even for opera, but for her first film, a nonsinging enactment of Medea for director Pier Paolo Pasolini. However bewitching Callas looked on the screen, and there was great disagreement about this, without music to ignite her imagination there was a hollow quality to her performance. Pasolini had used her as a pawn rather than a personality, and the film had at best a *succès d'estime*. No doubt Callas's disappointment was keen; she might well have hoped the film would be the springboard to an acting career, especially as a return to E.M.I.'s studio for an LP of Verdi arias just prior to filming *Medea* had ended inconclusively.

Filming *Medea*,
Turkey, 1969

Disillusioned by her experience with Pasolini and unready to attempt a return to the stage, Callas nevertheless was consumed with an overwhelming need to be active, to fit into an artistic niche, to forge a new identity. Thus, she accepted an invitation from the Curtis Institute of Music in Philadelphia to conduct a series of master classes. The experiment in January 1971 proved unsuccessful. The students were not as advanced or as well prepared as Callas had expected, and she withdrew after two days at the school.

Peter Mennin of New York's Juilliard School of Music persuaded her to reconsider the idea under more carefully planned circumstances. As a result, in the spring of 1971 she heard some three hundred young professionals for sessions the following fall and narrowed these down to twenty-five. The first classes were held from the middle of October through the middle of November. Callas approached her role as teacher with the same deep involvement she brought to her own singing. She did not speak from on high but as a friend or colleague who had been over the same ground and was anxious to help her students through the difficulties and pitfalls she had encountered. In her wide-ranging comments, she was soft-spoken, frank, and chary with praise. She placed great stress on fidelity to the printed page and on how, within its confines, a singer could create a living musical statement.

The class format was simple and effective. On a stage bare of all but a piano, stool, and table piled high with scores, a singer or singers performed an aria or scene in toto, and then Callas retraced the music phrase by phrase, and even note by note, often singing entire sections to illustrate her points. These provided extraordinary flashes, however uneven and scrappy, of the Callas vocal excitement. The repertory covered was largely standard, and Callas dealt with it in subjective terms as some of her comments illustrate:

To a soprano singing "Caro nome" from *Rigoletto:* "Gilda is a virgin but don't make it too cute because of what happens to her later. She sacrifices her life for love, don't forget."

To a soprano singing "Quel guardo il cavaliere" from *Don Pasquale:* "Donizetti has given you enough embellishments to bring this aria to life. Don't add any more, it makes it too sweet."

To a soprano singing "Salce, salce" from *Otello:* "This must be eerie, as though you have premonitions of death. It must seem to come from far back in your mind. You must give the public shivers."

To a soprano singing "D'amour l'ardente flamme" from *Le damnation de Faust:* "When you sing 'de sa main la caresse,' feel the caress of his hand. It's passion she feels but restrained. In those days there was restraint. I wish it were like that now. Now, it's all exposed."

To a baritone in "Cortigiani" from *Rigoletto:* "Be an animal when you sing this aria. Rigoletto wants to kill these courtiers, but is obliged to beg them. Thus, he hates himself as well."

To a bass singing Philip's monologue from *Don Carlo:* "Look at me with suffering. That's what I want. Remember, he is a king. Suffering is the same, but you must have a regal way with it."

Of course, there was detailed talk from Callas on matters purely of technique as well—breathing, phrasing, trills—as well as deportment: "A movement must have meaning. Otherwise, stand still. You must give the music exact expression but without moving an inch. The expression is on the face"; "Before you open your mouth, you should know exactly where a phrase is going and how long it is going to last"; "Don't just open your mouth, open your throat!"

It was all concentrated sharing, reflecting again the almost sacred nature of music to Callas. Yet behind this generous giving of herself, it seemed evident that the Juilliard classes were simultaneously serving a greater and somewhat ulterior purpose—the rebuilding of Callas's confidence before an audience. Here she could and did sing out without carrying the responsibility of performance and under the pretext of its being entirely spontaneous. Behind the scenes, Callas worked almost daily in her studio as a student herself with a demanding teacher, Metropolitan Opera coach and accompanist Alberta Masiello. Together they covered a vast amount of repertory. Among many of the scores studied, Callas went through *Lucia*, *Macbeth*, and *Forza del destino* completely. This intensive private schedule, coupled with the public Juilliard sessions, contributed to the courage she needed to face once again a recording microphone, though this time not for E.M.I. but the Dutch firm of Philips.

The sessions in London which began in December 1972 might never have taken place, however, had not Callas again found strength in another to meet her own needs. This time it came from an unlikely and surprising source—a singer with whom she had been closely linked during her Scala years as both colleague and adversary, Giuseppe di Stefano. They had renewed their friendship in the spring during Callas's second set of Juilliard classes, and the Philips recording of Verdi and Donizetti duets was undertaken, no doubt in large measure at the tenor's urging. Although his had been one of the most radiant and lovely of postwar lyric voices, indifferent singing and a continued abuse of his gifts sent his star into an early eclipse. A reunion with Callas, for whatever reason, was also a means of placing himself again in a musical and financial mainstream.

Prior to the Philips recording, the management of Teatro Regio in Turin invited Callas to make her debut in yet another role, that of stage director. In April 1973, Turin planned to inaugurate a modern theater, a replacement for its old house that had burned years before. A new production of Verdi's *Vespri* was decided upon, and Callas accepted the invitation to direct on the proviso that di Stefano be her codirector. When Turin accepted this condition, Gianandrea Gavazzeni, who was to conduct *Vespri*, withdrew from the production. Though he had often collaborated with Callas at Scala, admired her profusely, and was willing to work with her on *Vespri*, he refused to accept the presence of di Stefano.

The production was not a success. The press criticized the couple for their lame handling of the principals and for grouping the chorus in straight rows during crucial dramatic moments. For Callas, the venture must have been as frustrating as her episode with Pasolini. Zeffirelli feels "as a director in terms of the physical control of the stage she knew nothing. She can only teach what she knows. She has never seen how the chorus moves behind her because she is blind. She never knew what the rest of the stage was doing, she sensed it. She was never involved in the production, the making of it. She was there, singing, thinking of what she had to deliver. She must have known this production was going to be lousy. She had seen the designs, she knew what the ingredients were. This alone was enough to warn her. She didn't analytically follow—professionally or technically—what the making of a production was. She went, she always goes, by intuition. But here she needed more."

During the *Vespri* period, negotiations dissolved for a three-concert appearance in Tokyo the following month. She did go to Japan in May and with di Stefano, but it was to judge a contest and give a master class.

Behind the reasons for her not singing in Japan or elsewhere during her eight-year silence was the crossroads at which she found herself as a person. A state of voice is inexorably bound up with a state of mind. Her fears and her needs while she was away from the stage were great, and these above all prolonged her absence, as her own claustrophobic words from 1968 make abundantly clear:

"In life, before you do something, you must realize that there will be consequences. And if you're honest, you pay a big price, though it should be normal, honesty should be a part of you. But all honest or dishonest people have to know that whatever you do, you are going to pay a price. And I have found in my life by being honest that you are going to meet a lot of dishonest people, a lot of weak people who are going to try to pull you down. And then, my Lord, if you realize that I'm a woman, and I mean a *woman* with all her weaknesses, I'm undefended. I've been undefended all my life. But I have chosen to be honest, and I cannot help myself, I cannot be unfaithful to myself. 'Well,' I have thought, 'Maria if you are this way you will probably have to stand for a lot of things; you will probably be misunderstood, frequently misunderstood, hated, attacked.' I have been, and I have not been able to fight back. I have to sit back and take it in silence.

"Like Rome. God, I'm still feeling the result of Rome. I could not go on with that performance. I could not be killed that way. It would be stupidity. If I had had my vocal possibilities, if I hadn't been sick, I would have stood there. I've done that thousands of times at the Scala, everywhere. 'The tigress,' they call me. But I didn't have my voice in Rome. It was slipping all the time with an aggressive public. If I had been well I would have continued and I would have spit in their faces. If I could make my enemies—I would not kill them—but if I could make them come on their knees in front of me, I would, I can, and I must. But if one is not well how are you going to win the battle? Be crucified or killed? I'm not that foolish.

"Take Bing. Did he have to go and say, 'Oh, she's an impossible person.' Why? I'm quite sure he's met so many other impossible people. No, he got even with me for all the things he could not get even for with other people. That's what I call bad destiny. I was unlucky. I'm sure he just got so angry that he said, 'I'll get even with all her colleagues.' It's what I call, as I say, hard luck. Because my colleagues have hurt him much more, that's why he respects me. I am really sure that he quite sincerely loves me. But, he's a weak man. So, I suppose I paid the consequences for so many others, like

At home,
Paris, 1972

a glass that fills up. I was the thing that filled his glass up. It hurts. You hate it because it's unjust. The world is full of injustice. On the other hand if people love you, why do they love you? Not because I sang a beautiful aria or note. There must be more to it than that. What am I? Only a machine for singing? No, I am a human being. I need help too. Subconsciously I am admired for what is behind my art. But there is nothing special about my art. I am but one of many more or less capable instrumentalists. What I do musically is not done out of my bravura. I have to do it. It is a part of my job.

"Music has one set of standards. That is perfect musicianship first of all. After that you perform. There is only one language for music. Same thing with love. You love, you worship, you honor. They go together. You never say a lie. You do your best never to betray. Loyalty, of course. Gratitude, of course, without overdoing it. With dignity, whatever you do, with dignity. There is only one standard to everything. You are a musician? You have to know your music. I'm not doing anything special. The notes are there. They are written on the page. How can you not do them? If you don't there's something wrong with you. So what is so extraordinary about what I'm doing? A mother must be a good mother to her children, yes or no? There is no going away from that. It's her responsibility. She is not doing anything special. It *is* her duty. That's where I'm stiff as a German, if it can be called that. Everybody when he does something has a duty to perform. There is nothing extraordinary about how wonderful a mother is. She has got to be wonderful, otherwise don't have children. But if you do, be a good mother and don't expect anything in return.

"Life they say, is terrible. Of course, life is terrible if we make it that way. Life is hard. Yes, of course, life is hard, but you can't go around without shaving or cleaning yourself. Everything is wearying and tiring. But if we make it worse, how can we cope? There are certain things you have to do as a human being. It's not really all that difficult, but we create the difficulties, God, how many. We never take into consideration other people's feelings. We never think before we act. I have seen human beings do things that hurt so much you want to say, 'Can't you think before you do it?' Think and say, 'Well, if I do that, what consequences will there be to me, to that other person?' God gave us brains. We're not beasts. He gave us judgment. We have to use that to the best of our abilities. But we don't use it. We couldn't care less. We do what we want. We go about grabbing things with the least effort possible.

"I would like that too. Wouldn't I like to sit back and enjoy my celebrity, my money? Wouldn't I like to sit back and be comfortable? I can't. I have to help myself. I have known since my childhood that the people around me didn't have judgment, so I had to either do what they did or do what I knew I was supposed to do. And if you manage not to be pulled down, that's all to your credit. But then, you are criticized. You're hard, you're cruel, you're egotistical. That hurts. There is no defense, only a lot of hurt. You keep quiet and say, 'Well, let's see what happens tomorrow. Things can't always be like that.' You try to get used to it, if anyone can. This has gone on and on since I was a child, since I can remember. It's been a lonely life. My work is all alone. When I look at a score I know at once what I want from it. In your mind you have all these creative things, or interpretive, whatever you call it. You have to be alone to do all that. You cannot have distractions. The day is easy to live through. What about the evening? What about when you shut the door to your bedroom and are all alone? Damn it all, what does one do? Sit within four walls? I have been facing four walls all my life. I'm beginning to think I should get a big dog and have him around. It's the only thing. There's lots of times I can't sleep. I'm used to working at night. I'm used to thinking then. It's my job, my chemistry. But at night you get lots of funny ideas, pessimistic ideas, and I'd like to shake them. But can you go for a walk, really walk your feet off, get tired, do something? A woman can't do that. Take a train? Go some place when you get desperate? What does a woman do?

"It would be so nice to be able to have some honest shoulder to lean on. I had hoped that of my husband. I was so wrong. Glory went to his head. He was not all that bad in the beginning, or at least I hope not. My horoscope says I look through rose-colored glasses. But if you can't trust your husband or your mother, to whom do you turn? When I go back to Paris, you know who takes care of me and who I know will always be there? My maid Bruna, who adores me and who has been a nurse, sister, and mother to me. She is only two years older. When I was in the hospital she didn't want the nurse to touch me, for she was ashamed to humiliate me, to have a nurse clean me. Imagine that such a person should exist today, and that's my kind of person. They are very rare. But she shouldn't have been there. It should have been my mother and my sister. You think I don't think afterwards and say, 'Why?' When everyone should be proud of me. God, how many mothers would have adored to have a child like me? But, I'm alone. Friends are there to help, but they have their problems. And when you have a family and that family kicks you like mad, what do you do? Then my sister writes, 'Papa's, Mama's growing older.' Of course, they're growing older. So am I. So what do we have? Four homes, isolated from each other, mine and theirs. Miserably alone. At least I've accomplished something, it is true. That is to my credit. But I've accomplished it alone, and why should I now be alone at home? We should all be there helping the other. Friends can only help you to a certain point. On the other hand there are people who can make or ruin you, and I've never had support from the people I care for the most, and there are very few. I don't give myself here and there. Do you blame me? The less you give, the less you are hurt, and the people who have been the closest to me have hurt me the most.

"Don't make any illusions, happiness is not of my world. There are people born to be happy and people born to be unhappy. I am just not lucky. Yet, frequently I say, 'Why should this be? Am I that wrong? Am I that bad a person? What's wrong with being proud of me? Why should I be fought all the time when my main ambition is being honest. What's wrong with that? Is it such a sin? Is it a lot to ask not to be hurt by the few people around you?' So, I am always on the defense. I get aggressive. Since my childhood I've been aggressive. Do you blame me? But nobody has thought when they tear me down, 'How is this woman feeling? How is she taking it? Is there anyone to hold her hand? It must be hell!' Of course it's hell. That is why I am so exhausted when I go on the stage, why I have vocal difficulties. I become destructive instead of constructive because my faith is broken. When I have to go and persuade the public that everything is pure and honest and wonderful, a subconscious says, 'Are you kidding?'

"I thought I would become great to be able to perform better, under the best mental frame of mind. Well, it was a lie. It is not true. The more famous you become the more difficult things are, the more you are disliked, especially if you are not a crybaby. And the necessities of life are quite simple: You respect yourself, you want to be respected, you keep yourself well, you dress the best way possible. I've lost weight being hungry for two years. It was a matter of discipline. Nothing has come to me the easy way. But so long as the result was good I didn't care what the sacrifice was. But there must be a result, there must be something good to come out of it. I hate wasting my time. Frequently I have wasted my time on account of others, and there's never much help from others. Sooner or later they are going to fail you. Glory goes to people's heads. Not my head. Glory terrifies me. You are quite uncomfortable up there. But people around you get drunk. It is a wine which goes to their heads, and I have seen them always betray me for one reason or another. Mine is a big destiny. It's terrifying.

"But if there's one thing I have found in these years of sacrifice, it is that I wouldn't change for anything, for all the money in the world. You cannot. My religion is that, integrity, no matter what the price. You can't breathe otherwise. But there are people around you who are not like that, and that is what hurts. You feel like a strange animal that is out of place and misunderstood. I'm proud. I don't like to show my feelings. I want people to show their interest, but I never ask for anything for fear of being disillusioned. I don't like to lose.

"I wish I could have a medicine that could give me strength, mental and physical, especially physical. I started out very early in life, and I don't think my health can stand much more tension. It's all tension, you know. Whatever happens in life, it all comes down to that. I'd be pleased with three years, three good years coming back to what I was. If not, I've been gifted. I've been honored by everyone. So one magazine writes badly about me, that's nonsense. Let's face it, I am honored, adored, venerated, just a woman out of nothing, not going to bed with one and then the other, on the contrary saying 'No' to everyone. It is a miracle that I made a career. I'm something to have people proud of. But they're not. Dead weight. And you say 'What now, what next?' Anything to survive my dear. At my stage of the game, anything to survive."

Survival came in the form of an announcement in June 1973 that Callas with di Stefano would embark on a world concert tour beginning in London, September 22, and concluding in Japan in spring of 1974. In between would come appearances in Germany, Spain, France, Holland, and two months in the United States and Canada. While this was startling enough, it was more surprising that Callas would choose a recital format to pick up the pieces of her career, for though concerts had figured in her professional life from the years in Greece, they had never provided her with a comfortable or congenial forum, which she admitted and proved on many occasions. Her realm was the operatic theater; it alone afforded the proper scope for the totality of her art. Even more perplexing was that she consented to tour with a pianist rather than appear with orchestra; Callas's voice was not always a complete sound or experience without the texture, force, and overtones of an orchestra highlighting and intermingling with her timbre. Her voice could be admired and valued alone for its darkness and depth of color, but it was incontestably intensified and its beauty heightened by the contrasting metal of an orchestra.

When the London concert was announced, more than twenty-five thousand mail orders were received for some three thousand seats at Royal Festival Hall. The BBC obtained the right to televise the recital and E.M.I. permission to record it. Three days before, Callas canceled on the advice of her eye doctor. She has glaucoma which requires frequent medication, but the condition is not a new one. It seems more plausible that good sense made her reconsider another and less prominent starting point than London. On October 25, in Hamburg, Callas made her first public appearance as a singer in more than eight years. The program consisted of six duets with di Stefano, and each sang a single aria as an encore. Though the audience's welcome was prolonged and effusive, a principal German critic described her performance as no more than a reflection of former splendor, "the remnants of a vocal material, once exploited as though it were inexhaustible, of an inimitable way of singing that has lost all of its truly imperial power of expression. The brittle beginnings, the *mezza voce* that no longer carries, the desperate forcing, and the not always stable intonation made each number a moment of anxiety."

At this first concert nerves must have taken a tremendous toll, but by the fourth concert in Frankfurt it was painfully clear that nerves alone could not account for Callas's distressing singing. A great reduction in volume and a lack of top notes could have been countenanced, as they were in the Paris *Norma*, because there, one still had the compensation of her all-knowing musicality. But now there was only Callas's desperate attempt to stay afloat vocally with a voice that was broken. Yet, though the ability to sustain long phrases was gone and recitatives and flourishes were weak and imprecise, there *were* glints of her former magisterial sense of authority. Callas, however, was in no way helped by the off-pitch indifference of di Stefano and by the fuzzy accompaniments of eighty-two-year-old pianist Ivor Newton. The true tragedy was that di Stefano was risking nothing while Callas risked everything. To compromise her name and what it stood for was a dear price to pay for survival.

On November 26, the pair performed at last in London. If the city hoped for a miracle, it did not take place. If the public was demonstrative, its memories were rich. This was another, an unwise, Callas, an echo of the bright, luminous figure who had once blazed like a comet. A final parallel to Pasta is inescapable. In 1850, she had gone to England to be present at the debut of a pupil and had been persuaded to appear in scenes from *Anna Bolena*, having not sung publicly for ten years. Benjamin Lumley, an English theater manager, records "the spectacle was melancholy, not to say painful, to all who could feel with true artistic sympathy. She moved like a mighty shadow of the past before the eyes of the spectators, but it was the shadow of a shade." Yet there was one Pasta's voice spoke to that evening more than a century ago. Pauline Viardot was hearing her for the first time. With her eyes full of tears, she said to her companion, "You are right! It is like the Cenacolo of da Vinci in Milan—a wreck of a picture, but the picture is the greatest picture in the world."

Accepting applause, London, 1973, with Giuseppe di Stefano

THE GREAT YEARS

BY GERALD FITZGERALD

The woman in clumpy shoes, formless skirt, and buttoned-up sweater, a music score clutched under one arm, her right hand defiantly thrust into the air, is Maria Callas as she was in 1951. After four years of grueling work in dozens of Italian opera houses, the twenty-eight-year-old singer has at last exacted a full-time contract from Europe's most prestigious theater, La Scala of Milan. She is at work on the very first stage rehearsal of *I vespri siciliani.* This Verdi rarity, revived not only to mark the fiftieth anniversary of the composer's death, but to exhibit Callas's extraordinary vocal and dramatic talents, will open Scala's 1951–52 season.

Looks of amazement and confusion register on the faces of chorus members standing near Callas: Here was a dramatic soprano who could span a two-and-a-half-octave range. "My god," one of them recalls, "she came onstage sounding like our deepest contralto, Cloe Elmo. And before the evening was over, she took a high E-flat. And it was twice as strong as Toti Dal Monte's!"

Eighteen months earlier, Callas had sung two Aidas with Scala. Then, she had come in as a last-minute substitute for the indisposed Renata Tebaldi. Her performances caused no sensation, and no regular contract with the company materialized. With her official debut in *I vespri siciliani*, however, the diva all but claimed Scala as her own. She would rule its stage for nearly a decade.

Elena in *Vespri* was not new to the Callas repertory. She had sung the role the previous spring at the Florence May Festival. By chance, the very moment pictured here was seen by Lord Harewood in Florence, and his impressions capture Callas at that early period of her career:

"Act I of *Vespri* begins slowly; rival parties of occupying French and downtrodden Sicilians take up their positions on either side of the stage and glare at each other. The French have been boasting for some time of the privileges which belong by right to an army of occupation, when a female figure–the Sicilian Duchess Elena–is seen slowly crossing the square. Doubtless the music and the production helped to spotlight Elena, but, though Callas had not yet sung and was not even wearing her costume, one was straight away impressed by the natural dignity of her carriage, the air of quiet, innate authority which went with every movement. The French order her to sing for their entertainment, and mezza voce she starts a song, a slow cantabile melody; there is as complete control over the music as there had been over the stage. The song is a ballad, but it ends with the words 'Il vostro fato è in vostra man' [Your fate

Rehearsing act one of *Vespri,*
with Masini as Ninetta

is in your hand], delivered with concentrated meaning. The phrase is repeated with even more intensity, and suddenly the music becomes a cabaletta of electrifying force; the singer peals forth arpeggios and top notes and the French only wake up to the fact that they have permitted a patriotic demonstration under their very noses once it is under way. It was a completely convincing operatic moment, and Callas held the listeners in the palm of her hand to produce a tension that was almost unbearable until exhilaratingly released in the cabaletta."

Callas's success in Florence was duplicated in Milan. For her first Scala opening—there were to be five more in her future—she was supported by a distinguished array of colleagues. The sets and costumes were designed by Nicola Benois, son of the noted Russian scenic artist Alexandre Benois, who created many productions for Serge Diaghilev's Ballets Russes (including the world premiere of Igor Stravinsky's *Petrouchka*, with Vaslav Nijinsky and Tamara Karsavina). Herbert Graf, who had directed *Vespri* in Florence, also staged the opera in Milan.

Shown at left, in the ensemble that concludes *Vespri*'s fourth act, is the majestic Bulgarian bass Boris Christoff, bearded and robed in black as the Sicilian patriot Procida. (Callas was to appear infrequently with Christoff because of personality conflicts. Some years later, in Rome, they parted company permanently when the egocentric bass tried to keep the soprano from taking a solo curtain call during a performance of *Medea*.) To Callas's right stands the American tenor Eugene Conley, who sang Arrigo, and the Italian baritone Enzo Mascherini as Monforte, leader of the French and father of Arrigo, Elena's beloved.

At lower left, Callas, attired in Elena's bridal gown, pours forth all her youthful power in the act five Bolero, a display piece of awesome difficulty. As Scribe's melodramatic libretto has it, no sooner do Elena's wedding bells toll, than the Sicilians massacre the French oppressors to the man—including her groom's father. Even with so bloody a finale, it was a relaxed, demurely smiling Maria Callas [below] who accompanied Mascherini, conductor Victor de Sabata, then the music director of La Scala, and Christoff to accept the applause of the Milan public, a sound that would soon ring familiar in her ears.

Part of Maria Callas's first-season contract with La Scala stipulated she would sing Bellini's Norma. Already it had become the role with which she was most closely associated. Prior to her initial performance in Milan, on January 16, 1952, she had portrayed Norma in Florence, Venice, Rome, Buenos Aires, Rio de Janeiro, São Paulo, Mexico City, Palermo, and twice in Catania. The second Catania appearance was a special honor: Bellini had been born there and the performance marked the 150th anniversary of his birth.

Despite the recognition Callas had achieved with her previous Normas, the best Scala managed to give her was a lackluster staging dating from 1931 [right]. But even with such surroundings, Callas's performance electrified the Milanese.

Ten months later, on November 8, the soprano made her debut at the Royal Opera House in London. Again the role was Norma, and again she looked as fiercely dramatic as she had at La Scala [left], unflinchingly denouncing her faithless lover with the words "Trema per te, fellon" (Tremble for your life, you villain). Cecil Smith, an American critic resident in London, described the Covent Garden premiere: "Callas's fioriture were fabulous. The chromatic glissandi held no terrors for her in the cadenza at the end of 'Casta diva'... nor did the superhuman leap from middle F to a forte high C. One of the most stunning moments came at the end of the stretta to the Act II trio, when she held for twelve beats a stupendous, free high D. Among dramatic sopranos of my experience, I have heard this tone equalled only by Rosa Raisa. From this point onward, Miss Callas held her audience in abject slavery. She rewarded them by never letting them down, and by reaching a peak of eloquence in the infinitely moving closing scene of the opera."

Francesco Siciliani, who is now music director of Radio Italiana, recalls how Callas got her first chance to sing Norma. "One night in late 1947—I was then director of the Teatro San Carlo in Naples—I heard a broadcast of *Tristan und Isolde* from Venice. Realizing the soprano had an important voice, I phoned the Teatro la Fenice the next day and learned she was a Greek-American, a protégée of Tullio Serafin. For the moment, that was that.

"But in October of 1948, just after I moved to Florence to head the Teatro Comunale, Serafin called me from Rome. 'Come at once,' he begged. 'You must hear this girl. She is discouraged and has bought a ticket to return to America. Help me convince her to stay.' So, at his home I met Maria Callas. She was tall and heavy, but had an interesting face, real presence, expression, intelligence.

"With Serafin at the piano, she did her usual repertory for me—*Gioconda, Turandot, Aida, Tristan*. Parts of the voice were beautiful, others empty, and she used strange portamenti. During a pause, she said she had studied with Elvira de Hidalgo, which struck me as curious, for de Hidalgo had been a coloratura. 'I know coloratura pieces, too,' Callas explained, 'but I'm a dramatic soprano.' 'Well,' I asked, 'can we hear something of a different nature?' So she sang the aria from *I Puritani*, with the cabaletta. I was overwhelmed, and tears streamed down Serafin's cheeks. This was the kind of singer one read about in books from the nineteenth century—a real dramatic coloratura.

"'You're not leaving Italy,' I announced, phoning Pariso Votto, general manager of the Comunale in Florence. 'Look,' I said, 'let's forget we've scheduled *Butterfly* for opening night. I've found an extraordinary soprano and we must do *Norma*.'"

Six weeks later, with Serafin conducting, Callas sang Norma—the first step on a new vocal path. Over the years, Siciliani engaged Callas repeatedly, often for operas new to her repertory: *La traviata, I vespri siciliani*, Haydn's *Orfeo ed Euridice*, Cherubini's *Medea*, and Rossini's *Armida*. The last three Siciliani personally unearthed for her. Always, he made sure she worked with major conductors—Serafin, Gui, Kleiber. Few people did more to develop Callas's abilities. Only with her total conquest of Scala did her association with Florence end. Milan, jealous of Florence's musical rebirth, first stole Callas away, and then hired Siciliani for Scala's artistic staff.

Exactly seven weeks after Callas's Florence Norma, Serafin had her onstage in Venice singing a second bel canto role—Elvira in Bellini's *Puritani*. At the time, Callas had not yet perfected her Italian, speaking in the Veronese accent of her sponsor, Giovanni Battista Meneghini. Franco Zeffirelli relates one incident from that *Puritani*: "Maria had memorized the music in a few days, but not quite all the words. The prompter kept feeding her lines, but at one moment, in the aria 'Son vergin vezzosa,' instead of 'vezzosa'—charming—she sang 'viziosa'—you know, vicious—'I am a vicious virgin.' But even with these little mistakes, she put the whole world of opera in upheaval."

Singing "Casta diva" in act one
and during "Guerra" chorus in act four

Surprisingly enough, Constanze in Wolfgang Amadeus Mozart's *Die Entführung aus dem Serail* was introduced to the stage of La Scala by Maria Callas. The date: April 2, 1952. With the exception of Gluck's Alceste, all the other heroines she performed there–by Gluck, Spontini, Cherubini, Rossini, Bellini, Donizetti, Verdi, Ponchielli, and Giordano–were either created at the theater by the original interpreter or first sung there by another soprano.

Among her colleagues in the production was no less a Mozart stylist than the legendary basso Salvatore Baccaloni as Osmin [above, far left]. Adding to the pleasures of the event were Jonel Perlea's conducting, the exotic settings by Gianni Ratto–a young protégé of Giorgio Strehler at the Piccolo Teatro di Milano–and Leonor Fini's costumes, which helped conceal the Callas opulence [above, far right]. Nicola Benois, who for more than a quarter-century

headed La Scala's scenic department, remembers the visual elements as "extremely tasteful, somewhat like old prints in shades of sepia."

After her initial encounter with Constanze, however, Callas never again attempted a Mozart role, though she would have been well-suited to many of them. Critic Irving Kolodin once mused that she would make an ideal Queen of the Night. During the spring of 1971, at a public roundtable at the Juilliard School of Music in New York, she herself bluntly declared: "I find most of Mozart's music dull!" The auditorium was jammed with students and celebrities. In the third row sat Elisabeth Schwarzkopf, the supreme Mozart interpreter of the day. Hearing Callas's judgment, she blinked and quietly suppressed a smile.

But what Callas says is not what Callas does. However dull she may have found Mozart, Callas did not sing him in a dull way. At the Scala premiere of *Il ratto dal serraglio* (the opera was sung in Italian), her whirlwind rendition of "Marten aller Arten," one of the most arduous arias conceived for the voice, made the Milanese sit up and take notice. In 1957 she was to program this excerpt as a showcase for the gala inaugural concert of the Dallas Civic Opera. Constancy was never the vice of this Constanze.

St. Ambrose is patron saint of Milan, and on his feast day, December 7, the Teatro alla Scala traditionally begins its new season. In 1952, the day must truly have seemed ambrosian to Maria Callas. For the second consecutive year she had been chosen to perform a lead in a neglected Verdi opera–*Macbeth*. As with *I vespri siciliani* the year before, Victor de Sabata would conduct and Nicola Benois would design the production.

The director, Carl Ebert, had made a success of Verdi's *Macbeth* during the early 1930s in Berlin, staging a static, expressionistic conception of massive proportions. In Milan with Benois, he sought many of the same effects, constructing a twenty-foot-high drawbridge as an entrance to the castle in act one. For the ballet of the witches in the third act, Violetta Elvin was imported from the Sadler's Wells Ballet of London.

The Scala production marked Callas's first Lady Macbeth. A year earlier, she had almost sung the part under Arturo Toscanini's direction. Then, the Maestro had hoped to conduct *Macbeth* in Busseto, near the birthplace of Verdi. His daughter, Countess Wally Castelbarco–long a pillar of the Italian musical scene–knew of Callas's qualifications and arranged an audition for the singer. Toscanini found Callas ideal, but the project never materialized.

Those who heard Callas as Lady Macbeth at Scala–she did a total of five performances–experienced the exact vocal enactment of the part as prescribed by Verdi himself: "I would like her voice harsh, choked, dark. There are places that must not even be sung, but acted and declaimed with a veiled, black voice." Callas followed Verdi's instructions to the letter. As shown at right, she stands on the giant staircase of the castle in act one awaiting the return of her husband. She is calm, yet tense, determined that King Duncan will die and Scotland will be hers. Her eyes tell it all.

As Lady Macbeth, act one

As Lady Macbeth in act tw
with Mascherini, and
during Sleepwalking Scen

With goblet hoisted aloft in a toast, Callas prepares to sing Lady Macbeth's Drinking Song during the banquet scene [left and below left]. Still a woman of ample proportions, she nonetheless possessed all the requirements of theatrical projection—strong, clean-cut features with huge penetrating eyes (she was considered beautiful by many who knew her at the time), a statuesque frame, and long arms that gave even the simplest gesture power and meaning. Callas began the Brindisi incisively and cleanly, almost as pure bel canto. But as Macbeth [below right, Enzo Mascherini] imagined he saw the ghost of Banquo, she added pressure to her phrases in an attempt to hide her husband's guilt from their bewildered, almost spectral guests.

The climax of Callas's Lady Macbeth was achieved in the last act with the Sleepwalking Scene [bottom], in which guilt and terror haunt her shattered mind. Critic Peter Dragadze, writing of the Scala *Macbeth*, noted that "Callas's voice since last season has improved a great deal; the second passagio on high B-natural and C has now completely cleared, giving her an equally colored scale from top to bottom. Only Callas can give a role such as Lady Macbeth the drama, depth and feeling it requires. After her heart-rending Sleepwalking Scene, she was recalled for seven enthusiastic curtain calls, which for Scala is a lot."

La Gioconda occupies a special if curious position in the life of Maria Callas. In 1947, when still an unknown, she auditioned for the role in New York for the director of the Verona Arena. As a result, she was hired to make her Italian debut. The salary was poor, but the artistic conditions were excellent. Despite a minor misfortune during rehearsals—she sprained an ankle and had to be helped around the stage by her Enzo Grimaldi, a young American tenor also making his debut in Italy, Richard Tucker—this debut was a success. Callas's one great fear proved to be unfounded. Because opera in Verona begins at a late hour and ends well past midnight, she was worried no one would wait for the last act to hear her main aria, "Suicidio."

The Verona *Gioconda* also introduced her to two men who would figure significantly in her life: the renowned conductor Tullio Serafin, who was to become her artistic mentor, and Giovanni Battista Meneghini, a wealthy industrialist thirty years her senior who would become her patron, her friend, and ultimately, her husband.

During her career, Callas sang La Gioconda only twelve times. Her performances were limited to Verona and La Scala, where, during the 1952–53 season, she posed in Nicola Benois's act one set, an exact replica of the courtyard of the ducal palace in Venice [right]. Still, the role ranks as an important one in Callas's repertory. She recorded it twice, both times under the baton of Antonino Votto, and the 1952 version, on the Cetra-Soria label, introduced her art to the world at large. In America, where she had yet to sing, the Gioconda discs baffled opera lovers. How could so deep and dramatic a voice have also won fame as Lucia?

Maestro Votto, who conducted her Gioconda at Scala, calls her "the last great artist. When you think this woman was nearly blind, and often sang standing a good 150 feet from the podium. But her sensitivity! Even if she could not see, she sensed the music and always came in exactly with my downbeat. When we rehearsed, she was so precise, already note-perfect. But she had a habit that annoyed her colleagues: Even in rehearsal she always sang full voice and it obliged them to do so as well. Most singers are stupid and try to save themselves, but a rehearsal is a kind of hurdle. If in track you must run a mile, you don't practice by running half a mile. For over thirty years I was Arturo Toscanini's assistant, and from the very first rehearsal he demanded every nuance from the orchestra, just as if it were a full performance. The piano, the forte, the staccato, the legato—all from the start. And Callas did this, too. I remember we had a dress rehearsal in Cologne of *La sonnambula* at ten in the morning and she sang her entire role full voice; that night we did the premiere! She was not just a singer, but a complete artist. It's foolish to discuss her as a voice. She must be viewed totally—as a complex of music, drama, movement. There is no one like her today. She was an esthetic phenomenon."

For its 1953–54 season, La Scala planned to unearth a neglected rarity for Callas–Alessandro Scarlatti's *Mitridate Eupatore*. This, the management felt, would balance nicely with the soprano's other scheduled repertory: her first local Lucia di Lammermoor, the title role in Gluck's *Alceste*, and a Verdi heroine she would sing for the first time, Elisabetta in *Don Carlo*. But in the spring of 1953, Francesco Siciliani, manager of the Florence May Festival, revived Cherubini's long-forgotten *Medea* as a star vehicle for Callas, who mastered the taxing role in eight days. The public response to the Callas Medea was so strong that Scala scrapped its plans for *Mitridate* and substituted the Cherubini work as the second production of the new season.

For Margherita Wallmann, the last-minute switch was a nightmare. As director of the production, she was faced with the task of pulling everything together–sets, costumes, staging–for this unfamiliar work. "We had nothing!" she recalls. "The scenery in Florence, which I had not seen, was said to be a mishmash of styles. It would have been unthinkable to import such settings to La Scala."

At Miss Wallmann's suggestion, Scala finally engaged the noted Italian painter Salvatore Fiume to design the sets. The powerful image of the Argonauts landing at Corinth [above] is his drop curtain for act one. But, as the director recounts, Fiume came to the *Medea* production through an odd set of circumstances. "Originally, I had asked him to design *Alceste*, which I was to stage for Callas in the spring of 1954. He had created his very first sets and costumes for the theater only two seasons before when Nicola Benois, chief of

La Scala's scenic department, had convinced him to try his hand at it. But, being a painter, and an exceptionally strong one at that, Fiume did not grasp the style of Gluck—though repeatedly I tried to explain it to him. One day, as a symbol of King Admetus, he brought me a design for act one showing a huge warrior on horseback—like an enormous sculpture—with the entrance to the palace seen through the horse's legs. I pointed out that the king was supposed to be dying, not going out to battle, so Fiume tried to execute a new act one design. Now, to show the suffering of the dying Admetus, he painted a great wounded tiger, from the entrails of which issued the palace entrance. When I saw it, I was in total despair and at length asked La Scala to engage a new designer for *Alceste*. But suddenly, confronted with staging *Medea*, I realized that what Fiume had achieved in his designs for *Alceste* would work perfectly for *Medea*—for *Medea* is fantastic, primitive, and Cherubini's music verges on the romantic. Medea herself is from a savage tribe, so why not have a very savage decor onstage? So that problem was settled."

It was only one of many problems. "We didn't even have a conductor," recalls Miss Wallmann, "for our great music director, Victor de Sabata, had fallen seriously ill and was never again to conduct opera. By luck, however, Leonard Bernstein—he was young then and had never yet worked in a major opera house or even heard of Cherubini's *Medea*—happened to be in Italy winding up a concert tour. Somehow, our general manager, Antonio Ghiringhelli, persuaded him to make his debut at La Scala conducting our *Medea*.

"We sent him the score—a first edition, printed in 1798—and because the pages were decomposing, they gave off dust and it made tears stream down his face. He coughed and sneezed all through the rehearsals. But despite this painful allergy and the fatigue from his long tour, he fell in love with Cherubini's music and quickly memorized it. And he came to a perfect understanding with Callas—even to cutting one of her major arias. He even elicited a sense of humor from her. Callas was always very serious, but one day, when a tempo he took seemed too slow to her, she jokingly told him: 'Now, Lennie, if you want me to be a great Medea, you must be a great Medio'—a play on words that roughly meant 'conduct like a god.' Thank heaven they adored each other.

"Bernstein did wonders with the orchestra. We only had five full days of rehearsal onstage. He worried how I could handle the finale, when an immense temple is consumed in flames even though the entire chorus must continue singing until the curtains fall. 'Don't worry,' I explained. 'At La Scala we have all the supers we need. They will do the running, rushing, and escaping. Your chorus will be there in place singing—perhaps covered by smoke, but you will hear them.' It was all so new to him.

"As for Maria, she was extraordinary. At that time, she had just begun to lose weight, but not too much. Her figure was still powerful. She really looked like one of the caryatides on the Acropolis, those great women who stand like pillars supporting the temple. She had enormous impulse in her gestures—you *felt* her strength. She dominated. For Medea, her physique was an advantage, which gave the character a quality of antiquity. Her portrayal lost this special kind of presence when she became too thin.

"Since Medea is a stranger in Corinth, an ominous Colchian princess who practices black arts, in my directing I let Maria roam free from the other characters onstage. The chorus I grouped in blocks, while Maria often stayed front center, a world apart from all else that was going on. I believe Medea inspired Maria very deeply. She identified with the role. She herself was torn between America,

Greece, and Italy—like Medea, a wanderer without a real home. And like Medea, when it was necessary, she found the strength to cut long-held ties, to go on and survive. This takes courage. Real courage. During her early years at La Scala, you know, she was still a very young woman, and married to a much older man. I am sure that certain sexual frustrations found an outlet in her work—unfulfilled passions were released in her singing and acting. When this was no longer a problem for her, she was not the same artist.

"But at the time of our *Medea* she was at her peak. She had splendid long red hair—flaming red. In the last act, when she must murder her children, she lay supine as the curtains parted—head down diagonally on the high staircase of the temple—a great blood-red cloak and her fiery hair spread out around her, a symbol of the grisly deeds to come. Holocaust has been ordained. Never moving, gazing into the stormy night sky, she sang her first line, 'Numi, venite a me, inferni Dei!' [Deities, come to me, infernal gods!]. When we first tried the scene in rehearsal, Maria protested: 'Margherita, I can't sing in such a position. It's impossible!' And she broke down and cried. I was upset for her and told Luigi Oldani, the secretary general of La Scala, 'I'd better change this, even though it is very beautiful. Maria is suffering and I don't want her to be unhappy.' But Oldani replied, 'Don't change a thing. She is a very ambitious woman and has an unerring theatrical instinct. She will do it. You will see.' And in a few days, there was no more crying. Maria did the scene exactly as I asked. Unforgettably."

Leonard Bernstein remembers what happened at Scala when the final curtain fell: "The place was out of its mind. Callas? She was pure electricity."

Fiume sketches for acts two and three [above]; Callas during finale [below]

TEATRO ALLA SCALA

LUNEDÌ 18 GENNAIO 1954 - alle ore 21 precise
PRIMA RAPPRESENTAZIONE

LUCIA DI
LAMMERMOOR

Dramma tragico in tre atti di S. CAMMARANO
Musica di
GAETANO DONIZETTI
NUOVO ALLESTIMENTO

HERBERT v. KARAJAN

"Question: Which Is Mad, the Callas Lucia or Her Frenzied Public?" So read the headline on Claudia Cassidy's review of Callas's first appearance in *Lucia di Lammermoor* in Chicago. The year was 1954. Describing how Callas had bewitched her audience with the Mad Scene, Cassidy wrote: "Near pandemonium broke out. There was an avalanche of applause, a roar of cheers growing steadily hoarser, and a standing ovation, and the aisles were full of men pushing as close to the stage as possible. I am sure they wished for bouquets to throw, a carriage to pull through the streets. Myself, I wish they had had both."

Invariably, wherever Callas sang Lucia, the public reacted with the same fervor. But, beginning with her first appearance in the role, in Mexico City in 1952, it was her dramatic vocalism, not her acting, that earned Callas her triumphs. For unlike her other major roles, Callas never had the opportunity to build a detailed visual realization of Lucia with a director such as Visconti or Zeffirelli. With the exception of one production staged especially for her at Scala, her Lucias were always performed with stock sets and run-of-the-mill directors. It was not until 1958, with the Dallas Civic Opera, that she finally appeared in a major staging of the opera, a Zeffirelli production originally created for Joan Sutherland at Covent Garden. For the Dallas performances, Zeffirelli was present, but Lucia's costumes were not. Callas was obliged to perform in costumes intended for a member of the chorus. On opening night, she muffed her high E-flats, much to her dismay. No sooner had the curtains closed than she sang the recalcitrant note five times in succession to prove to herself—and to those within earshot—that she could capture it. But her days as Lucia were over. She never again attempted the role.

The Scala production, however, was one of the supreme nights of Callas's career. It had its premiere on January 18, 1954, at a time when Callas could sustain an E-flat in alt for ten seconds or more. Her stage director and conductor in Milan was Herbert von Karajan, who asked Nicola Benois to execute the decor, but the designer begged off when he heard the conductor's unorthodox scenic concept. Explaining that he felt uncomfortable with such ideas, Benois proposed Gianni Ratto for the job. Under Karajan's constant surveillance, Ratto turned out bare, stylized sets with moody, dim lighting and murky rear projections [the act two Sextet is shown below]. Benois remembers that Karajan demanded and got an additional number of lighting rehearsals to achieve the gloom he sought.

While Callas relished making music with Karajan—who is part Greek—she detested his visual production. Still, he conducted Donizetti's score superbly. After the cadenza of the Mad Scene, the audience stood to applaud Callas, raining red

As Lucia, act one,
and in act two, with
Modesti, Villa, di Stefano,
Panerai, Zampieri

carnations onto the stage during her solo curtain calls, a triumph repeated six times that year.

In the fall of 1955, the Scala production was taken to the Berlin Festival. By then, the rapport between Callas and Karajan had led to a subtlety of phrasing not even Milan had experienced. The Germans were literally bowled over by the romantic beauty of Donizetti's score and the performance given it. English critic Desmond Shawe-Taylor, who witnessed the premiere, wrote: "Miss Callas' performance did not end with the Mad Scene; through ten minutes of solo curtain calls she remained with consummate art half within the stage character, with her air of wondering simplicity, her flawless miming of unworthiness, her subtle variation in the tempo of successive appearances and in the depth of her curtseys, and her elaborate byplay with the roses which fell from the gallery (poetic, chivalrous Berlin!)—one of which, with such a gesture and such capital aim, she flung to the delighted flautist! Oh yes, an artist to the fingertips: the real royal thing."

If in *Lucia di Lammermoor* Callas proved herself a vocal revelation, for scenic action literally all she had to rely on was personal magnetism. This she had in abundance, and it remains one of the most inexplicable of her qualities. Sandro Sequi, the Italian stage director, was a student during the decade of her prime. Determined on a career in the theater, Sequi watched Callas performances not only to enjoy her gifts, but to try to understand them. "Certain artists are gifted with something special," says Sequi, "and Callas had that kind of theatrical quality one sees today in Nureyev, Plisetskaya, Brando, Olivier. Magnani had it, too. Yet they are all quite individual, unlike each other in every respect. After watching Callas many times on stage in many roles, I realized she had a secret few theater people know. But to explain this, I must go back a bit in my own life.

"As a teen-ager, I studied dancing with Clotilde and Alexandre Sakharoff, who were very famous in Europe during the twenties and thirties—he was a pupil of Isadora Duncan. In his lessons, Sakharoff always stressed using the brain to send tension to every muscle of the body—a tension of the mind, the intelligence, which would travel to every limb, to the fingers, the toes, the face, everywhere. But then there must be a sudden relaxation, which gives the impression of a break of energy, a kind of fall. Sakharoff would demonstrate a gesture of the most terrible intensity, then end it. The effect was extraordinary, a kind of climax, like when people die.

"This alternation of tension and relaxation can exert an incredible hold over the public. I believe this was the key to Callas's magnetism, why her singing and acting were so compelling. Think of the movements of her arms in the Mad Scene of *Lucia* [left and right]. They were like the wings of a great eagle, a marvelous bird. When they went up, and she often moved them very slowly, they seemed heavy—not airy like a dancer's arms, but weighted. Then, she reached the climax of a musical phrase, her arms relaxed and flowed into the next gesture, until she reached a new musical peak, and then again calm. There was a continuous line to her singing and movements, which were really very simple.

"Onstage, when an artist must convey great power or energy, he cannot do so constantly. If he did, the performer would seem hard, tough. Callas never was. Hell's fire one moment, she could be sweetly tender the next. All in an instant—the very thing Sakharoff had shown me. I doubt it was a technique she used consciously. Everything about her struck me as natural and instinctive, never intellectual.

"To sing opera requires a tremendous amount of energy, and it might seem twice the drain on the physique of a singer to coordinate the voice with the body. But the opposite is true, as Callas proved. Both things can go together, indeed, must go together. That is why Callas is remembered as no other singer, however beautifully others may have sung. For me, she was extremely stylized and classic, yet at the same time human—but a humanity on a higher plain of existence, almost sublime. Realism was foreign to her, and that is why she was the greatest of opera singers. After all, opera is the least realistic of theater forms. To my mind, Callas was wasted in verismo roles, even Tosca, no matter how brilliantly she could act such roles. Verismo made her smaller than she was. Her greater genius was revealed in *Norma, Sonnambula, Lucia*. This was the classic Callas."

During the Mad Scene, *Lucia*

On April 4, 1954, Christoph Willibald von Gluck's *Alceste* was staged at La Scala for the first time in the theater's 176-year history. The opera itself predated Scala by eleven years. For the artists involved with introducing this masterpiece to Milan—conductor Carlo Maria Giulini, director-choreographer Margherita Wallmann, designer Piero Zuffi, and the title heroine, Maria Callas—the production became a labor of love and deep involvement. During its nearly two centuries, Scala had lavished a wealth of talent and means on many great—and not so great—works, but almost to the exclusion of Gluck.

Prior to the 1954 *Alceste*, stagings of the composer's operas were few and far between, though some were of exceptional merit. *Orfeo ed Euridice* had been given in a total of eight seasons, conducted most often by Arturo Toscanini, and later by Antonio Guarnieri, Jonel Perlea, and Wilhelm Furtwängler. In 1911, there had been a single production of *Armida*, led by Tullio Serafin; in 1937, a single production of *Ifigenia in Tauride*, under Victor de Sabata. Nothing else.

Maestro Giulini, who under Sir Georg Solti is now principal guest conductor of the Chicago Symphony and has abandoned the opera house in favor of the concert platform, put in five seasons at Scala as a permanent member of its artistic staff. Between 1951 and 1956, he conducted fifteen works there, ranging from the riches of Monteverdi to the banalities of Cilèa. Among the performances of which he has fondest memories are *L'Italiana in Algeri* and *La cenerentola*, in which he collaborated with Giulietta Simionato and Franco Zeffirelli, and the celebrated Visconti-de Nobili-Callas production of *La traviata*.

But for Giulini, *Alceste* represented "something sacred. I edited the score so carefully, going back to the original text of Calzabigi, but using Gluck's later French musical revision. Maria Callas made the ideal protagonist and approached her role in a way that was absolute, complete. For me, she was *il melodramma*—total rapport between word, music, and action. She gave value to every demand of expression. From her first entrance with her children [left], she had an amazing capacity to sustain attention even when standing motionless. In my entire experience in the theater, I know of no artist like Callas. It is no fabricated legend: She had something that was different.

"During the many performances I did with Callas—not only *Alceste*, but *La traviata*, a triumph, and *Il barbiere di Siviglia*, a fiasco—she maintained an incredible sense of responsibility to her work. At rehearsals, she absorbed everything with unbelievable rapidity. She not only grasped the musical phrases as

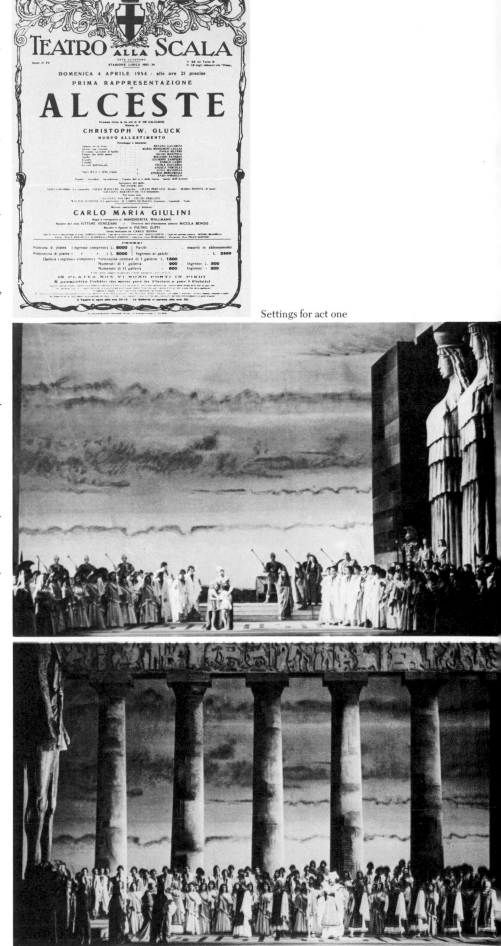

Settings for act one

you demonstrated them to her, she made them her own. To work with her was to work in profundity.

"We never limited our work merely to getting the music together, to establishing the tempos. We always went far beyond that. We searched for the meaning of each word, the value of each note, of each pause. We looked for the reasons a phrase might go one way rather than another. These things are fundamental to great art and were vital to her. They are the only basis on which to perform a role such as Alceste.

"Gluck's vocal demands, of course, are classic and stately, and because of Callas's attitude, she endeavored to make her voice serve the needs of his music. In a way she was more like an instrumentalist than a singer—I mean, naturally, the general run of singers. Think of a violinist who owns a glorious Stradivarius. If he possesses the technique, he can play Bach, Mozart, Beethoven, Brahms, or Berg. But each must be played in a different way, in its own period and style.

"Maria knew this is equally true of the voice, and not only did she seek to capture the spirit of a composer's music, she sought to convey the heart of the character she was to portray. When an artist prepares so rare and difficult an opera as *Alceste*, which requires many weeks of rehearsal, he comes to live in the climate of the work itself. He listens to the orchestra, the instrumentation, to the lines of all the singers and the chorus. A little world creates itself around the artist as the music is reborn.

"In this way Maria discovered the world of Gluck and came fully to understand the quality of her role. Even though it is a far more controlled kind of part than say, Violetta or Norma, for Maria it was no less intense, no less strong or deep or interesting. Alceste is far more interior than exterior, and in building her characterization, and this is the miracle of Maria, she created a long, stupendous line, an unbroken arch. Every musical phrase, word, and gesture was developed with the logic indicated in Gluck's score.

"I know she loved singing Alceste, and she did it with immense humility, humanity, and passion. But at this point I must make one point clear. Offstage Maria is really a very simple woman of humble background. Alceste, however, is a great queen, a figure of classic nobility. Yet, through some mystic transformation, Callas transmitted all Alceste's royal stature. To my mind it is useless to search for an explanation. It is a kind of genius. From the moment Maria would step on the stage, she materially became the character she was to play.

"Callas could have been—and I don't say this is true—the most egotistical, selfish, cruel woman alive, yet onstage she could convince an audience she was the most selfless, generous, loving of creatures. These were her qualities as Alceste—a selfless wife, generous to the point of sacrificing her own life to save her husband. I feel sure that if in his day Gluck had had Callas as an interpreter, he would have seen his ideal realized."

Shown here, with Paolo Silveri as the High Priest [left], Callas's Alceste offers gifts to placate the gods who demand Admetus's life.

With Silveri, scene two

Margherita Wallmann, who directed the 1954 production of *Alceste* at La Scala, learned the Gluck tradition from the late conductor Bruno Walter, for whom she had staged *Alceste* and *Orfeo ed Euridice* many years before. She points out that, "Most of Gluck's operas are based on ancient Greek tragedies, so the producer must strive to create the feeling of space that exists in the immense theater at Epidaurus, where many of these dramas were born.

"In Milan, my designer for *Alceste*, Piero Zuffi, and I were greatly concerned with the proportions of the Scala stage. With the large chorus, Gluck almost becomes four-dimensional. Zuffi, who often worked with Giorgio Strehler at the Piccolo Teatro di Milano, understood stage construction and was so helpful in every detail. He did not utilize many colors, but if one studies the architecture of his sets, one discovers the true, classic structure of Gluck and his *Alceste*. In effect, Gluck was re-creating ancient Greek theater, seeking, as they had, to express eternal human values.

"These are what Maria Callas brought to her Alceste. She was regal, yet submissive to her destiny, and very sweet, very loving. Even as Norma, I never saw her display such tenderness with the children as she did in *Alceste*.

"Before I ever met her, I saw her by chance one night in a restaurant. At one moment she removed her glasses, and I was fascinated by her huge, dark eyes. They haunted me, for I felt I had seen them before. One day I realized where. They are exactly like those of the famous statue of the charioteer of Auriga at Delphi. I believe Greek subjects stirred deep emotions in Maria. Her origins, her ancestry. Thus, when I would demonstrate a classic gesture to her, it did not come out as an imitation, but as something her own. These were born in her, part of her heritage. In *Alceste*, *Medea*, and even in *Norma*, all her movements were so real, so true, so convincing.

"Before one rehearsal for *Alceste*, I told Maria not to arrive at the theater until noon, because from ten that morning I had to do staging with the chorus. At twelve, I would be free to block her positions onstage and to work with her on her interpretation. But when I arrived at ten, to my surprise, there sat Maria. 'But, dear,' I said, 'you don't have to come for another two hours.' She replied, 'I want to watch you work with the chorus. That way I will get in the right mood and know what I must do.'

"What other major artist can you name who would sit for two hours in an empty auditorium observing a chorus rehearse just to understand the overall quality of a production? But this, of course, is one of the many things that went into making Maria the incomparable artist she was."

On these pages, Callas is shown in the dramatic moment when the temple trembles and Alceste's subjects flee in terror. The Queen is abandoned even by the High Priest, who fears the wrath of the gods. Left alone, Alceste laments the fate of her doomed husband, then sings the celebrated aria "Divinités du Styx" (Gods of the River Styx) in which she defies the deities of death. Resolving to save Admetus, she offers to give her own life so that he may live.

As Alceste, with Silveri

Alceste quietly informs the distraught Admetus [top, Renato Gavarini with Callas] of her pledge to die so he may live. But the gods are so moved by her sacrifice they grant life to both husband and wife. In Gluck's day, operas frequently ended with long ceremonial ballets; in *Alceste*, love's victory is celebrated by dance [above]. Callas, being myopic, could see little of the choreography as she sat on the throne with Admetus, and at the dress rehearsal turned her head for a moment to smile at a friend, La Scala photographer Erio Piccagliani, who was in the wings to take a close-up of the soprano [right]. The smile is pure Callas and was meant for Piccagliani alone.

Throughout the 1953–54 season, Callas lost weight in a physical transformation that seemed almost miraculous. For her director in *Alceste*, Margherita Wallmann [shown above with tenor Gavarini], Callas's slenderizing was a godsend: It meant she could devise scenic effects that would not otherwise have been possible. In Wallmann's words. "For the act two finale, when Alceste gives herself in death to spare Admetus, I wanted her body to be borne aloft into the temple as the curtain closed. But Maria, because she had always been fat, had never in her life been lifted over anyone's head, and at the first rehearsal she was really afraid to try. To convince her she would be safe, I myself acted out the scene. Of course, Maria then agreed to do it. In the performance, as she was carried up the temple steps, her body tilted back slightly so that her beautiful long red hair flowed down behind her. The effect was stunning."

For conductor Carlo Maria Giulini, Callas's amazing loss of weight was accompanied by a refinement in her artistry: "She became another woman and a new world of expression opened to her. Potentials held in the shadows emerged. In every sense, she had been transformed."

Seated in her dressing room at La Scala, Maria Callas awaits the call to go onstage [left]. It is April 12, 1954, and she is about to perform in a work new to her repertory: Verdi's *Don Carlo*. Callas, her artistic credentials thoroughly established at La Scala, is calm: The theater promises to become an artistic haven where her talents can fully develop. Already she knows that her next season will surpass all that has gone before in her career. She has truly arrived.

Dressed as Elisabetta di Valois, wife of the aging King Philip II of Spain, Callas wears huge rings to ornament her fingers. Her costume, according to designer Nicola Benois, was inspired by the paintings of Velázquez; made of black, silver, and white, it was intended "to suggest the drama of a woman cruelly struck by fate." It almost seems Callas has already entered the interior life of Elisabetta. Only a short while later, her very posture and expression will be virtually duplicated onstage when, as Queen Elisabetta, she secretly meets with her stepson and former fiancé, Don Carlo [right].

Callas had learned the part of Elisabetta nearly four years earlier. For the 1950–51 season, two houses—the Teatro San Carlo in Naples and the Teatro dell'Opera in Rome—had engaged her for the role. Jaundice, however, had forced her to abandon rehearsals and retire temporarily from the stage. Thus, her debut in the role did not take place until the Scala performances.

The critics praised her characterization's dramatic power and her vocal confidence. Some felt she lacked a certain requisite sweetness and would have been better suited to the role of the fiery Princess Eboli (in the Scala production, the role was taken by Ebe Stignani). In any event, after five performances of *Don Carlo* at Scala, Callas never again appeared in the opera.

On the following pages, her Elisabetta is seen in the great auto-da-fé scene, where she is splendidly gowned in silver and white. Surrounding her, clockwise, are Don Carlo (Mario Ortica), Rodrigo (Enzo Mascherini), King Philip (Nicola Rossi-Lemeni), and the court. They are awaiting the burning of heretics. "It was a terrible, black moment in Spain's history, a time when even kings wept," comments Benois. "This is what we hoped to capture in our production."

As Elisabetta di Valois, with Ortica; [next pages] with Mascherini, Ortica, Rossi-Lemeni

In his study, King Philip finds Don Carlo's portrait in his wife's jewel box and confronts the Queen [above, Rossi-Lemeni with Callas]. Accused of adultery, Elisabetta faints, and Rodrigo and Eboli come to her aid [right, Mascherini and Stignani]. Rossi-Lemeni, who thinks Callas did this revival of *Don Carlo* to fill time between appearances as Alceste, found her an exemplary colleague. "She frequently asked practical advice about her acting. If I suggested a gesture or pose she liked, she'd modestly say, 'Now, you gave me something I should have thought of myself.' If she disagreed, of course, she didn't utilize it. But she always carefully considered ideas.

"I met Maria in 1946 in Chicago. I was there to help launch a new opera company with a *Turandot* starring Maria, Mafalda Favero, Galliano Masini, and myself. The venture folded and I went to New York, where Giovanni Zenatello hired me to sing Méphistophélès in *Faust* at the Verona Arena. Knowing he needed a Gioconda, I suggested Maria. For friends in Chicago, she always was ready to sing, at a party, after dinner. Amazing—so strong physically and spiritually, so certain of her future. I knew in a big outdoor theater like Verona's, this girl, with her courage and huge voice, would make a tremendous impact."

Rossi-Lemeni, who later was Tullio Serafin's son-in-law, worked with the conductor and Callas often. "For me, Callas was always Callas, whether as Isolde, Gioconda, or Norma. Her personal projection was so potent that even if it didn't belong to a role, it looked right and became valid. The public must believe an artist is lost in his portrayal. To do this, one needs more than technique; one must be born with a special gift. Callas was.

"Despite Maria's power, she often doubted herself and grew anxious, fearing failure. She could never rest because of the great obligation she felt to her work. Her husband, Meneghini, always stood in the wings whispering encouragement: 'Go on, Maria! There's no one like you. You're the greatest in the world!' Somehow this helped pull her through crises. Meneghini once told me that when she woke, their day depended on odd croaking noises she made in her throat—not vocalises. If it felt right, she was happy; if not, she suffered, even if she later sang well. So mighty and so weak, that was Maria."

Don Carlo, act three, with Rossi-Lemeni [above]

and Mascherini and Stignani [right]

When Maria Callas appeared for rehearsals at La Scala in November 1954–direct from her American debut with the Chicago Lyric Theater–she was a woman totally transformed. So changed was her appearance that many of her colleagues failed to recognize her. The new Callas had the figure of a ballerina and her red hair had been lightened to blonde to impart a softer stage appearance. (It was a short-lived effort and Callas soon adopted the natural chestnut-brown she maintains to this day.)

With five operas on her schedule–four of them new productions–the 1954–55 season at Scala was to be Callas's busiest and most varied. It would also be her first collaboration with two major figures from the world of the legitimate theater and film–Luchino Visconti and Franco Zeffirelli. Under their direction, Callas would refine her natural gifts as an actress until they equaled her qualities as a musician and singer.

For the third time in four years Callas was to open the Scala season. The opera, Gaspare Spontini's *La vestale*, had not been staged in Milan for a quarter-century, and it would mark two important debuts: that of Visconti who, as the son of a noble Milanese family, had practically grown up in box four on the theater's first tier but had never directed an opera, and that of a young tenor named Franco Corelli, making his first Scala appearance.

Visconti, who describes *Vestale* as "a neoclassic *Norma* but with a happy ending," remembers what he first felt working with Callas: "What do I recall of her during rehearsals? Beauty. Something beautiful. Intensity, expression, everything. She was a monstrous phenomenon. Almost a sickness–a kind of actress that has passed for all time."

During *Vestale* rehearsal

Arturo Toscanini, who played the cello in La Scala's orchestra at the world premiere of Verdi's *Otello* and who later served as the theater's artistic director and chief conductor, came to Milan during preparations for *La vestale*. Since the war, Toscanini had returned to Scala to conduct concerts but never an opera. Visconti remembers the eighty-seven-year-old Maestro's visit.

"At the time, the small theater—La Piccola Scala—was under construction. The plan was for Maestro to inaugurate it with *Falstaff*, which he wanted me to stage. Often I went to his home for lunch to discuss this, and one day he expressed the wish to watch one of my rehearsals. I was delighted and when he arrived I put him in the best box. But he spotted Victor de Sabata in the orchestra section and went down to greet him. Antonino Votto, our conductor for *Vestale*, and Maria then came offstage to pay their respects to Toscanini and de Sabata [left].

"Later, Maestro called me to him, saying, 'I like very much what you do, but you must understand that my eyesight is poor. I find this Callas woman very good, a beautiful voice and an interesting artist, but her diction is unintelligible. With the tenor I understand every word. This is important, for opera is theater, and the words are more important than the music.' I was stupefied—surely Toscanini could not mean this—and I explained that Maria was a Greek-American and did not speak perfect Italian. But Toscanini held to his point. 'No! No!' he said. 'You *must* hear every word, otherwise it is a concert.'

"You see, Toscanini was a man of the theater. He came from a century when people attended opera as we do movies and spoken theater. Can you imagine anyone today watching a film, not understanding a word but being fully satisfied?"

Toscanini [seated], Votto, de Sabata, Callas; Bianchi [far left], Oldani, Corti, Mola

Visconti's custom is to work closely with his designer. "I made Piero Zuffi redo the *Vestale* sketches at least twenty times," he laughs today. During his research, Visconti took inspiration from the paintings of Appiani, whose imperial, neoclassic style corresponded exactly with Spontini's music. Colors were cold–"like white marble, moon-struck marble." Because *Vestale* is an early nineteenth-century opera and at that time singers came to the proscenium to perform, Visconti had the stage floor built forward. Thus, when the curtains opened, Callas was first seen veiled, leaning motionless against one of the enormous pillars that flank Scala's stage and which had become part of Zuffi's setting.

Many of the gestures Visconti had Callas and Corelli use were derived from poses found in the paintings of Canova, Ingres, and David. "Maria was marvelous," Visconti relates. "I had already admired her for many years–from the days when she first did Kundry and Norma in Rome. Every night she sang I secured a certain box and shouted like a mad fanatic when she took her bows. I sent her flowers, and finally we met. She was fat, but beautiful onstage. I loved her fatness, which made her so commanding. She was already distinctive then. Her gestures thrilled you. Where did she learn them? On her own. But with *La vestale*, we began systematically to perfect them [left and right]. We selected some from the great French tragediennes, some from Greek drama, for this was the kind of actress she could be–classic. Today, some famous singers try to imitate what Maria did, but they only make fools of themselves. Maria looked a certain way with her long neck, body, arms, fingers. She can never be copied.

"At some point, Maria began to fall in love with me. It was a stupid thing, all in her mind. But like so many Greeks, she has a possessive streak, and there were many terrible jealous scenes. She hated Corelli because he was handsome. It made her nervous–she was wary of beautiful people. She was always watching to see I didn't give him more attention than I gave her. And she disliked the baritone, Enzo Sordello–who knows why?–and did not want to do a scene with him in the last act. 'Look, Maria,' I told her, 'we can't change the baritone or the opera just to please you!'

"But I could forgive her anything because she did all I asked so scrupulously, so precisely, so beautifully. What I demanded, she rendered, never adding anything of her own. Sometimes during a rehearsal I'd say, 'Come on, Maria, do a little by yourself, do something you like.' But then she'd ask, 'What should I do? How am I to place this hand? I don't know where to put it!' The simple fact was, because of this crazy infatuation, she wanted to have me command her every step."

Visconti working on *Vestale*,
with Callas and, standing far right, Votto

During their work, Visconti extracted more than he had ever expected from Callas. "*La vestale* is difficult to stage, for it needs great style," he explains. "This Maria gave it. For me, she was a wonderful instrument which could be played as I wished and which responded in an inspired way. How different from contending with a singer of the old school, such as Ebe Stignani [seen at the right, the heavyset and hatted woman behind Callas]. As the High Priestess, Stignani was hopeless with her two stock gestures, worse than a scrubwoman onstage. Unbearable! She was the antithesis of Maria, who absorbed and grew from day to day. How, I don't know. By some uncanny theatrical instinct, if put on the right course, she always exceeded your hopes. How beautiful she and Corelli looked during the love duet in the temple, the sacred flame flickering on the altar. Pure physical beauty, figures of neoclassicism reborn."

The next four pages recapture the massive triumphal scene in which Giulia performs the ceremony of placing a wreath on the brow of the victorious Roman general Licinius, whom she loves. First the scene is shown in rehearsal, with Visconti kneeling to the side of Corelli to observe Callas as she pretends to hold the wreath. At stage center is Nicola Rossi-Lemeni, who sang the High Priest; at the far right stands the monolithic Stignani. The second photo captures the same moment in all the pomp and glory of the Zuffi-Visconti decor. "I'm not in that one," quips the director. "My costume wasn't ready."

The spectacle awed the Milanese with its succession of sweeping stage pictures, including a poignant funeral procession with weeping priestesses carrying garlands of white roses. Toscanini sat in a stage box, and, during a bow, Callas took a carnation a fan had thrown her and gave it to the shy old Maestro. The house went wild. Once again, Callas's uncanny theatrical instinct was at work.

Preparing *Vestale*, with Stignani [in rear];
[next pages] with Visconti, Corelli, Rossi-Lemeni,
and Stignani, in rehearsal and performance

Each autumn, La Scala pastes large sepia-colored posters on billboards outside the theater to announce the coming season's repertory and roster of artists. When workmen put up the 1954–55 edition, it listed a total of twenty-eight works, but Giordano's *Andrea Chénier* was not among them.

Antonio Ghiringhelli, who at the time was general manager of Scala, explains: "Originally, we had scheduled *Il trovatore*, with Mario del Monaco, Maria Callas, Ebe Stignani, and Aldo Protti. But del Monaco suddenly decided he was too sick to sing Manrico. Nevertheless, he felt well enough to do Andrea Chénier." A bemused smile crossed Ghiringhelli's face as he recounted the incident, betraying the ease he at last feels, free from such caprices. "What could we do? We made a substitution."

By that point in her career, Callas knew her true métier was bel canto and had little interest in verismo roles. However, to help the theater and fill out contracted time, she took on the role of Maddalena di Coigny, learning it in five days.

An existing production, created in 1948 for Mirto Picchi and Renata Tebaldi, was taken out of mothballs, and the public was duly informed of the change. The Milanese dote on rumors about their opera house, and the switch in schedule engendered a full quota. Some held that del Monaco was afraid to sing Manrico, which requires two fortissimo high-C's in the aria "Di quella pira." Others said Callas, intent on usurping the repertory of Tebaldi—her principal competition as leading soprano of the theater—had instigated the change of opera.

Chénier, the poet of the French Revolution, was del Monaco's most powerful role, and at the premiere, on January 8, 1955, he brought down the house with the brooding "Improvviso" [left].

Had the opera been *Il trovatore*, Callas might well have walked off with the show, for Leonora was one of her bel canto specialties. But even if Maddalena was not a role requiring her rarefied vocal skills, at certain moments it permitted Callas to display her gifts as an actress. As the young daughter of an aristocratic family that is ruined by the Revolution, Maddalena must go from ado-

Del Monaco as Chénier

lescent playfulness and innocence to womanly compassion. As Callas listened to Chénier's "Improvviso," in which the poet insults the aristocracy and describes the misery of the peasants, her eyes showed this change from girl to woman [right].

In retrospect, Callas's generosity in coming to the aid of Scala in a moment of crisis turned out to be a mistake. *Andrea Chénier* is, from first act to last, a tenor vehicle. The soprano's music contains only one dramatic high point—the third act aria "La mamma morta." It begins with a poignant cello solo, and Callas mirrored its tonal color in her voice as she began the first, recitative-like lines of the aria. For those who understood what she was doing, it was a moment of revelation.

But in the music of composers such as Giordano and Mascagni, the Italian public expects a certain animal power and visceral vocal punch, not niceties of musical phrasing. The two previous Scala Maddalenas, Renata Tebaldi and Maria Caniglia, had in no way altered these expectations. Thus the audience was unprepared for Callas's approach, which created intensity by other means. They were equally unprepared to accept in a verismo role the transformation that Callas's voice was undergoing at that moment (her first *Sonnambula* was two months away). For whatever reason—perhaps the great weight loss, perhaps the added emphasis on bel canto repertory, perhaps just natural vocal development—Callas's sound was becoming lighter in texture, more transparent, somewhat less powerful in volume.

To make matters worse, Callas let a climactic high-B get out of control, and it wobbled wildly. This was exactly what her detractors, especially the Tebaldi faction in the top gallery, had been waiting for. At the conclusion of "La mamma morta," open hostility erupted in the theater. Adding to the din was the claque, with which Callas had always refused to deal—her ego demanded real, not paid, applause. As hoots and whistles combined with the applause of Callas's admirers, the soprano maintained her composure. It was some measure of compensation that, at the opera's conclusion, Giordano's widow went backstage to express her personal appreciation to Callas and del Monaco.

The clash between the partisans of Tebaldi and Callas had at last come to a head. According to Luchino Visconti, it was an argument that raged between the fans, not between the singers themselves. "They went about their work and paid no mind to each other," he says. Ghiringhelli, in an attempt to quiet the warring factions, had learned to schedule his repertory so that the two sopranos would appear during different periods. Still, this did not quell the dispute, nor did a published comment from Callas, whether invented by a reporter or true, help the situation: "If the time comes when my dear friend Renata Tebaldi sings Norma or Lucia one night, then Violetta, La Gioconda, or Medea the next—then and only then will we be rivals. Otherwise it is like comparing champagne with cognac. No—with Coca-Cola." In any event, Tebaldi soon left Scala to establish an impenetrable beachhead at the Metropolitan Opera in New York. When Callas followed her there, she found the overriding preference to be for Coke.

As Maddalena di Coigny

Andrea Chénier in Milan and *Medea* in Rome
served as preludes to one of Callas's most brilliant
performances in the bel canto literature–Amina in
La sonnambula, which opened at La Scala on
March 5, 1955. Through the sorcery of director
Luchino Visconti and designer Piero Tosi, Callas
seemed a reincarnation of the legendary nineteenth-century ballerina Maria Taglioni as she
made her entrance, high on a bridge [right], singing with a style that reached back to Pasta.

For Callas, the role of Amina had special significance. Her voice teacher, Elvira de Hidalgo,
had herself been a celebrated Amina, singing the
role at the Metropolitan Opera in 1910. Thirty
years later, when Callas graduated from the
Athens Conservatory, de Hidalgo chose to stage
Suor Angelica for her. Paired with the short Puccini work was act one of *Sonnambula*, for which
she had selected another of her students. "I recall," says de Hidalgo, "how aware and envious
Maria was of my pupil who sang Amina." With the
Scala production, Callas at last had her chance to
triumph over that long-ago rival.

Piero Tosi can recount every episode of the
Scala production. "Callas was never that capricious
myth created by the press. In the theater she was a
soldier, never asking questions or making a fuss.
She would put on her costume, let me pull her hair
back in a band, then go on stage barefoot; she even
wore a very tight corset. Gina Lollobrigida didn't
have a waist like that–twenty-two inches. All the
while, Callas was eating rich foods at Biffi Scala and
boxes of *marrons glacés*. She'd call our old ward-
robe lady to measure her waist and then to pull in
the corset. I tell you it would kill a film star–and
Callas had to sing!"

Visconti made Callas's Amina no peasant girl, but the evocation of a bejeweled nineteenth-century prima donna *performing* the role.

Here, she awaits her fiancé, resplendently gowned in white silk, a necklace of pale blue opals, a flower crown of pink, mauve, and lilac.

Piero Tosi recalls the impression Callas created during the sleepwalking scene in act two. "It's a strange thing. Offstage, Maria is tall and strong, even a little rigid, but the moment she stepped onstage, there was a metamorphosis. She looked small, with an incredible grace. Her steps were like those of a ballerina, and when she stood still, she took a dancer's fifth position. Of course, Luchino had coached her in these details, but it was *how* she did them. For me, though the critics hated it, the second act was the most beautiful of all–the Count's room at the inn, with neo-Gothic wood beams–the kind of wood that by night gives off the color of pale violet. The set and mood were almost metaphysical. Half the stage was illuminated by the moon, the other half obscured in shadow–zones of light. Callas entered from the rear, a sylphide tripping on a moonbeam. She crossed the stage on the diagonal of light, singing her dream of her fiancé, pretending to ascend the church steps for the wedding. She was enchanting. When the Count touched her shoulder, she fell to the floor, but very softly, with her legs crossed like a Margot Fonteyn [top right, with Giuseppe Modesti]. Later, she had to lie on a divan and her pose was exactly period Louis-Philippe. Pure 1830. When the villagers arrived with lanterns, the mood faded and the spell was broken [right]. One of the things the critics complained of was that I had dressed the villagers like ladies and gentlemen–the women in shades of pink, pearl, and gray, and the men in black, with white gloves. But Luchino and I had intended to evoke a lost, divine, melancholy era. Critics never understand."

Visconti's memories are no less vivid. "To start with, Maria's infatuation had not abated and she seemed more possessive than ever. She couldn't bear for me to pay attention to anyone else, especially to Leonard Bernstein, our conductor, who was so amusing, such a wonderful friend. We were together a lot, and Maria spied on us even when we went outside the theater to have a coffee or take a little walk. Once, Lennie and I went to visit her at her hotel because she had a painful carbuncle on her neck. When the moment came to leave, we said 'Ciao, Maria. Get well!' and headed for the door. 'You stay here!' she commanded me. 'I don't want you going off again with Lennie!' My God! In those days, she sometimes could be an absolute birdbrain. Yet onstage, she would amaze me. For in truth, the character of Amina is nothing like Maria herself. She made her into a marvelous night bird.

"I always kept a handkerchief in my pocket with a drop of a particular English perfume on it, and Maria loved the scent. She told me always to place the handkerchief on the divan on which she had to lie down during the inn scene. 'That way I'll be able to walk directly to it with my eyes closed.' And so that's how we accomplished this effect. Luckily, no musician in the orchestra ever decided to wear the same perfume or one night she might have walked right off the stage and into the pit."

In *Sonnambula*, act two, with
Modesti [top right] , Ratti [right]

In his settings for *La sonnambula*, Tosi tried to create the illusion of flat period prints—like old postcards or lithographs. He did not want volume or dimension on-stage and he used his decor and lighting accordingly. Even costumes became mere areas of color flattened by light. In the mill scene of the first and last acts, he used chilly colors, blues and greens. Nothing was realistic.

In the unreal ambience of the final act, Tosi recalls, Callas imparted a particularly startling effect to the sleepwalking scene on the bridge. "At the dress rehearsal, as the lights dimmed for her entrance, Callas was seen in silhouette, the lake and the mountains behind her. She looked like a shadow, a specter floating upwards. When she came to the broken plank on the bridge—where she must simulate falling and all the chorus gasps in horror—I watched her closely. Though she seemed to fall, I saw that she actually remained absolutely still. Yet she had caused the sensation of a fall—the fall of a ghost.

"I was fascinated. I had to know how she did it and so, at the premiere, I stood in the wings near her as she ascended the bridge. Slowly, she began to fill her lungs with air, and this gave an illusion of flight, of floating upward, to the audience. Then, when she had to fall, she quickly exhaled all her breath. What can you say? She was a theatrical wizard and knew all the tricks."

By the time Callas had descended among the villagers, the lighting had dimmed to near blackness. Without the audience seeing it, a tomb had been placed onstage. As the lights gradually rose to illuminate the tomb, Callas knelt by it, never moving, to sing the elegiac "Ah, non credea" [left].

Visconti remembers that Callas always wanted him nearby in the wings as she performed "Ah, non credea," to tell her later if her tone had been pure, her phrasing good, whether she had made any mistakes. "I had to lead her to the stage before each act and prod her to go on. Then she would beg me, 'Please take me to this point,' and we'd go two feet nearer the open stage. But it was in this final act that she was most uncertain of herself."

In the opera's finale, Amina awakens and is reunited with her fiancé. In Visconti's production, as Callas began the jubilant cabaletta "Ah, non giunge," the lights on stage and in the auditorium—even Scala's great central chandelier—rose to full intensity. Callas, no longer Amina, stood front stage center, the great prima donna at her moment of triumph—the queen of La Scala [above]. Even before she finished the piece the audience had begun shouting and applauding. "It was more than bel canto brilliance," Tosi recalls. "It was magic. She drove the public crazy."

As Amina, act three; with Valletti [above];
[next pages] *Sonnambula* curtain call

On April 15, 1955, the curtains of La Scala rose on one of the most charming comedies ever to grace its stage—Rossini's *Il Turco in Italia*, designed and staged by Franco Zeffirelli, then at the dawn of his career. The prima donna of the evening was Maria Callas. As Fiorilla, Callas was being seen in a comic role in Milan for the first time. One of the decorative curtains from the production [above] depicted the Turk and Fiorilla, Vesuvius smoldering in the background.

During her opening aria, Fiorilla extols the virtues of promiscuity to a group of her friends [above]. Not only does the flirtatious girl have an old husband, she also has a young lover and is soon to pursue the wealthy Turk. No one in Milan needed to be reminded that Callas herself had an old husband and while her fidelity was not in question at that time, she shared other qualities with the volatile Fiorilla. It made for all the more fun.

Zeffirelli recalls the production with affection despite the problem he had in turning the tragedienne Callas into a comedienne. "Offstage, in those days, Maria was not a very funny lady," he explains. "She was always taking herself so damned seriously. To make Fiorilla come alive I had to invent clever byplay for her. Well, as everyone knew, Callas was greedy for jewelry. She had a diamond necklace and an emerald collar and after every premiere her husband

added a new souvenir to her collection. So I covered the Turk—Nicola Rossi-Lemeni played him—with many jewels. I told Maria as soon as Fiorilla sees him she must not be frightened but fascinated by this new fool with his splendid ornaments. Whenever the Turk offered her his hand, Maria would take it and examine his rings [above]. She was adorable doing it, really very funny. At one point she even danced a little tarantella and at another took off her shoe to hit her rival, Zaida. But there was one problem. Rossini left a line, 'Che Turca impertinente! Osa a Fiorilla l'amante disputar!' [That impertinent Turkish girl! Daring to vie for Fiorilla's lover!], as a kind of ad lib without music. Maria said, 'I want to speak it to prove I can act.' But she was embarrassingly bad and finally our conductor, Gianandrea Gavazzeni, added some music under the line. Then Maria did it perfectly, with marvelous charm and humor.

"Our *Turco* was so refreshing, so lovely. From the beginning Maria knew it was going to be a hit. She had an instinct about such things. She knew the cast was good—Valletti, Rossi-Lemeni, Stabile; she'd looked at my designs and couldn't wait to do it. And whatever others may say, she never paid attention to her own status as a prima donna. In the moment of truth, she is a great friend as well as a great artist. I took my father, who was crippled, to the opening night of *Turco*. He was so moved by the whole evening. After the performance, Maria was in her dressing room surrounded by society people, fans, reporters, photographers. But when I entered, the first thing she said was, 'Your father liked it?' I said yes and he would come to greet her later for it was hard for him to cross the stage. At once, Maria took my hand, left the others behind, and led me to find my father—this old man. She kissed him and thanked him for coming to the performance. You see, Maria does what comes straight from the heart, a marvelous heart for all her mistakes."

Franco Zeffirelli recalls another incident about his staging of *Il Turco in Italia*. "After Maria saw the film *Roman Holiday*, she decided she wanted to look like Audrey Hepburn. She got slimmer and slimmer. During rehearsals we had a little argument because she kept tightening her corset and then would ask me to have the tailor take in the waist even more. She'd say, 'I suffered so much to get thin and now you put me onstage and make me look fat!' So I would have the seams pulled in and the waistline lowered to please her. And she always insisted on rehearsing in her costumes to get their feel—a wonderful thing.

"Maria was captivating in her Neapolitan dresses. One, which she was to wear in the second act, had something of a Spanish flavor, and I couldn't find the shade of velvet I wanted in any fabric shop; yet it was always right in front of my eyes: the material in which the chairs of Scala are upholstered, a lovely rich red. For her skirt, I used the same red silk that covers the walls of the parterre boxes. They couldn't have been more perfect or appropriate.

"During the last act, when Fiorilla arrives on a street in disguise to spy on the Turk and Zaida, Maria was dressed very raggy, but precious raggy. The costume was gold lamé overlaid with a yellow veil, which made a wonderful effect. She looked golden like the sun [left and below]. I made her shawl with my own hands. First I dyed it, then added decorations. It was so stiff when I brought it to her she couldn't wear it. 'What do you expect me to do with this?' she asked. I told her to warm it with the heat of her body and then it would soften. It did, but it also kept a nice crisp quality, a sculptured effect. Maria came to love it, flinging it all over the place in jealousy, fighting—so tempestuously funny. She had the public roaring with delight."

Throughout the action of *Il Turco in Italia* a poet wanders in search of a subject for an opera buffa libretto, which he finds in Fiorilla's antics. Shown at right as the sage old poet is baritone Mariano Stabile, who had made his debut at La Scala thirty-four years earlier in the title role of *Falstaff*.

On the night of May 28, 1955, as Carlo Maria Giulini softly brought to a close the poignant prelude to act one of *La traviata*, then plunged his orchestra into the festive allegro that signals the curtain to rise on Violetta's party, the conductor's eyes shifted instantly to the stage: "My heart skipped a beat. I was overwhelmed by the beauty of what stood before me," he says. "The most emotional, exquisite decor I have seen in my entire life. Every detail of Lila de Nobili's extraordinary sets and costumes made me feel I was materially entering another world, a world of incredible immediacy. The illusion of art—or should I say artifice, for theater is artifice—vanished. I had the same sensation every time I conducted this production—over twenty times in two seasons. For me, reality was onstage. What stood behind me, the audience, auditorium, La Scala itself, seemed artifice. Only that which transpired on stage was truth, life itself."

Luchino Visconti staged this *Traviata* for Callas. "Only for her, not for myself. I did it to serve Callas, for one *must* serve a Callas. Lila de Nobili and I changed the period of the story to the *fin de siècle*, about 1875. Why? Because Maria would look wonderful in costumes of that era. She was tall and slender, and in a gown with a tight bodice, a bustle, and long train, she would be a vision [left]. For my direction, I sought to make her a little of Duse, a little of Rachel, a little of Bernhardt. But more than anyone, I thought of Duse."

The production was to have a decided impact on operatic staging, influencing many directors and designers just starting their careers. For Sandro Sequi, "Visconti taught us you must believe what you see, but that truth must be filtered through art. And while everything in his *Traviata* looked extremely realistic, in fact it was not. For most theater people in Italy, de Nobili is the world's greatest scenic designer, because of her marvelous capacity to crystallize a mood. Her work gives the illusion of truth, but with the quality of a painting, a sense of poetic distance. She can impart a feeling beyond reality. I remember the great chandelier in act one [below], which in fact was not real but painted, with pieces of silk, gauze, and tulle around it. When illuminated, it became a living picture. The same was true of the large oriental vases and screens she made for that scene—there wasn't an authentic detail of oriental art on them. Yet one saw them and believed they were real. The entire production had a hint of decadence, which was right. Visconti and de Nobili summoned up an unforgettable dream of the *belle époque*."

Painstaking weeks of rehearsal went into the Callas-Visconti-de Nobili-Giulini production of *La traviata*. The conductor explains how Callas labored to accomplish what was asked of her. "In performance, she sang and acted with an ease as though she were in her

As Violetta Valéry, act one

own home, not in the theater. And this was vital for our vision of Violetta, for the audience had to believe everything she did. In the first act, Callas was dressed and moved very much like the other courtesans, except she had this mysterious aura that made her different from all the others. It was not that she was better lighted or had more to do; she simply possessed this unique magnetism.

"Our conception was that love was a thing Violetta had never known, even something she shied away from. She realized that if she fell in love, she would lose her lucidity, her cold capacity to play with life. True love would endanger her existence of selfish pleasure. This is a woman who lives egotistically, taking from others, never giving of herself.

"For me, this *Traviata* will always remain a special memory. Long before I began musical rehearsals with the soloists, chorus, and orchestra, before Visconti began his staging with the cast, we worked alone with Maria over an extended period. We three arrived at her characterization, with a complete rapport between words, music, and action. Visconti—apart from the fact he is a genius of the theater—has incredible sensitivity to romantic Italian opera. Each of Maria's gestures he determined solely on musical values. We concentrated much attention on Violetta's state of mind, trying to penetrate the psyche of this fragile feminine creature. In doing this, we discovered a thousand delicate nuances. I'm sure that anyone who saw Maria in this *Traviata* could no more forget her than forget the beauty of Greta Garbo in *Camille*. One was upset, moved.

"As for Callas's singing, I had conducted a single *Traviata* with her four years before at Bergamo—my first experience in the theater. She came at the last minute as a replacement for Renata Tebaldi, who had sung the premiere. We scarcely had time to go over the score with the piano before the performance. Of course, Maria sang magnificently—she was immense then—but her Violetta at La Scala was something else. Very interior, so tender. As she, Visconti, and I went step by step through our preparations, she found new colors in her voice, new values in her musical expression, all through a new understanding of Violetta's innermost being. Everything came into rapport. Let me assure you, it was slow, fatiguing, meticulous work, not done to win popular success but for theater in its deepest expression.

"Maria did not know the meaning of caprice or routine, even if she

had to repeat a thing a hundred times. She was one of the few performers I have known–singers, instrumentalists, conductors–for whom the last performance was as important, as fresh, as exciting as the first. With others, and this is the woe of the theater, after opening night and a few repeat performances, everything starts to go down in quality, to get stale. But with Maria, I assure you the eighteenth *Traviata* was as engrossing and intense as the premiere. Some nights, of course, were more favorable than others. No singer is a machine. But one thing remained constant: Maria had a dedication to her work and to the theater, and she had the desire to give to the public. You felt her inspiration not only in the big moments, the famous arias and duets, but also when you heard her call the name of her maid in a recitative. It could break your heart."

Visconti's memories tally with Giulini's, but include the moment when Giuseppe di Stefano joined rehearsals to be taught the intimate love play the director had conceived for Violetta and Alfredo. The work proved a tedious bore to the tenor; he began showing up late, or not at all. "Maria grew furious over his behavior," recounts Visconti. "'It's a lack of respect for me, a lack of regard, and *also* for you!' she fumed. I said I didn't give a damn if the fool came late. We'd act out his scenes together, we two; worse for him if he didn't learn anything. It was no insult to me."

Piero Tosi, who had designed the Callas-Visconti *Sonnambula* that had opened two months earlier, watched the performance of *Traviata* with an artist's eye. "De Nobili's first set, with its funereal colors of black, gold, and deep red, filled the air with a premonition of Violetta's death. Visconti gave each chorister a sharply defined character, each courtesan an individual personality. Gastone he made a mincing homosexual. The disorder and confusion of the stage action was that of a real party, a rowdy one. Since the set had an offstage pavilion, Violetta's guests could exit for dinner and return naturally. During the duet 'Un dì, felice,' the lovers were alone, Callas in a black satin gown and long white gloves, a bouquet of violets in one hand. As Alfredo declared his love, she slowly backed away from him toward the proscenium, from where all the soft stage lighting came, gracefully moving her long train to permit her retreat. Her white-gloved arms were stretched out behind her, in caution. Finally, standing like this, she was embraced by Alfredo. In surrender, the bouquet fell to the floor. It was unforgettably touching. Theatrical beauty.

"After the guests departed, the abandoned room looked like a cemetery–the great floral arrangements no longer fresh, the table a mess, napkins and fans on the floor, chairs in disorder. Then the maid Annina entered to extinguish the chandelier and candles as Callas huddled by the fireplace, wrapped in a shawl and lit only by the flames. Removing her jewels and the pins from her long hair, which fell to her shoulders, she sang 'Ah, fors'è lui.' Rising for the cabaletta finale, 'Follie! Follie!' she moved to the table, sat, threw back her head, and kicked off her shoes– the image of Zola's Nana. Then the voice of Alfredo interrupts her song. It is a sound she doesn't understand. Is it in her heart, her mind? Or is it real? Vainly she searches for the voice, running toward the veranda. You could feel her heartbeat at that moment."

When the curtains fell, the audience roared its approval. But di Stefano had had enough. After their radiant bows [left], the tenor finished the opera and the next morning left Milan, never again to appear in *Traviata* with Maria Callas or to work with Luchino Visconti.

As contrast to the feverish, haunted atmosphere of Violetta's salon in act one, de Nobili and Visconti made the garden scene of the second act tranquil, all blues and greens. Again, however, the quality was rich, like that of a painting. Thick foliage helped dwarf the enormity of the Scala stage, lending the drama a feeling of utmost intimacy. In the rear, a massive three-story country villa loomed mutely, its windows and portals covered with awnings and shutters to close out the heat of summer. On the left of the stage stood a small greenhouse, while strewn about were various gardening tools—a wheelbarrow, rake, spade, water can, hose. To the rear of this, a large grill gate flanked by vine-covered pillars. Casually placed to the right, a grouping of outdoor furniture—wicker chairs, a divan and table, and an umbrella to ward off the sun. Nearby, a fountain for birds. The scene was as a poet might imagine a late nineteenth-century villa near Paris.

The perfect realization of the decor was no accident. As is her custom, de Nobili—aided by a few trusted assistants—painted every inch of it. Thus the set was itself a painting. Giulini recounts that at the dress rehearsal de Nobili was still at work onstage. To his amusement, as the curtains rose none of the invited guests in the theater realized what she was doing, for, in her smock, she looked like one of Violetta's maids puttering about in the garden.

If in the first act Visconti had made Callas a reincarnation of Duse, in the second he made her Bernhardt. Her costume was inspired by a photograph of one worn by the actress in *La dame aux camélias*, which Visconti had found during his research. De Nobili echoed the warm white tone of the gown in the flowers that adorned the garden, and delicate pale-green ribbons and lace decorated the costume. As Callas came on stage searching for Alfredo, she wore a bonnet tied with silk bows; in her hand, she carried a parasol. The picture of serenity and joy, Violetta is a woman changed by love.

But her happiness is soon cut short by a visit from Alfredo's father. Giulini remembers the fear and timidity with which Callas greeted Giorgio Germont [above and far right, Ettore Bastianini], but also how, when the old man affronted her, she asserted her rights with dignity.

Act two *Traviata*, with Bastianini as Germont

For many people, including Visconti and Giulini, the core of *Traviata* lies in the second-act duet between Violetta and the elder Germont. Giulini says, "The brilliance with which Callas had depicted the courtesan's selfish desire for pleasure in the first act made all the more moving her transformation into a woman consumed by love in the second. This contrast in emotions is what Maria, Luchino, and I had sought during our long rehearsals. Callas, using every vocal, musical, and dramatic device at her command, fully revealed Violetta's capacity to give, her infinite ability to dedicate herself to another – even to the point of making a complete sacrifice of herself, of leaving the only true love she has ever known. It was incredible how, during this long duet, Callas drew an unending line of differing moods and feelings. And as Germont, Ettore Bastianini showed that he recognized not only Violetta's human qualities, but also the genuine value of her love for his son. Even today, as I remember them seated in the garden, I am deeply moved."

In the photographs on the opposite page, Germont tells Violetta her liaison with his son endangers not only Alfredo's future, but also that of his younger sister, whose impending marriage would be compromised by scandal. Callas's Violetta, not wanting to hear the truth, drops her hand from her throat and grasps the arm of her chair, as if to gain support. But Germont continues his persuasive narration, and Callas soon betrays the surrender Violetta has yet to make by letting her right hand fall limply in her lap. As Germont reminds Violetta that Alfredo may in time tire of her, Callas clasps her face in dismay, murmuring, "It's true, it's true." On this page [below], Violetta bows to the father's demands in the tender "Ah! Dite alla giovine," which Callas sang with her face inclined to the floor, her voice a mere whisper that somehow filled the theater. Piero Tosi remembers the moment: "Incredible. So emotional, yet so intimate. She scarcely seemed to be singing, yet everyone heard."

In her biography of Sarah Bernhardt, *Madame Sarah*, Cornelia Otis Skinner wrote: "Many actresses have played the role of Dumas *fils*' lovely and repentant sinner and most actresses have over-emoted. The secret of Bernhardt's success was in the disarming simplicity of her approach. She played Marguerite Gauthier with an exquisite frailty, a poetic pathos that was almost unbearable."

The very characteristics that Bernhardt brought to Marguerite, Callas brought to her operatic incarnation, Violetta. And just as during her long years on stage, Bernhardt was known as "The Divine Sarah," so Callas came to be called "La Divina." Nicola Benois, who has spent a lifetime watching famous artists come and go, says:"The world needs the arts and its artists and there are those few who work in the arts who seem to have been touched by some divinity. I remember Nijinsky. He was one. There was no way to explain his talent except by attributing it to some god. The same with Callas. From the first time I saw her–she was fat then–I felt something mystic about her. But after her wondrous physical transformation, we came to call her La Divina.

"We may have joked among ourselves when we first said it, but we had reason to call her that. Callas had something inimitable, something amazing, something other artists didn't have–no matter how splendid their talents in many other regards. I've seen only one other artist who could register such a range of expressions–Chaliapin. There were motives that stirred Callas that lesser mortals do not possess. Yes, she was truly divine."

Something of this greatness is seen in the photographs on these pages: How her hand clasps the arm of Ettore Bastianini, anguish in her face as she implores Germont, "Qual figlia m'abbracciate, forte così sarò" (Embrace me as your own daughter, so I will find strength) [left]; how she falls to her knees crying she will die of grief, after which Germont lifts her to her feet, commanding her to live [right]; how she bids Germont farewell, saying her final breath of life will be for Alfredo [next four pages].

Traviata, act two, with Bastianini
[also on following pages]

Having won his point, the elder Germont leaves. Violetta, overcome with grief, crosses to the table. First, she dashes off a letter to Flora, the courtesan friend from former days, accepting a party invitation, for now Violetta must resume her old way of life. But she can no longer delay the painful moment: She must write a note of farewell to Alfredo. As she calls on heaven to give her strength, sorrow distorts her face. In Visconti's words, "At this moment, Violetta is all but dead. While Maria sat at the table, she made not one move we had not prepared in rehearsal—how she cried, how she grasped her brow, how she put the pen in the inkwell, how she held her hand as she wrote, everything. No singing, only acting as the orchestra accompanied the long pantomime [left]. Some members of the audience wept as they watched Callas in this scene."

Among those who wept was Piero Tosi. "So great was Callas's presence at this moment, the scenery existed no more. You saw only her. Nothing remained but Violetta and her anguish. But then, Alfredo suddenly entered the garden, at first not seeing Violetta, going instead to the gate—as if from a premonition that his father might arrive. Whatever the reason, he gave the feeling he knew something was wrong. Turning as he stood by the gate, he gazed lovingly at Violetta as she finished the note. Then, just as Verdi intended, Visconti's staging whipped up a terrible suspense as Alfredo questioned Violetta about the contents of the note and Violetta agitatedly tried to hide from him what she had written. Upset, Alfredo moved away from her to the left of the stage, by a little hassock. Slowly, with her arms outstretched, Callas walked toward him. As the lovers enfolded each other, overcome with passion, he sank onto the hassock, she to her knees, pouring out her heart in the invocation 'Amami, Alfredo' [Love me, Alfredo]. Callas sang not to the public but with her face to the floor, all but buried in Alfredo's embrace [below]. Her cry was that of a desperate soul, one that wished to annul itself. Then, in tears, she ran from the garden."

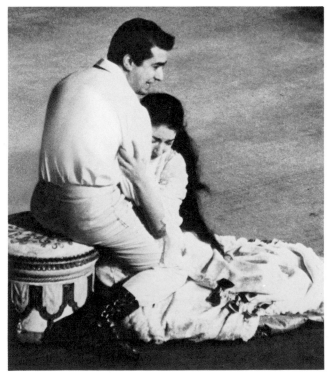

Traviata, act two, with di Stefano   131

In act three of *Traviata*–Flora's party–Callas was attired in a tight-fitting gown of bright red satin encrusted with rubies, a collar of rubies encircling her neck, a ruby bracelet on one of her long white-gloved arms [left]. Once more, Violetta has become the most glamorous of Parisian courtesans, her façade cold and hard. But in a private moment, she mourns her loss of Alfredo [below].

De Nobili's set was a winter garden with the atmosphere of a hothouse; everywhere were lush tropical plants. The women wore rich colors, the men formal black. Conductor Giulini recounts that, "At one performance, as a joke, Callas's husband, Battista Meneghini, went onstage as a super, dressed as a toreador. When Maria spotted him, she was furious, but then she laughed. Of course, the audience saw nothing of this for Maria had great self-control and revealed only what she wanted the public to see."

Throughout the rehearsals and the performances, Visconti encountered now familiar problems with his diva, whose demands for his time and attention bordered on the manic: "During the act-one prelude, Maria would insist I stay onstage with her almost to the moment the curtain had to rise. One night, as the music was about to end, I told her, 'Look, Maria, I don't want to be caught here onstage talking to the whores!' But she wouldn't let me go. 'No, no,' she begged, 'stay just a second more.' Lord, she nearly drove me crazy at times.

"A week or so after the premiere, I had to return to Rome. I stopped by the theater to say good-bye and thank her for the unparalleled performance she had given. It was during the intermission of act three and, after long, sweet farewells, I went downstairs to Biffi Scala to join some friends for dinner before my departure. A minute later, Maria walked into the restaurant in full stage makeup, her red ball gown half covered by a cloak. 'Fool!' I said. 'Go away! What are you doing here dressed like that?' She looked so sad and she embraced me, saying 'I had to see you once more and tell you good-bye again.' So genuine. How could you not give her your heart? But the incident could have been much worse–suppose she'd changed her costume and entered Biffi's in the nightgown Violetta wears in the last act?"

Alfredo, who has learned that Violetta is to attend Flora's party, shows up at the festivities first, recklessly gambling at cards and pretending to ignore his mistress when she arrives on the arm of a handsome baron. When the others go off to dinner, Violetta sends for Alfredo. He, misunderstanding the reasons for her desertion, refuses to listen and accuses her of infidelity [above]. Confused by his words, Violetta hides her true motives by telling him she now loves the baron [right]. Piero Tosi remembers that the confrontation between the lovers ended on a staircase at the right of the stage. "As Alfredo called all the guests from the dining room, he seized Violetta by the arm and violently dragged her down the steps to the opposite corner of the stage. There,

denouncing her before their shocked friends, he took his winnings from the gambling table and threw them at her as payment for any debt he might owe. Callas never moved. She stood transfixed, with her arms outstretched as if crucified, like some great statue of grief [left]. Then, as Alfredo's anger reached its climax, he compounded his insult by hurling Violetta to the confetti-strewn floor [below]. Here, totally degraded by the man she still loves, the forsaken woman sang the great ensemble finale."

Director Sandro Sequi's old teacher, Alexandre Sakharoff, never saw Callas in the Visconti staging of *Traviata* at La Scala, but he did see her in other roles in Rome. "He was amazed that such an actress could exist in opera," says Sequi. "He told me she reminded him of Sarah Bernhardt, whom he had seen many times in many plays and for whom he had a kind of mania. Bernhardt was extremely stylized–she never screamed and ranted onstage–and in *La dame aux camélias*, when Armand threw the money at her, she froze like a statue of sorrow. This was exactly the effect Callas achieved in the same scene in *Traviata* as Visconti staged it for her."

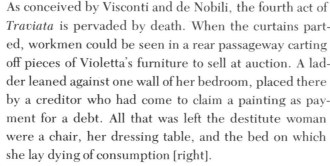

As conceived by Visconti and de Nobili, the fourth act of *Traviata* is pervaded by death. When the curtains parted, workmen could be seen in a rear passageway carting off pieces of Violetta's furniture to sell at auction. A ladder leaned against one wall of her bedroom, placed there by a creditor who had come to claim a painting as payment for a debt. All that was left the destitute woman were a chair, her dressing table, and the bed on which she lay dying of consumption [right].

"It was frightening," says Piero Tosi. "When Callas rose from the bed, she looked like a cadaver, some decadent manikin from a wax museum—no longer a human being, but a living corpse. And she sang with a thread of a voice, so weak, so ill, so touching. With great effort she reached the dressing table, where she read Germont's letter and sang 'Addio, del passato' [left].

"Then you saw the lights of the carnival crowd as it passed outside the windows. On the wall were shadows of the celebrants at play. For Violetta, the world had become nothing but shadows. The Paris she once knew was no more. In Callas's every gesture, death seemed imminent. Even during the joyful reunion with Alfredo, she was so wan and frail that she scarcely moved.

"After the lovers sang of their dream of living together in happiness far from the city—'Parigi, o cara'—Violetta was seized by a desperate need to leave the deathtrap in which she found herself. She called her maid to bring some clothes and began a terrible struggle to dress. When Callas put on the long cloak and little bonnet Annina gave her, she looked even more grotesque—the cloak was askew and the bonnet crooked, its poor ribbons hanging loose, for she lacked the strength to tie them. It was a pathetic sight. Then came the moment when she tried to put on her gloves. But she couldn't because her fingers had already grown stiff and rigid with approaching death. Only then did Violetta realize there was no escape, and in this awareness Callas let forth with overwhelming intensity the outcry 'Gran Dio! Morir sì giovine' [Great God! To die so young]. She was stupendous, this broken, suffering, distorted skeleton of a woman vainly fighting to live.

"For the moment of death, Visconti called upon all of Callas's genius as an actress. After accepting her fate and giving Alfredo a locket containing her portrait, Violetta spoke the famous concluding lines. Radiantly, she told Alfredo that her pains had ceased, that her old strength had returned, that new life was being born, and, on the words 'Oh, joy!' she died, her great eyes wide open, fixed in a senseless stare into the audience. As the curtains fell, her dead eyes continued to stare blankly into space. For once, an entire audience shared Alfredo's shock and grief. They too had felt death."

De Nobili's act four sketch and set for *Traviata*

"Addio del passato"

Of the twenty-three roles Maria Callas sang at La Scala, she fell flat on her face in only one: Rosina.

"In no way was Maria suited to this role," states Elvira de Hidalgo. Her teacher's verdict is reinforced by virtually everyone who saw the performance or was involved with it. The conductor, Carlo Maria Giulini, says, "Her personality was wrong, her conception misguided. She made Rosina a kind of Carmen." The Count Almaviva, Luigi Alva, who was making his debut on the big Scala stage, feels, "For all Maria's intelligence and musicality, she never caught the freshness of Rosina's nature. She used too much pepper, exaggerating gestures. This, coupled with her horrible costumes, made everything she did look ridiculous." The Don Basilio, Nicola Rossi-Lemeni, adds, "*Il barbiere* is an ensemble work, not a prima donna vehicle. Maria was aggressive, a viper, acting as though Rosina had the whole situation wrapped up in her hands. But no single artist can shift the emphasis from Figaro and all the other colorful characters so beautifully balanced by Rossini. Maria was totally out of the picture!"

The production, no masterpiece when new in 1952, had decor by Mario Vellani Marchi and indifferent staging by Carlo Piccinato. Giulini, who was ill and conducted only as a favor to Victor de Sabata, says nothing was properly rehearsed. "I conducted every performance with my head down so I wouldn't see what was happening onstage."

At left, Tito Gobbi (Figaro) with Alva in act one, and Callas, Anna Maria Canali (Berta), Melichore Luise (Dr. Bartolo), Rossi-Lemeni, and Alva in the act two finale. At right, Callas's Rosina, which reaped radishes, not roses, from habitués of Scala's top balcony.

The night of February 16, 1956, the premiere of La Scala's revival of *Il barbiere di Siviglia*, provided Milanese operagoers with what they liked best–a fiasco. And even better, it was Callas's. Maestro Giulini explains the curious attitude of the Scala audience. "This *Barbiere* is the worst memory of my life in the theater. I don't feel it was a fiasco for Maria alone, but for all of us concerned with the performance. It was an artistic mistake, utterly routine, thrown together, with nothing given deep study or preparation.

"In Milan, people think the boundaries of music extend from Via Verdi to Via Filodrammatici. Beyond this little rectangle lies a desert, a wasteland. The world must come to La Scala. The world revolves around La Scala. An utterly provincial notion. Sadly, most of the patrons of Scala never even want to hear an opera performed well. They arrive at their seats hoping with all their hearts that something will go wrong. The audience is jaded, annoyed, bored, so it prays for a scandal. It's an old story. How many times did Toscanini fight this mentality? He worked for years at Scala because he was its absolute lord and could practice his art as he pleased. To him the public meant nothing.

"In this hostile climate, most conductors, singers, choristers, and orchestral players feel like gladiators, glad to survive, but sad to have to do so by being involved in a deadly contest. At La Scala, just as in the Circus Maximus, blood must be shed. It does not matter who perishes, just that one or the other dies. The performer stands in peril every moment. This is especially true with operas with long traditions, such as *Barbiere*, *Rigoletto*, *Traviata*, and *Trovatore*. And since the public can't actually kill an artist, it invents other means to accomplish destruction. It may be by disrespect–jeering, talking during the music, walking out. Or it may be, and this is perhaps even worse, by conceding success. Success at La Scala is always without joy, without love, without gratitude. The best thing a public can say to an artist is thank you. Not bravo. This already implies a judgment.

"One especially sensed the warlike climate of the Scala audience during the Callas era. When her Rosina was whistled and hissed, people went home content. This even though Maria was the prize of the theater, greatly admired, even to the point of idolatry. As such, she became a target. In some ways she provoked such reactions. Her bows, for example, showed a certain insolence, her iron will to vanquish. This went against the grain, so when the public had the chance to show her any discourtesy, or could bother her, it did so with the greatest of pleasure. With *Alceste*, Maria and I earned respect, esteem, probably because the audience was afraid to expose its ignorance about the work. I feel certain, however, that Maria's greatest triumphs at La Scala–even her incomparable Violetta–left something of a bitter taste in her mouth."

Here Callas's Rosina is shown in act two with Luise's Bartolo [left], Gobbi's Figaro [top left], and Alva's Almaviva [top right].

Il barbiere di Siviglia, act two,
with Luise, Gobbi, and Alva

After conducting *Il barbiere di Sivig-lia*, Carlo Maria Giulini never again led an opera at La Scala, and rarely elsewhere. In contrast, Luigi Alva was just launching his career in Milan, where he sings to this day. "To be a newcomer amid such oper-atic giants as Callas, Gobbi, and Rossi-Lemeni was frightening," he confesses.

"Callas impressed me, for even though she was a great diva, she was so concerned about her work, punc-tual at every rehearsal, giving so much in her singing. At the pre-miere I tried to express my gratitude for the faith she had shown in a beginner. 'No, no, Alva,' she said. 'There is nothing to thank me for. I see how serious you are and your desire to do well. That gives me great pleasure. We need people like you in the theater.'

"In act three, during the lesson scene, she sang brilliantly, with me at the keyboard and old Bartolo doz-ing off [left]. In fact, all her singing was good. She only needed what I needed: a director of the quality of Visconti or Zeffirelli. Comedy was not her métier, and we were left to our own devices. For veterans like Gobbi and Rossi-Lemeni, this was nothing. Luckily, I had once done the opera in Trieste, so I had some-thing to base my acting on."

Rossi-Lemeni, despite Giu-lini's words, recalls "the conducting was wonderful, Alva splendid, Gobbi incomparable. And I had an incredible triumph with Basilio. Too incredible. Of course I tried to do my best, but the applause after 'La calunnia' was exaggerated. I am sure it was a polemic, a protest against Maria's Rosina. She was very dis-turbed by it, so when we took our curtain calls, she found a moment to retaliate. She bowed not to the pub-lic but to me. Maria was never at a loss to think of something."

Lesson scene in *Barbiere*,
with Alva and Luise

Sarah Bernhardt inspired Victorien Sardou to write two plays that have survived as opera librettos but are forgotten in the legitimate theater, *Fedora* and *La Tosca*. Both texts were tailor-made for the actress's magnetic style, and year after year she turned them into box-office gold on tours throughout the world. "There is but one Sarah and Sardou is her prophet," raved a captivated critic, which provoked a more cynical scribe to question his spelling of prophet. George Bernard Shaw termed these Bernhardt vehicles "sheer Sardoudledom"; still she thrived on such melodramatic claptrap. Today, without Bernhardt, these relics from a more flamboyant era are kept alive only through the music of Giordano and Puccini.

Both Giordano's *Fedora* and Puccini's *Tosca* were in the repertory of Maria Callas. Oddly, she never performed Tosca or any other Puccini role at La Scala during her career there. Fedora, however, she did only in Milan, during the spring of 1956. Since the leading characters of *Fedora* are Russian, Scala invited Russians—Nicola Benois and Tatiana Pavlova—to create the decor and staging. Benois says, "Maria worked closely with Pavlova to learn the Russian school of acting, absorbing all that was pertinent to her role as expressed by Giordano and all that was applicable to her own personality. Maria had the knack of taking everything she could get from an associate. With the help of Pavlova, herself a great actress in both Russia and Italy, she created a Fedora rich in range, depth, and authenticity. Being Eastern Orthodox may have given Maria some special kinship for this role. On the stage, she became Russian 100 percent.

"For my first set, I envisioned a mythical Russia—where mushrooms grow on rooftops and strawberries by every door. No room ever existed like the one I designed [below]. Sheer imagination combined many elements of life before the Revolution, all painted in vivid colors. With Maria's costumes, too, I felt free to draw on fantasy. During the era of *Fedora*, the late nineteenth century, noble women no longer wore the kokoshnik, a kind of half crown. But on Maria a kokoshnik would make a wonderful theatrical effect, and in an opera totally based on theatrical effects this was reason enough to give her one."

At left, amid grief-stricken servants, Fedora (Callas) learns her fiancé is a victim of nihilist bullets.

As Princess Fedora Romazoff

In act two, Fedora gives a party in Paris to obtain proof against Loris Ipanoff, murderer of her fiancé [above, Callas with Franco Corelli].

As a pianist plays a nocturne for her guests, Fedora interrogates the nobleman, who is infatuated with her, drawing forth a confession.

Loris admits the crime, and Fedora entices him to return later that night [left]. After her guests depart, she dispatches an incriminating letter to the Tsar's secret police in St. Petersburg [bottom left] and instructs spies to assassinate Loris when he leaves her house. Loris unsuspectingly arrives for the rendezvous and only then Fedora learns the murder was not political: Her fiancé was the lover of Loris's wife! Fedora rages against the dead man and begs Loris not to leave lest he himself be killed. Now *they* become lovers. But the letter Fedora had sent to Russia is to cause the deaths of Loris's brother and mother, and ultimately, to drive Fedora to commit suicide.

When Callas sang Fedora, protest filled the musical press. Conductor Gianandrea Gavazzeni explains the controversy: "Some critics wrote that Maria was unsuited for verismo declamation. Others feared that Giordano's unvocal writing and heavy orchestration would tax her resources. Teodoro Celli, in particular, felt the project to be out of her artistic realm. In my opinion, however, Maria proved them all wrong. I found her tremendous, and she had a personal triumph with the public.

"In truth, Maria's unique qualities were what made her Fedora so fascinating. Not only did she bring uncommon musical discipline and an enormous sense of style to the part, she superimposed on the text a thousand tints and inflections. This in itself was rare to hear in a verismo work. I especially recall the strange vocal colors she found for the lines Fedora semispeaks as she dies. They were haunting. I'm afraid the critics came to the theater with their reviews already written in their heads. Most of what critics write is prefabricated."

Franco Corelli, who sang Loris, says, "No one can imagine what it meant to me, a virtual beginner on the stage, only in my second year at La Scala, to work with Callas. I learned so much—how to improve myself. Maria was extremely thoughtful with me and tried to

In *Fedora*, act two

make everything easy. And she did. She herself was so involved in the opera that she involved me too. I felt it a duty to respond, to work deeply, as never before, in a way I really did not fully comprehend, but which I strongly sensed. For the last act, Maria and I worked out many of the little dramatic details without our director, Tatiana Pavlova.

"Act three is set in Switzerland, and begins as a romantic idyll, with Fedora and Loris strolling into the garden of their chalet. We had a charming little pantomime in which Maria sat in a swing and I pushed her. Very lovely. Then a letter arrives that makes Loris realize Fedora is the mysterious woman who has persecuted him and his family [top right]. This scene demanded believable action, so I asked Maria if I could seize her by the hair during my anger. She loved the idea and put a hundred pins in her beautiful chignon to hold it in place.

"Thus, the moment when Fedora's guilt was revealed, Maria fell to her knees, pleading for mercy. I pulled her head back and denounced her to her face, then dragged her across the stage by her hair. Violently! At this point, as I turned away, covering my face with my hands, she drank poison from a large crucifix she had worn throughout the opera. In Fedora's time, you see, the nobility kept poison concealed on their persons in case of danger. When I realized what she had done, in shock I tried to carry her into the chalet, but as we reached the steps, she was so near death I gently sank there with her in my arms. Here Maria uttered those final lines so movingly –'Loris, I feel cold. Warm me in your embrace. Give me a little of your love...your lips' [right].

"We had rehearsed four weeks to achieve such effects. Hard work, but worth it for the exceptional results. The full value of the opera came forth. This *Fedora* could have been filmed as it was–perfect. Maria had helped me so much during rehearsal that in performance we completely interlocked. That's the only word for it. Interlocked."

In act three, with Corelli

TEATRO ALLA SCALA

STAGIONE LIRICA 1956-57

DOMENICA 14 APRILE 1957 · alle ore 21 precise
SERATA DI GALA
PER LA 'GIORNATA DELLE NAZIONI' ALLA XXXV FIERA DI MILANO
PRIMA RAPPRESENTAZIONE

ANNA BOLENA
Tragedia in tre atti di F. ROMANI
Musica di
GAETANO DONIZETTI
NUOVO ALLESTIMENTO

GIANANDREA GAVAZZENI

Regia di
LUCHINO VISCONTI
Scene e figurini di
NICOLA BENOIS

Anna Bolena, the story of Henry VIII and his second wife, Anne Boleyn, had gathered dust until the fall of 1956, when Donizetti's birthplace, Bergamo, resurrected it as a tribute to the composer. The performance, sung by talented young artists, was witnessed by another of Bergamo's musical sons, Scala conductor Gianandrea Gavazzeni, together with Luigi Oldani. In Gavazzeni's words: "We recognized at once it would be an ideal vehicle for Maria Callas, both musically and theatrically. Many years before, the great conductor Gino Marinuzzi had told me *Anna Bolena* was an opera to revive the day the right soprano came along.

"Luckily, Luchino Visconti showed interest in directing the production when Scala offered it to him. That winter we began to plan. For nearly two weeks I met with him daily at his home in Rome, playing the score over and over on the piano and discussing the libretto's tragic qualities. It was rewarding work. Visconti came into immediate accord with Nicola Benois on all aspects of the designs. And we had an excellent cast to back up Callas–Nicola Rossi-Lemeni as Henry VIII, Giulietta Simionato as Jane Seymour, and Gianni Raimondi as Percy. Indeed, it was exceptional."

Visconti also remembers the production with pleasure. "It was rather beautiful, if I do say so myself. But not sublime as everyone else has said. It had atmosphere. Benois and I used only black, white, and gray–like the gray of London–for the sets. The castle interiors, such as the broad staircase down which Callas made her entrance [below], were filled with enormous portraits. The colors of the costumes–Jane Seymour, the king's new love, wore red, for example, and the guards scarlet and yellow–played off these somber sets.

"But for *Anna Bolena*, you need more than sets and costumes. You need Callas. Each day I went with her to the tailor to watch over every detail of her gowns, which were in all shades and nuances of blue. Her jewels were huge [left]. They had to be to go with everything about her–her eyes, head, features, her stature. And believe me, onstage Callas had stature."

Next pages: courtyard of Windsor Castle,
with Rossi-Lemeni (Henry VIII), Callas (Anna),
Clabassi (Rochefort), and Raimondi (Percy)

"Callas's costumes in *Bolena*," relates Nicola Benois, "were literally sculpted on her figure. The elegance she had developed over the years so enhanced her esthetic effect that Luchino and I did everything we could to emphasize her presence onstage. How she walked in her gowns! Like a queen. All her costumes were inspired by Holbein's portraits of Anne Boleyn, but no single detail was authentic. Nor in the sets were specifics copied from any of Henry VIII's castles. Luchino gave me precise documentation from history, but he did not seek reality.

"I confess that, after all my years in the theater, to collaborate with Luchino was like attending an academy. He is not only a director, he is a man of knowledge, culture, and taste. Doubtless this comes from his heritage. He is a true aristocrat, not only by title, but by nature.

"Our entire production of *Anna Bolena* became a trick of perspective, an optical illusion. Some scenes seemed very deep set, even 125 feet, but none were really more than 35. I believe illusion to be the greatest merit of the designer's art. Today, this might seem an outmoded ideal, but for me it holds true and beautiful. Consider what opera is. A totally artificial form of theater. No one speaks, they sing, and this is not life. If you say 'Open the window,' you are talking about a real window. But if to a beautiful melody you sing 'Open the window,' it has already become something else. Music transforms. It creates another sphere. And just as it gives extension to words, so it extends all the dimensions of theater. Operatic scenery must have a sung quality, must exist in another space, be doubly poetic, doubly romantic. Nothing is real in opera, however true the human values it expresses and intensifies. Most important, scenery must capture the spirit of the music it accompanies. In *Anna Bolena*, Luchino and I discovered Henry VIII's time through Donizetti's score. Had the opera been composed by Schoenberg, Gershwin, or Britten, we would have done something quite different."

The Visconti-Benois *Bolena* set a new standard for interpreting operas of the early Romantic Era. At the premiere, on April 14, 1957, the audience applauded each set as it appeared. Director Sandro Sequi says: "I was deeply impressed by what I saw. While it was in the great, old tradition of La Scala, the production was executed through a screen of time—absolutely correct in taste and judgment. Only in this way can works of the Romantic epoch come alive today. Imagine *Anna Bolena*, or any opera from its era, staged with historical accuracy. It would be like some cheap, fake movie."

Shown here, Anna (Callas) is shaken by an unexpected reunion with Percy, a former suitor summoned to court by the king. At top left, Rochefort (Clabassi); left, Percy and Henry VIII (Raimondi and Rossi-Lemeni).

When the final curtain fell at the premiere of *Anna Bolena*, Maria Callas set the record for solo curtain calls at La Scala: The applause continued for twenty-four minutes. No critic could dispute her triumph: It was the apex of her career to date.

Ironically, exactly a year later in a revival of *Bolena*, the same public that had called her back for bow after bow would snub her coldly, finding merit only in her colleagues. The 1958 performance marked Callas's first appearance in Italy since the notorious Rome *Norma*, when hoarseness had forced her to withdraw after the first act. For months, the Italian press had been busy attacking her, refusing to believe she had been ill and insisting she had insulted both the Roman public and the President of Italy, who had been in the theater that night. By the time of the *Bolena* performance, Callas had been tried in absentia and unanimously pronounced guilty.

Piero Tosi witnessed the singer's return as the doomed Anna: "Such hate had been stirred up against her that protesters were in the square outside La Scala, where an entire militia of armed police stood guard. It was like the Risorgimento. Inside the theater, plainclothesmen watched corridors, foyers, boxes. Backstage, more police.

"To avoid an incident during Anna's entrance, Visconti hid Callas amid choristers. For two scenes, the public reacted to her like ice, shouting approval to the others—Cesare Siepi, the Henry VIII in this performance, Simionato, and Raimondi. But in the third scene, which takes place in the great gallery of the castle [top left], the king discovers his wife with Percy and orders her arrested for adultery. Here the role of Anna really gets moving in the exciting ensemble finale. As two guards came to seize her, Callas violently pushed them aside and hurled herself to the front of

As Anna Bolena, with Raimondi, Siepi, and Simionato

the stage, spitting her lines directly at the audience: 'Giudici? Ad Anna? Giudici?' [Judges? For Anna? Judges?] It wasn't theater any more, it was reality. Callas was defending herself, all but saying 'If this is my trial, judge me... but remember, I am your Queen!'

"She dared her accusers and stared them down, dramatically surpassing anything she had ever done, singing with scorching brilliance. When the curtain fell, the audience went mad. An uproar, sheer lunacy. Then Callas swept forth for her bows, inflated with her power, her victory, her magnificence. And every time she came forth, she grew more, more, more. You could not dream what she did. It was a show within a show."

When the curtains rose on act two, the public in her thrall, Callas joined Simionato for the duet in which Jane remorsefully admits she is Anna's rival for the throne. Those who were in the audience that night, and especially those connected with the production—Gavazzeni, Visconti, Benois, Simionato—remember it as one of the most exciting moments they ever experienced in the theater.

But Callas could do more than excite. She could profoundly move her public, as she did during the final scene. Tosi has this memory: "It was Benois's finest set, the Tower of London, a deep subterranean chamber with barred windows near the high ceiling through which harsh light glared. Below, all was in obscurity until, little by little, the shadows lifted and soldiers could be distinguished, their hats silhouetted in a dim gold light, as if in a painting by Rembrandt. Then the light rose a bit more and women of the court who had followed their queen to prison grew visible. From their shadows, Callas at last came into sight, but never moving, seeming unable to rise. The audience did not dare breathe, cough, stir. There was absolute silence except for Callas's voice in a prayerful song that went on and on. Here Visconti showed his genius, for he never intruded on this sound, so perfect, so expressive. Callas's stillness created incredible tension while her voice, human yet crystallized, seemed almost an object. What one saw and heard were indivisible.

"After the cabaletta in which Anna goes to her death cursing Seymour and the king, the applause seemed endless. I was crazy with excitement and ran to the stage door to see if the people outside would try to kill Callas as she left the theater. The police remained, guns ready, holding back the crowd. When Simionato came out, everyone clapped. She had sung fabulously. Then one by one, the other singers. Finally, Callas emerged. She wore a long black chiffon dress and all her diamonds, her face stark white. Stunning. Now began the third show as she slowly walked through the long loggia to Biffi Scala where her limousine was waiting. The police were baffled, not knowing what to do, for the crowd was cheering. As people had left the theater, word of her triumph had spread. After Callas drove away, none of us could go home to sleep and we milled around for hours in a kind of shock and ecstasy."

158

After Anna Bolena, *with patrons of La Scala—Tina Biffi and Carla Del Bò Novaro*

Immediately after the premiere of *Anna Bolena*, director Luchino Visconti and designer Nicola Benois abandoned romantic images to turn their attention to the classical values of *Ifigenia in Tauride*. Once more, the *raison d'être* of their effort was Maria Callas. Three years earlier, she had proven her supremacy in Gluck as Alceste. Despite the splendor and success of the new production of *Ifigenia*, given its premiere on June 1, 1957, it was scrapped after only four performances.

Benois describes his work with Visconti: "For the opera's single set, we looked to the Bibienas, the master theater designers of Gluck's era. Our costumes were inspired by paintings of Tiepolo. If our approach sounds anachronistic for a legend set in ancient Greece, it was in perfect harmony with the music, my cardinal rule as a scenographer. Of all the sketches I have drawn in my career, this one came closest to perfection when produced on the stage." Indeed, the portal where Callas stands [right] is an exact realization of the vaulting arches in Benois's original design [above].

TEATRO ALLA SCALA

LUNEDI 3 GIUGNO 1957 - alle ore 21 precise
SECONDA RAPPRESENTAZIONE

IFIGENIA
IN
TAURIDE

Opera in due parti di N. F. GUILLARD de EURIPIDE
Musica di
CRISTOPH W. GLUCK
NUOVO ALLESTIMENTO

NINO SANZOGNO

Ifigenia in Tauride brought to a close the remarkable theatrical alliance of Maria Callas and Luchino Visconti, though as the two artists worked on this, their fifth collaboration, neither realized it would be their last. Unrelated circumstances brought their joint endeavors to an end. In 1960, Visconti was slated to direct Callas in a Scala revival of Donizetti's *Poliuto*, but shortly before rehearsals were to begin, a play he had staged–*L'Arialda*–was censored by the government. Refusing to work in any state-supported theater, he withdrew from *Poliuto*.

"Afterward, I would occasionally discuss possible projects with Maria," says Visconti, "but nothing came of them. I suggested Carmen, Salome, the Marschallin. She always refused. She said she was afraid to do Carmen because she didn't know how to dance like a gypsy. I told her, 'Who cares about your dancing. Sing! That's the thing.' As for Salome, she was afraid to disrobe onstage during the Dance of the Seven Veils. Why I don't know, because the first time I saw her, as Kundry in *Parsifal*, when she was still enormous, she was half naked in the second act, covered with yards and yards of transparent chiffon–a marvelous temptress, like an odalisque. On her head was a little tambourine hat that plopped down on her forehead every time she hit a high note. She would just bat it back in place. The Marschallin didn't interest her, perhaps because it had to be sung in German. In any event, after *Ifigenia* we could never seem to agree on what to do together.

"As a matter of fact, we really didn't agree about *Ifigenia*. As always, I conceived my production to make Maria look as glorious as possible. But she didn't understand my idea at all. 'Why are you doing it like this?' she asked. 'It's a Greek story and I'm a Greek woman, so I want to look Greek onstage!' I said, 'My dear, the Greece you are talking about is too far off. This opera must look like a Tiepolo fresco come to life.' But still she fussed, wanting to look Greek."

Ifigenia is a priestess of barbarous Scythians who seeks to bring an end to human sacrifices. Callas, through her commanding presence and posture, created a character of profound dignity and compassion. The fact that the text provided Ifigenia no amorous interest did not in the least diminish Callas's expressive authority. At the moment when she recognized her brother, Orestes [Dino Dondi, left and right], Callas was able to impart four simultaneous meanings to one simple word, *fratello* (brother): One heard an all-encompassing sister love, a sadness at their having been parted so long, a happiness at having found him, and fear for his imminent sacrificial death. This ability to infuse words with meaning brought Ifigenia vibrantly to life and gave each scene in which she appeared the dramatic force Gluck intended. Even when Callas did not sing, when she simply crossed the stage in despair and grief, she sustained intensity, that pure dynamic style which made her ideal for classical heroines [next pages].

Visconti adds: "Maria did exactly what I asked. As the curtains lifted, a storm was raging and she had to pace frantically across the stage. She wore a majestic gown with many folds of rich silk brocade and an enormous train, over which she had a large cloak of deep red. Her hair was crowned with huge pearls, and loops of pearls hung from her neck, encompassing her bosom. At a certain moment she ascended a high stair, then raced down the steep steps, her cloak flying wildly in the wind. Every night she hit her high note on the eighth step, so extraordinarily coordinated was her music and movement. She was like a circus horse, conditioned to pull off any theatrical stunt she was taught. Whatever Maria may have thought of our *Ifigenia*, in my opinion it was the most beautiful production we did together. After this I staged many operas without her–in Spoleto, London, Rome, Vienna. But what I did with Maria was always something apart, existing unto itself, created for her alone."

With Dondi as Orestes

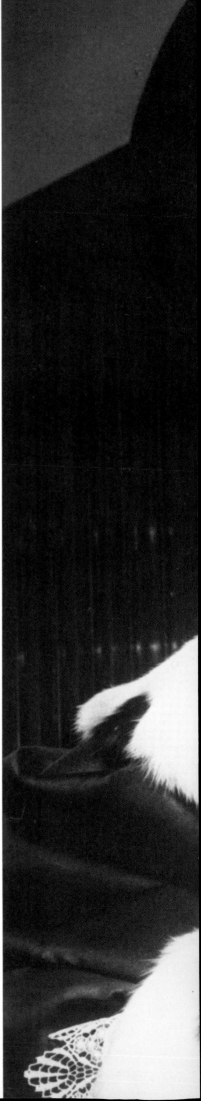

When *Un ballo in maschera* had its world premiere, in 1859, a dispute arose as to where the action of the story should unfold. For the new production planned for the opening night of the 1957–58 season at La Scala, the same issue was raised. The management of the theater insisted on Boston. The producers, however, preferred Sweden. Director Margherita Wallmann explains: "Since the libretto deals with regicide, a touchy subject in Verdi's day, the censors had forced him to change the historical site, the Stockholm of Gustav II, to a fictitious, far-off Boston. So the king became a governor. Personally, I felt we should respect Verdi's original dramatic concept, for he composed his score with the elegance of a royal court in mind, and Gustav's taste was very Parisian. But finally we had to give in. Gianandrea Gavazzeni, our conductor, pointed out that if Verdi could accept Boston, so could we.

"With my designer, Nicola Benois, I sought an acceptable way to put Puritans onstage without conflicting too much with Verdi's music. We decided to show a primitive New World, with little luxury. To avoid heaviness, Benois hung many banners, flags, and tapestries in his decor, constructing all the sets of wood, for early America was carved from its forests [below, scene one of act one, the governor's office]. This did impart some sense of lightness, but I still feel our approach was a compromise."

Benois speaks of how he and Wallmann saw Amelia, the role Maria Callas would sing: "Margherita conceived her as a great lady from London, which meant her costumes could have elegance [right]. But we also wanted to show she was fascinated to be among Indians. In her home, in act three, there hung a huge rug that Amelia had purchased from a local tribe, and her costume was trimmed with fur ornaments made by the natives."

As Amelia

Act three of *Ballo* was the first Verdi that Callas—then a student in Athens—sang in public. In 1947, after an audition at La Scala, she was promised a debut as Amelia. Instead, the role went to another artist, leaving a tearful Callas. She waited ten years to sing the role there, and she never sang it elsewhere.

Maestro Gavazzeni describes Callas's Amelia: "Her sense for the words was not only Verdi's, but the Verdi of *Ballo*, where the music literally bursts into life from the text. She captured the extreme desperation of a woman whose fate cannot be resolved. One of Callas's great gifts was to differentiate styles of expression—Rossini from Bellini, Donizetti from Verdi. Even Verdi from Verdi. Musically, I felt she was born with some kind of sixth sense. She had a strange, burning inner quality. You only need hear a note or two to recognize her voice. She was always different, yet always herself."

Amelia, wife of Renato, is infatuated with Riccardo. An Indian mystic, Ulrica [top, Giulietta Simionato], advises her to end this dilemma by seeking a magic herb that grows at the foot of the gallows, where Riccardo meets Amelia and makes her confess her passion. Renato [right, Ettore Bastianini] finds them and takes his wife home. He then tells her she must die for infidelity [far right]. In the final scene, a brilliant masked ball at the governor's palace, Renato plunges a dagger into Riccardo (Giuseppe di Stefano). As Amelia comforts the dying man, he pardons his assassin [next pages].

With Simionato [above]; Bastianini [right]; and [next pages] di Stefano

Il pirata might have occupied a more enduring position
in the Callas repertory had it come at a different moment in her career. But by May 19, 1958, when this
obscure Bellini work was resurrected by La Scala, the
singer had become enmeshed in an unfortunate series
of circumstances which hurt her professionally. For all
the work and diligence she had given to Scala through
the years, the theater had not defended her publicly, as
it might have, when fatigue forced her to refuse an extra and uncontracted performance with the company at
the Edinburgh Festival. Scala's lack of support outraged
Callas's sense of justice and fair play, and her husband
began a feud with Antonio Ghiringhelli, Scala's general
manager.

Had Edinburgh been the only incident, Callas
might have persuaded the press of her integrity in the
affair. But almost immediately after it, impresario Kurt
Herbert Adler canceled Callas's contract with the San
Francisco Opera when physical exhaustion prevented
her from arriving on schedule for her West Coast
debut. Not even a much acclaimed concert that
launched the Dallas Civic Opera or a splendid opening
night at Scala in *Un ballo in maschera* kept the press
from taking any and all opportunities to attack her. The
last thing Callas needed was to get a fever and sore
throat the day before the *Norma* that was to inaugurate
the 1957–58 season in Rome. She canceled after the
first act, no substitute was on hand to carry on, and
once more Callas was made a scapegoat in the news.

When she returned to Scala in the spring of 1958,
after a successful series of Violettas, Lucias, and Toscas
at the Metropolitan Opera, she won back the Milan
public with an inspired first-night *Anna Bolena*. But
the management of the theater seemed disenchanted
with its star diva, perhaps fearful that Rome–where the
state subsidies are allotted–was still angry over the

As Imogene

Norma walkout. Whatever the reason, during rehearsals of *Il pirata*, Ghiringhelli made no conciliatory move toward Callas and did nothing to squelch rumors that the opera would mark her last appearances at Scala. Clearly, Callas was no longer wanted, and Meneghini announced that, after his wife's contracted appearances, she would return to Scala only under a new management.

Despite everything, Callas worked on *Il pirata* with her accustomed intensity. Fortunately, she was surrounded by sympathetic colleagues: Franco Corelli as Gualtiero, the pirate of the opera's title, and Ettore Bastianini as her husband, Ernesto. Antonino Votto conducted, Piero Zuffi did the decor, and Franco Enriquez, who had staged Callas's Covent Garden debut in 1952, directed. As things turned out, the production did not attain distinction with its particularly mediocre sets. At the premiere, Corelli and Bastianini were in fine voice, but Callas did not hit her vocal stride until the dramatic final scene, the score's strongest musical section.

At the last performance, on May 31, 1958, Callas again seized the words of the libretto to score a personal point, just as she had done a few weeks before as Anna Bolena. It was the kind of theatrical audacity only Callas would dare.

The heroine, Imogene, knows that her pirate-lover must die. Following a long grief-stricken aria, she must launch into an exciting cabaletta finale in which Imogene imagines she sees the scaffold on which the pirate is to be executed—"Là...vedete...il palco funesto" (There, behold, the disastrous scaffold). By coincidence, the Italian word *palco* means both a scaffold and a theater box. As Callas came to the line, she strode toward the left of the stage and, with scorn in her eyes and a gesture of disdain, she pointed into Antonio Ghiringhelli's darkened box—her own "palco funesto."

The double entendre was not lost on the audience and it triggered an exultant ovation. The public, fearing it might never hear Callas again, called her forth repeatedly for bows. But without warning, Scala's huge fire curtain was abruptly lowered, cutting the singer off from the audience. Meanwhile, in the auditorium, security guards materialized as if from nowhere to hustle everyone from the theater. This had been Callas's 157th performance at Scala. She was not to sing there again for two and a half years. When she did return, it would be more as a guest than as its absolute mistress. But, after that final *Pirata*, as the beleaguered Callas stepped from the stage door, hundreds of admirers crowded around her, throwing flowers in her path to demonstrate their love and esteem.

With Corelli as Gualtiero

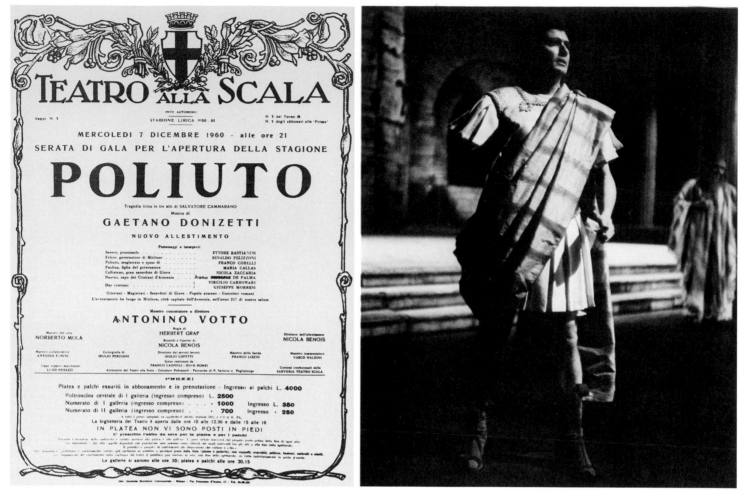

Poliuto, Donizetti's musical adaptation of Corneille's *Polyeucte*, never established itself in the repertory after its world premiere at the Paris Opéra in 1840 under its French title, *Les Martyrs*. From time to time revivals of this opera would crop up in Italy, usually to show off a star tenor, but the score was invariably returned to the shelf.

All the same, when *Poliuto* was announced to open the 1960–61 season at La Scala, it drew a packed house–the best-dressed, worst-behaved audience in the theater's 183-year history. Among the celebrities present: Prince Rainier and Princess Grace of Monaco, strategically displayed in a proscenium box; the Begum Aga Khan; Aristotle Onassis with assorted cronies from the Jet Set; columnist Elsa Maxwell; and the bejeweled leaders of Milanese society. None, of course, had come to hear *Poliuto*. What had drawn this glittering assembly was that celebrity among celebrities, Maria Callas, who had not sung at Scala for two seasons and was making her return in a new role, Paolina, her last such on any stage.

According to Antonino Votto, who conducted *Poliuto*, "At this moment in Maria's career, Paolina permitted a perfect exhibition of her gifts. Nowhere in the score did she face the exposed vocal problems found in *Lucia*, *Sonnambula*, or *Anna Bolena*. To my ear, her performance went extremely well." Franco Corelli, who sang the title role, totally agrees with the conductor. In contrast, most critics wrote that Callas sounded hollow and hesitant, and expressed disappointment that the role did not provide enough dramatic challenge to draw a major portrayal from her. The public in the upper gallery, however, rejoiced to have its diva back under any conditions, and, at her first entrance, their cheering halted the music. Below, the gilded first-nighters reacted with far less enthusiasm: They had come to gawk at a star, not to appreciate the art that had made her a star.

For the designer of *Poliuto*, Nicola Benois, the production proved a difficult task. "Visconti and I had planned every detail, but he withdrew from the project, leaving the direction to Herbert Graf, who had to prepare a staging at the last minute. Despite these problems, Maria was no trouble–simple, human, and sympathetic during rehearsals, always ready with a smile. But she badly needed a strong hand to guide her, to give her courage–the hand of Luchino. For some time she had begun to distance herself from theater life, injured by backstage politics and by gossip in the press. I know this tormented her, made her suffer psychologically. She was hurt by all that had befallen her glorious career. No wonder at times her voice no longer functioned as it should have. Before all else Maria is an artist, and things were done to her that would have destroyed anyone of weaker character."

Shown above, Poliuto (Corelli) and Nearco (Piero de Palma) attend a clandestine religious service in a deserted cave near Melitene. At right, Poliuto's wife, Paolina (Callas), follows her husband to confirm her suspicion that he has converted to Christianity. On the next pages, Paolina and Poliuto witness the return of the Roman proconsul Severo (Ettore Bastianini), formerly Paolina's lover.

Next pages: the Square of Melitene
(Callas, Corelli, and Bastianini)

During act two of *Poliuto*, Severo finds Paolina in the atrium of her father's house; he has come in the hope of renewing the love they once shared [above]. Paolina, who married Poliuto when Severo had been reported killed in battle, is a faithful wife; she sends the proconsul away. Meanwhile, a pagan priest arouses Poliuto's jealousy, informing him that Severo and Paolina have met in private. Later, during a pagan ritual in the Temple of Jove, the Christian leader Nearco is led in under arrest. Severo demands the names of his followers and Paolina is terrified Poliuto will be implicated [right]. When Nearco is threatened with torture, Poliuto steps forward to declare his new faith. At this Severo condemns his rival to death. Paolina falls at Severo's feet begging mercy for her husband, but her action incites Poliuto to such anger he overturns the altar by which they were married. Guards take him to prison as Paolina's father drags his daughter away.

For his production of *Poliuto*, says designer Benois, "I wanted to capture the style of Gonzaga. The sets were sepia, the costumes very colorful. In that period at Scala, we took time to discuss the esthetic ideals of each opera, seeking the proper sense of style. There was deep commitment for the needs of the art we served.

"Herbert von Karajan saw *Poliuto* and was very enthusiastic about it, finding the conception ideal. He actually thought my sets were constructed, for even from the front row they looked three-dimensional. He refused to believe me when I told him each scene was a painted flat. Finally, I took him backstage to let him touch the canvas. 'It's a miracle!' he exclaimed. 'In Vienna and Salzburg we spend a fortune to build sets to achieve what you do with paint and canvas.'

"During Donizetti's day, no theater had space backstage for huge constructions, so designers were obliged to learn how to create a sense of volume on flat surfaces. My *Poliuto*, alas, will be one of the very last productions of this kind. A recent law in Italy decreed that artisans in scenery shops must retire at age sixty-five. That has forced all the old master craftsmen out, men who through years of experience could take a designer's sketch and translate it into a marvelous stage picture. The young men who have taken their place lack the training and technique to do this. This is sad. Careers of singers and dancers are limited by age, but a painter can continue until he is ninety. Think of Picasso or Chagall. This stupid law represents a tremendous loss for opera, the senseless end to a great tradition of theater."

With Bastianini and de Palma

Act three of *Poliuto*, with Corelli

The finale of Donizetti's *Poliuto* takes place in a cell beneath the Colosseum where Poliuto and other Christians are to be fed to lions. The distraught Paolina comes to plead with her husband to refute his new religion [left]. Though she fails in this, she does convince him of her love. Then, inspired by his serenity in the face of death, she decides to join him in martyrdom [above]. When trumpets signal the Christians to step forth into the arena, Paolina and Poliuto slowly mount the stairs together, certain of the paradise that awaits them.

Franco Corelli describes the scene: "Through high barred windows the audience could see the pagan mob that had gathered in the Colosseum to witness the slaughter. Below, where Maria and I stood, it was quite dark except for a very bright spotlight on us. For the final hymn, as we climbed the steps to our death, except for this light on us, the stage was plunged in blackness. A beautiful effect.

"Maria sang her music with such wonderful legato line and phrasing, keeping her voice very clear and high, and as it should be, she made the character of Paolina sweet and gentle. While this was by no means an easy role, it did not ask of Maria the great dramatic outbursts of a Norma or a Medea. Never did she force her voice or seem to worry about making a big tone. She was only concerned in doing justice to her music. Today, when I listen to pirated recordings of this *Poliuto*, I cannot help asking myself, 'Where is there a soprano like Maria today?'"

As the second event of its 1961–62 season, La Scala announced a new production of *Medea*. In fact, it was new only to the Milanese. Three years earlier, a virtual duplicate, created for Maria Callas by director Alexis Minotis and designer Vannis Tsarouchis, had its premiere at the Dallas Civic Opera. When Scala undertook *Medea*, the theater lured the same team. The result was a similar production, although the settings had to be totally rebuilt and new elements added to accommodate the stage's great depth and large proscenium opening.

Minotis, husband of the late Katina Paxinou, did many Greek tragedies with the actress–*Oedipus Rex*, *Electra*, *Agamemnon*–seeking to recapture the style of expression and gesture used in the time of Aeschylus, Sophocles, and Euripides, working laboriously to uncover long-lost methods. One day in Dallas, he was startled to see Callas do a movement he and Paxinou had been discussing for future use. Callas was kneeling in a frenzy, beating the floor to summon the gods. Minotis asked her why she had done it. "I felt it would be the right thing to do for this moment in the drama," she answered.

How she felt this, Minotis cannot explain. As a girl in Greece, Callas never saw the classic tragedies. She was too involved with her music, and, once the Germans occupied the country, most theatrical activity was curtailed. There were–or so Minotis thinks–things that simply flowed in her blood.

Other than Callas, Minotis, and Tsarouchis, the only other constant in the Dallas and Milan *Medea*s was Jon Vickers's Jason. The conductor was new to Cherubini's score, Thomas Schippers. During rehearsals of Medea's mysterious act-one entrance, a problem arose for Callas and Schippers. "The Corinthians are seized by confusion as Medea arrives, her face covered by a shroud," explains Schippers. "No one knows who she is until she shows her face, saying 'Io? Medea!' [preceding page and above]. From the podium to where Maria stood far back on the stage, it was quite a distance, and our first two measures of music seemed impossible to coordinate. The orchestra had one chord to play on the 'de' of 'Medea,' nothing else, but it was always off. Maria said, 'It's easy. I sing "Io?" then you count two-three-four and hit the chord while I uncover my face.' But my two-three-four during the pause, where no tempo is marked, could not be the same as hers. Her timing was dramatic, something she felt. Finally I suggested she either gesture to me when to come in or take off her shroud from my beat. After several more tries, she decided it best to follow me."

At the premiere, on December 11, 1961, one of those incidents that have so contributed to the Callas legend took place during the act-one duet in which Medea begs Jason to return to her and their children [right]. "As Maria started the section 'Dei tuoi figli,'" Schippers recalls, "the audience seemed to feel her singing was not going well–I didn't agree–and from the

In Medea with Tosini (Glauce),
Ghiaurov (Creon), and Vickers (Jason)

top of the gallery came an awful hissing sound, like a typhoon, that covered the entire auditorium. Maria continued and finally reached the point in the text where Medea denounces Jason with the word 'Crudel!' The orchestra must follow this word with two forte chords, then wait for her to sing a second 'Crudel!' before it can continue playing. But after the first 'Crudel!' Maria completely stopped singing, creating a long fermata, a suspense-filled pause. I watched in disbelief as she glared up into the auditorium and took in every pair of eyes in the theater, as if to say, 'Now, look! This has been my stage and will be mine as long as I want it. If you hate me now, I hate you just as much!' I saw this, I felt it. Then Maria sang her second 'Crudel!' directly at the public, squashing it into silence. Never in my life have I seen anyone dare such a thing in the theater. Never. And there was not a murmur of protest against her after that.

"I was paralyzed. The hissing had not upset me because I myself have been booed. It was Maria's stopping that threw me—I had no idea when she was going to start again. She controlled the whole thing." When she did start, on the words "Ho dato tutto a te" (I gave everything to you) Callas shook her fist at the gallery.

Carol Fox, who for twenty years has guided the Lyric Opera of Chicago, first saw the Callas Medea in Venice in 1954, eight months before she and Lawrence Kelly presented the soprano in her American debut. A singer herself, Miss Fox was puzzled by, and disagreed with, the Callas vocal method, but she could not resist the artistry with which it was employed. "I don't think Judith Anderson was one bit better than Callas as Medea. I'm not comparing them actress for actress, or suggesting that Maria could have done what Anderson did or vice versa. What I mean is the results Maria achieved with her singing and acting were in every way comparable to what Anderson did with her artistic means. Maria's interpretive ability was simply staggering. In this she left all the competition far behind."

Callas is shown here in the act-two confrontation between Medea and Creon (Nicolai Ghiaurov). While an angry mob calls for her blood, the sorceress hysterically begs the King to let her remain one more day in Corinth to be with her two young sons. Moved by the mother's plea, Creon yields to her request, but tells her she is thereafter banished from his realm.

Act two of *Medea*, with Ghiaurov

During Medea's act-two duet with Jason, Callas often looked more like a member of the Martha Graham Dance Company than an opera singer. Her face and gestures summoned myriad images: supplication, so Jason would let her see their sons [above and right]; guile and duplicity the instant he turned his back; then joy and gratitude as he acceded to her request [next pages].

Vickers has mused on the Callas phenomenon: "After the war, an enormous revolution took place in opera because of two people: Wieland Wagner, who totally changed the approach and emphasis of the physical aspects of stage direction, and Maria Callas, who took her talent almost to the point of masochism to serve her work and find its meaning. There are some who think they are following in her shoes, but, believe me, they don't know which direction she was going. I not only learned a great deal about the stage from her, I learned how the public image of an artist can be unjustly distorted. She was a superb colleague, giving you something to work with and wanting you to give it back. She never tried to steal the limelight or upstage anyone. In the Dallas *Medea*, she showed Teresa Berganza, who was exceedingly young and beautiful, how to act the old maid, Neris. Teresa watched what Maria did, then made the role her own. With Neris's aria, Berganza stopped the show. And Maria never moved a hair or a finger until the applause finished. That's generosity."

With Vickers as Jason
[also on following pages]

Neris [above, Giulietta Simionato] comforts Medea, who starts when she hears Jason's wedding march [below]. While the ceremony is held in the temple, nothing can quell Medea's pain [right].

In act three [next pages], Medea's maternal love wars with her desire for retaliation. Weeping, she asks the gods if they keep her from what she must do [top left]. When Neris enters saying that Glauce has accepted the mantle and diadem Medea sent, Medea savagely admits their magic powers [bottom left]. She then sends her sons into the temple to save them from her wrath. But the furies drive her on and, grasping the dagger [right], Medea follows them into the temple to fulfill her accursed fate.

On pages following, Callas's last Scala bow, with Simionato and Vickers.

After her last Medea at La Scala, on June 3, 1962, the better part of two years passed before Maria Callas again stepped onto the stage of an opera house. She filled her time with a few concerts in Europe, a few recording dates, and a lot of leisure in the company of some of the world's wealthiest and most socially prominent figures. Her residence was now an elegant apartment in Paris; her chief companion, Aristotle Onassis.

At various intervals, rumors would reach print announcing her return to opera—as Anna Bolena in London, Orfeo in Dallas, Medea in New York. When Callas finally did return, it was as Floria Tosca at the Royal Opera House, Covent Garden. This theater had always treated her with respect and kindness. Never in London had she undergone the indignities she suffered in Rome, Milan, and New York. Beginning with her Covent Garden debut a dozen years before, there had existed a kind of love affair between Callas and the British public.

The circumstances that brought Callas back to the stage on January 21, 1964, are best told by the man who conceived and directed the Covent Garden *Tosca*, Franco Zeffirelli. "It took a long time to convince her, and besides my own efforts, most of the credit belongs to the late Sir David Webster, who was the general manager of the Royal Opera House. He literally followed Maria all over the world until she accepted. He did everything he could to make it come true. But before she gave him her final word, Maria phoned me, saying, 'Franco, I'll do it if you will help me.' I had never staged *Tosca* before. In fact, I had refused several offers to direct it because I needed in the soprano a personality who could comprehend my approach. Callas was the one.

"To begin with, you have to understand what Puccini sought to express when he composed this opera. Take the very first chords, those associated with Baron Scarpia. The sound is solemn, pompous, big with a grandeur that is found in no other score of Puccini. It is the splendor of Rome, with its overwhelming proportions, its Vatican-like magnitude. Puccini depicts the size of the city throughout *Tosca*. He felt it tremendously.

"With my set designer, Renzo Mongiardino, I wanted to capture this sense of immensity on the stage, to put the characters of the opera in proportion to the gigantic, baroque architecture of Rome. Therefore, instead of doing an entire church, we decided to do only a side nave, so that the base of the great columns would be much higher than the singers. Our nave and altar were not accurate reconstructions from the Church of Sant'Andrea della Valle, which is specified in Puccini's libretto. When that particular church was built, a standard of architecture already had been established by Bernini and Borromini. To achieve the impression of that style onstage, we had to do just a little part of the church. This was overpowering in itself.

"For my conception of Tosca—and how quickly Maria grasped the idea and brought it to life—I wanted her played as an exuberant, warm-hearted, rather sloppy, casual woman, a kind of Magnani of her time. She was not to be sophisticated and elegant. How I hate the posey-lady, grand-diva Tosca who arrives with four-dozen roses, a walking stick, wearing a large hat with

OPERA
ROYAL HOUSE
COVENT GARDEN

THE ROYAL OPERA HOUSE, COVENT GARDEN LTD.
IN ASSOCIATION WITH THE ARTS COUNCIL OF GREAT BRITAIN

presents

THE
COVENT GARDEN OPERA

in

a new production of

TOSCA

Opera in Three Acts by GIACOMO PUCCINI

Text by GIACOSA and ILLICA

after the play by Sardou   (Property of G. Ricordi & Co.)

Producer: FRANCO ZEFFIRELLI

Sets by RENZO MONGIARDINO   Costumes by MARCEL ESCOFFIER

with

MARIA CALLAS

RENATO CIONI   TITO GOBBI
ERIC GARRETT   VICTOR GODFREY

Conductor: CARLO FELICE CILLARIO

on January 21st, 24th, 27th, 30th, February 1st, 5th

Tosca's entrance, with Cioni as Cavaradossi

feathers, gloves—impeccably dressed as if she were going to visit the Queen or the Pope. Tosca was never like that!

"The first act takes place on a beautiful summer morning. Because Tosca is a singer and a Roman, she wakes up late. Rushing to the church to see her lover, Mario Cavaradossi [Renato Cioni], who is painting an altar there, she stops to buy some flowers for the Madonna—instinctively, impulsively, what she likes, daisies, carnations, zinnias, a colorful, confused bunch of flowers that she carries lightly, with no formality, in her hand. She arrives and is like a ray of sunlight in the dark church, very feminine in a lace veil and yards of peach chiffon. She was free—no corset or brassiere, for in that period dresses were cut to give women support.

"But when Cavaradossi keeps Tosca waiting outside a locked door while he helps the political prisoner Angelotti hide, she grows wildly jealous. She storms into the church, screaming at her lover. She makes a big scene, looking all over the place, behind things, in corners, to see if some rival, another woman, is hiding from her. She is ready to slap Cavaradossi, to scratch his face—she is a real Roman woman, not a controlled, composed lady. Only when Tosca is convinced that Cavaradossi is alone does she begin to calm down. *This* is what Sardou and Puccini wanted.

"Tosca is very religious, but she is also a fleshly woman, a kind of victim of her senses. Even though she is in a church, she begins to talk about making love with Cavaradossi, about a rendezvous at their little house in the country. She giggles and laughs and hugs and kisses him [right], then pulls herself together, saying, 'No, don't touch me in front of the Madonna!' But she is very sensual. The way I think of it, they might have had it right there in the church. If Angelotti had not been hiding nearby and desperately in need of help, Cavaradossi would have. Tosca was ready. They could have—the church was closed.

"But then Tosca sees the blue-eyed Mary Magdalene her lover has painted and has another jealous fit. It takes all Cavaradossi's persuasion to prove again that he loves only her, to regain her trust [next pages]. Well, Maria carried it off, creating this magnetic, temperamental creature. From her entrance to her exit, she held the audience absolutely breathless."

With Cioni [also next pages]

No sooner does Tosca depart than Cavaradossi and Angelotti flee, the prisoner carrying a bundle of women's clothes hidden in the church by his sister, the beautiful Marchesa Attavanti, to serve as his disguise. A sacristan immediately enters with choirboys in tow. They have come to rehearse a cantata. Zeffirelli gives the scene: "British youngsters are so well-trained musically that they never have to watch the conductor. So I had them play real brats, running everywhere, uncontrollable. Two climbed on Cavaradossi's scaffold and started a fight over his designs. Right on cue, one boy lost the papers so they fell like snow through the air as Baron Scarpia made his frightening entrance. 'An uproar in church? Where is respect?' he brusquely demands, paralyzing the children in their tracks.

"It was the best entrance I ever gave anyone. The lights dimmed slightly, as though a cloud hovered over the church. Tito Gobbi had all the angles of Scarpia just right—Mr. Scarpia, whose clothes were made in Vienna, impeccably groomed, pre-Revolutionary in style. A dirty, ruthless man who plays at being elegant, beautiful—his hands clean, his nails polished. No petty little suburban police chief, but elegant, noble, even graceful—still, the steel hand in the velvet glove.

"Tosca then returns, looking for Cavaradossi. Not wanting to betray her purpose, she falls to her knees pretending to pray. Scarpia kneels beside her. He is looking for evidence and he begins whispering in her ear, subtly playing on her emotions [top left]. First, he praises her art and piety, then suggests all are not so pure. Has not Cavaradossi put the face of Angelotti's sister in the portrait of Mary Magdalene? Does the painter not use the church for his assignations with this woman?

"Tosca, unable to bear another word, jumps to her feet, demanding proof. 'Is this the tool of a painter?' asks Scarpia, coolly handing her a large lace fan he has found on the floor—part of the disguise that Angelotti accidentally dropped as he fled the church. Tosca studies it [bottom left] and, recognizing the insignia of the Attavanti family, is convinced her lover has betrayed her. At this moment, Callas's face literally broke with the strain. It was so real how she portrayed Tosca's anguish [right]."

With Gobbi as Scarpia

Holding the fan, Tosca weeps believing Cavaradossi to be unfaithful [top left]. Poisoned by jealousy, she swears to catch him with his new mistress [above]. "In church?" asks Scarpia hypocritically. "God will forgive me, for He sees my tears," she replies [left].

"Maria did not do the conventional and throw the fan at the painting of Mary Magdalene in Tosca's moment of revenge," recalls Zef-firelli. "Instead she almost collapsed from emotion, and the efficient Scarpia retrieved this valuable piece of evidence from her hand. Now Tosca, completely crushed, a broken woman, reels across the stage to a basin of holy water, grasping it for support. Scarpia follows her there, offering his hand. For a long while she hesitates, but finally she takes it because she needs help—from anyone, even Scarpia.

But Scarpia's hand is like touching something cold, damp, repulsive—like an octopus [above]. Shaken, Tosca runs from Scarpia, up the altar steps to look again at the blue-eyed Magdalene. As she leans on the balustrade, her hands inadvertently fall on Cavaradossi's smock, which the painter had left behind as he fled. With her lover's clothing clutched in her hands, Tosca is consumed by anger and pain. She despairingly throws the smock to the ground and rushes offstage in tears. As she did each of these things, Maria showed the woman Tosca is.

"All the while, the church has been filling with worshipers awaiting Mass. In the *Te Deum* [right], Puccini evoked the great power of the Church, but the scene is difficult to direct. Scarpia must deliver his diabolical monologue while the stage is filled with people, while a large religious procession is in progress. To isolate him, I cut the set diagonally so that he stood at the tightest angle at the left, behind a huge pillar. There, as if in cinema close-up, Gobbi voiced Scarpia's determination to capture the rebels and have Tosca in the bargain [far right]. As with Maria, Tito was dramatic perfection."

Baron Scarpia's private chamber in the Palazzo Farnese is the setting for the second act of *Tosca*. In Zeffirelli's words: "I made the set seem like hell, with ominous shadows cast on the wall from the light of a roaring fireplace. Puccini constructed this act so dramatically. For me, the action is exactly like what takes place in the arena during a bullfight.

"Each of the characters in his own turn is the bull and the matador. Scarpia starts out so confident of himself. He is Chief of Police and controls all Rome—which for him means virtually the world. And at the end, he is dead on the floor, stabbed by Tosca. Cavaradossi, too, is so healthy, handsome, arrogant when he is brought in for questioning by Scarpia [above]. Little by little, he is destroyed; the police torture him, beat him, and when the poor boy is finally dragged from the room, he is covered with blood, almost a corpse.

"As for Tosca, she arrives the reigning diva, having just sung a cantata for the Queen of Naples. She is dressed in her finest attire. But as Scarpia bargains with her for Cavaradossi's life, her glory and beauty begin to peel away. First, Scarpia helps her remove her stole. Then she takes off her gloves. At last, as Scarpia chases and tries to rape the terrified woman, her hair becomes unpinned and she loses some of her jewels. She ends up disheveled, a murderess; she is no longer the woman we saw enter so magnificently. It is a very exciting second act, the best ever in opera.

"My costume designer, Marcel Escoffier, and I decided we did not want Maria to appear gaudy in this act. At the same time, she had to look like a great diva, like a woman who would be invited to sing at court. She had to be elegant, very elegant. So we made her an Empire gown of rich red velvets—reds of many different shades, panels sewn together so one part was bright, another less so. From the distance it looked like one piece. The gown had a long train and gold embroidery, real and of the period. Her jewels—she wore a necklace, earrings, and a tiara—were all rubies and diamonds, but nothing flashy.

"The truly sensational thing was her stole—six feet long and six feet wide. It cost well over $2,000. We found it at an Indian shop in London, a unique place. It wasn't a filmy sari; it was a heavily embroidered solid gold-metal fabric. And what use Maria made of it! She spent hours before the mirror in her dressing room deciding how to wear it. For her entrance, she wrapped herself in it, then, using only one gesture, she opened it so that it fell back [right]. What she could do with a costume! I remember well how moments later she removed her gloves. It took her three minutes to take off two gloves, caressing them, putting them in order, pretending that nothing in the world was more important. With such elegance, such grace."

Act two of Tosca,
Cioni and Gobbi [above]

Scarpia has furnished his huge office with some of the amenities of home. "He is," says Zeffirelli, "a precise man when it comes to business affairs, so on the right side of the stage stood his desk—papers, pens, everything in perfect order. To the left of the stage, however, he had established his private domain. Near the fireplace were elaborate tapestry chairs, a table beautifully set with silver and crystal, and a large couch covered with a fur throw, with pillows and cushions. Here, he would have his officers bring some woman who feared for her life, or a prostitute, instructing the men not to disturb him for an hour or so. That's really all he had in mind for Tosca. To have her. Not for love, but for animal pleasure. The man is an absolute bastard."

When Tito Gobbi portrayed Scarpia in London, it was the first complete staged *Tosca* he had done with Callas. "I found in Maria all the answers to my problems as an actor and this made me love and adore her. From the start of my career, my friends always kidded me, calling me the lawyer because of the way I think. I always ask why. For me every action in the theater must have a reason and I must know the meaning. So I always felt frustrated when colleagues did things without reason or showed no response to my acting. Most performances came out 80 percent. What could I do? Just try to do my best.

"With Maria, I discovered an artist who also asked why and who understood what it means to be an actor. We reached 100 percent together. There was action and reaction, give and take, collaboration for the good of the performance. She was Tosca and I was Scarpia. Not Maria and Tito. We never tried to direct each other, but we watched each other and spoke with our eyes to discover what could happen. Everything came spontaneously. If something unexpected occurred—one night Maria accidentally fell down—we absorbed it into the drama. No one in the audience knew we hadn't planned it that way. We adjusted. We felt totally free to realize our parts.

"Franco Zeffirelli wanted this. He left us at liberty and shifted the supporting cast so it played off what we did. And for once there was the right distance maintained between Tosca and Scarpia—not too close, not too far. I hate doing this opera when the soprano stays across the stage from me. Nothing can happen. Maria was just right. We balanced this proportion and kept everything clear, never covering over each other's actions.

"Maria was Tosca every second of the performance. The way she moved and sang, the way she listened to colleagues when *they* sang. She filled dramatic pauses with her presence, her ability to sustain tension. She was genuine, authentic, without the old clichés. Better than Callas we will never see."

After Cavaradossi is led away, Tosca senses that she and her lover are in peril, but does not realize the potential for cruelty of their captor. To hide her fear, she pretends calm. But the game is a deadly one and Scarpia the only player who enjoys it. When Tosca refuses to tell him what she knows, he sadistically describes to her how Cavaradossi is being tortured—a spiked vise tightened on his head [left]. Now will Tosca speak?

When Tosca begs Scarpia for pity, he replies that only she can save Cavaradossi. Tosca submits but asks that she first be permitted to speak with her lover. "In my staging," Zeffirelli explains, "Scarpia banged on the floor with his foot and a trapdoor opened. Maria knelt down, peering into the torture chamber, her features lit by the torchlight coming from the inferno below. She called to Cavaradossi and he told her to keep silent, to have courage. When Tosca rose and Scarpia demanded her confession, she was once again resolute: 'I know nothing,' she exclaimed."

Refused again, Scarpia orders his henchmen to recommence the torture. "But you are killing him," Tosca cries out in desperation. "Your silence is killing him," laughs her tormentor, and he calls to his men to "open the door so she can hear him groan."

Tosca, now nearly hysterical, implores her lover to allow her to talk. Again, Cavaradossi says no. But their exchange has convinced Scarpia that Tosca has information. Determined to find out what it is, he signals his men to carry the torture to the very limit. A bloodcurdling cry that follows destroys Tosca. "Look in the well in our garden," she blurts out. "Is Angelotti there?" "Yes!" An officer enters to say that Cavaradossi has fainted. "Assassin!" Tosca screams at Scarpia. Then, realizing she is still at his mercy, she asks to see the victim.

The half-conscious, blood-spattered Cavaradossi is carried in by an officer and Tosca helps lead him gently to the couch [above]. Tenderly enfolding him, she tells him "this villain will pay for his crimes." The painter asks weakly if she has confessed. "No, my love," she lies [right].

This sweet scene is too much for Scarpia. "Go look in the well in their garden!" he shouts to his men. In disbelief, Cavaradossi turns on Tosca, cursing her for betraying his cause. But at this very moment a report is brought to Scarpia: The revolutionary forces have won a great battle at Marengo. Staggering from the couch, Cavaradossi shouts, "Victory! Victory!" and prophesies the downfall of tyrants such as Scarpia. The police chief has heard enough and orders his men to take the rebel away.

"In a rage," recounts Zeffirelli, "Maria attacked the officers who were dragging Cavaradossi out, wildly beating them with her clenched fists. She had become an avenging fury! But what was her might against such forces? As the door closed, Tosca found herself trapped, alone with Scarpia, who seemed totally undisturbed by such violence. 'My poor supper,' he laments, 'has been interrupted.' And casually he walked toward his table."

Tosca, act two, with Cioni

With all the suavity at his command, Scarpia pours Tosca some wine. But she comes straight to the point: "How much? Your price?" [left]. Frozen with fear, she hears Scarpia admit he can be bought, but not with money. In payment for Cavaradossi's life, he wants Tosca herself. Tosca grabs her stole and starts for the door, but Scarpia blocks her way. "Go," he tells her calmly. "You are free. But if you hope for help from the Queen, you hope in vain. She cannot pardon a corpse!" [below]. Tosca stares into his eyes with a mixture of scorn and disbelief. "How you loathe me," he says, smiling. "Oh, God!" Tosca explodes, not hiding her hatred [right]. "And this is why I desire you," retorts Scarpia as he begins to track her around the room. In terror and revulsion, Tosca tries to elude his grasp.

Tito Gobbi tells how he and Callas did the rape scene the first time they tried it. "I pursued her, but she knew she couldn't get away and in her frenzy, instead of running from me, she finally ran toward me, this poor frail woman, and began beating me on my big chest with her fists. A last desperate effort to hurt me, to wound me. When I saw how futile her action was, I burst into sadistic laughter, looking down into her agonized face [top left]. Then, with all my force, I grasped her hands and opened them up, then spread her arms, literally crucifying her [right]. Maria knew at once what I was doing and responded with such suffering. It was a totally spontaneous thing that happened between us. But we kept it in every performance because it was born in a moment of theatrical inspiration and was too good to lose.

"After this, Maria fell on her knees [bottom left]. Now Scarpia tells her: 'You hear that drum? It's the march of the condemned. Down there in the darkness a gallows is being built. By your wish, your lover has only an hour to live!' Then Maria sang 'Vissi d'arte,' but for once the aria didn't break the drama, for she sustained the atmosphere we had built even in her soliloquy."

Franco Zeffirelli says, "Maria grabbed her stole from an armchair, clutching it to her as she sang the aria. At the dress rehearsal, we had a terrible moment. Maria was leaning against Scarpia's desk and her long hair—actually a fall—caught fire from the candles. She didn't realize it. People ran onstage to put out the fire. But she went on singing. Never stopped."

Gobbi recalls another moment: "Scarpia agrees to write a safe-conduct for Cavaradossi as payment for Tosca. At that moment I tried to caress Maria, but she grew rigid, like stone, refusing any concession until she got the permit. I went to write out the document and when I asked by what port she wanted to depart, she replied 'Civitavecchia,' coming close to watch me, her hand touching the desk. I looked at her with lust, running my feather quill all the way up and down her beautiful long white arm. Maria froze, petrified. Stupendous. Now everyone asks me to retain this bit of action, but it can never be the same without Maria to respond."

With Gobbi as Scarpia

"After Maria sang 'Vissi d'arte'" [above], recounts Zeffirelli, "I had an inspiration which we developed together. I gave her the idea, but Maria made it beautiful, made it work. Increasingly nervous, Tosca must find something to do. Impulsively, she goes to the table, pours a glass of wine, drinks it hurriedly, and the moment she brings down the glass her hand bounces back. She has seen the knife.

For a moment, Maria stood transfixed, then down, down, down, ever so slowly, it must have taken a full minute, her hand reached toward the table and the knife. It was the biggest cinematic close-up you could achieve on the stage. Mesmerizing!"

"When Scarpia finished writing the permit," Zeffirelli continues, "he rose from the desk and hurried toward Tosca saying, 'Ah, at last you are mine.' In a flash Maria had the knife in the air and plunged it into him [above]. At one rehearsal, she was so into the part that she accidentally hurt Tito. The knife was supposed to be retractable—you know, the blade was supposed to slide back into the handle. But that time it didn't. Tito yelled 'My God!' and then went on with the scene.

"Now it is Tosca's turn to track Scarpia. 'Here is Tosca's kiss,' she cries [top right]. 'Your blood chokes you? Killed by a woman? Look at me! I am Tosca, oh, Scarpia!' [middle right]. After a final lunge, Scarpia falls back, Tosca venomously commanding him, 'Die, damn you! Die! Die! Die!' [right].

"When Tosca sees that Scarpia lies motionless, she stares at his corpse, traumatized with disbelief. Still clutching the knife tightly, her other hand clenched into a fist, she mutters, 'He's dead. Now I forgive him.' [below]. She is overcome with the horror of what she has done."

Tosca does not linger long over Scarpia's corpse, for she has but one purpose in life: to save Cavaradossi. Rushing to the desk, she searches madly for the document she needs. But it is not to be found.

Glancing for a moment at Scarpia, whom she fears even in death, Tosca is gripped by a new horror—the permit is clutched in the dead man's hand [top left]. Thus, even now, Scarpia torments her. Tosca struggles to extract the paper from her victim's rigid, unyielding fingers [middle left]. When Callas let the hand fall, Gobbi made it hit the floor with a hollow thud. Callas shuddered, looking at Scarpia in ironic disbelief, then spoke Tosca's most famous line: "E avanti a lui tremava tutta Roma!" (And before him all Rome trembled!) Though Puccini specified eleven sung notes—middle C-sharp—for these words, the tradition is to declaim them. Callas would vary from performance to performance how she did the passage, depending on her mood, sometimes singing, sometimes speaking.

Zeffirelli describes these moments: "Tosca's instinct is to run off, but she cannot accept being a cold-blooded murderess. Not only is she a good Catholic, she is also a diva, a great actress. The candles, the crucifix are a kind of religious and theatrical gesture. For herself, if not for Scarpia, she feels compelled to stage some sort of scene of repentance [bottom left].

"Here, I didn't have to direct at all, for Puccini indicates every step, every action in the score. The music directs. There is a chord for the moment when Tosca must wrest the passport from Scarpia's hand, a chord for the first candle, a chord for the second, and then the drums for the crucifix. Everything is given precisely. As Maria played the scene, Tosca suffered deeply. The whole strange ceremony of the candles is a painful experience for her. All through the theater you could hear her panting and whimpering" [right].

Gobbi points out that limited sight made the scene technically difficult for Callas. "The poor girl could see nothing. The stage was plunged into darkness except for a few candles. Under my breath I would whisper—go left, go straight, to the front, to the back. It's really a miracle how she ever did it."

For Tosca's exit, Zeffirelli resisted the usual slow, melodramatic withdrawal. "No, grabbing her stole, she ran out as fast as she could, swallowed by total darkness. The lights had dimmed, only two candles remained burning, Scarpia lay dead on the floor. Nothing else. And the curtain fell."

Tosca, act two finale

As with the proportions of the church in act one, Zeffirelli imparted the tremendous size of the prison in act three by showing only a portion of it and by cutting it diagonally across the stage. "We built an immense rounded tower of huge stones, with no details from the Castel Sant'Angelo, but all its grim power. A long, steep flight of steps led up to a sentry bridge.

"From the first notes, Puccini's music is tragic, and Cavaradossi knows he is going to die. When Tosca arrives, however, she is radiant, certain all will turn out as she wants. She is crazy with hope: Scarpia is dead and now they can escape to start life anew. Not wanting to deprive her of a few minutes of joy, Cavaradossi humors her [left]. This makes the scene so poignant.

"As Tosca watches the 'mock' execution of her lover, she becomes almost manic—cracking jokes, sure of victory, hysterical: 'How handsome my Mario is!' The guns fire and Cavaradossi falls. 'There! Die! What an actor!' she laughs. Maria edged toward his body, giggling with glee, saying 'Don't move! Stay still!' Then she learns the ironic truth: The execution was real.

"Maria wore the same dress as in act two, but with a big gray cape. As the alarm sounded, a sleeping soldier—played by an acrobat—woke. Half-dressed, he started to chase her. She ran like a bird all over the stage, then up the steps, the soldier at her heels. He nearly caught her at the top but got tangled in the long train of her dress. This gave Maria the chance to throw her cape over his face and make him fall backward down the stairs, blocking the police who had joined the pursuit below.

"Maria now had only a moment to sing her last line, 'O Scarpia, avanti a Dio!' [Oh Scarpia, God will judge us!] [right]. As she was still singing, another soldier ran from a side bridge and lunged at her. But she was too quick and she jumped. The soldier missed her by a hair.

"Maria wasn't one of those Toscas who lift their skirts and look where they are jumping. She just flew off into space. She was everything I ever hoped my Tosca would be. She could not have given more to me, the public, or Puccini."

Act three of *Tosca,* with Cioni

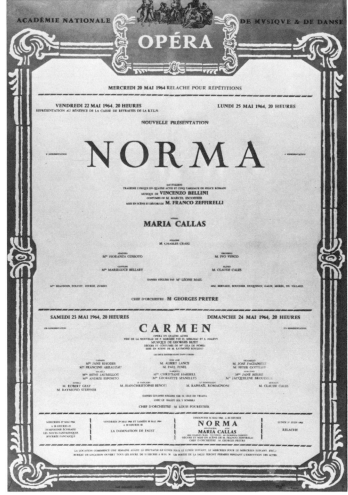

Rehearsing "Casta diva"
in Paris with Zeffirelli

Encouraged by the reception accorded her comeback as Tosca, Callas accepted an engagement for eight performances of *Norma* at the Théâtre National de l'Opéra during May and June of 1964. Callas had performed only once before at the Paris Opéra—a gala benefit in 1958 for the Legion of Honor. Thus, though Callas herself had become a familiar figure on the boulevards, frequenting the salons of haute couture and fashionable supper clubs, her art was known in Paris principally through records.

Supporting Callas in the new Paris production of *Norma* were Franco Zeffirelli as set designer and stage director, Marcel Escoffier as costume designer, and Georges Prêtre, then her preferred conductor. Zeffirelli speaks of Callas's work in Paris: "At the time, some people remarked that the voice of gold had turned to bronze. Well, I think bronze is also a noble metal and that Maria was right in wanting to do *Norma*. The impact she made! Incredible! It really did not matter whether her voice was in good shape. What if she cracked a few high notes? She could have avoided that so easily by taking optional lower ones or by leaving them out completely. Most people would not even have known the difference, and those who did, if they really understood who Callas was, would not have cared in the least.

"I begged Maria to be prudent, to avoid unreasonable vocal challenges. But she refused, saying 'I can't, Franco. I won't do what Anna Moffo does in *Traviata*. I won't skim through my music. I have to take chances, even if it means a disaster and the end of my career. I must try for all the notes even if I miss some.' No one could have convinced her otherwise. At one performance, she broke on a critical high-C in the last act, in a way I have never heard in my life. The public gasped in open horror, and, in panic, the orchestra stopped. Maria, furious with herself, started the phrase again and this time got the note square on. Bravery! She was determined to get it, and she was right; you can't leave your audience with a sour taste. After a performance, whether good or bad, Maria always showed a very positive attitude. She knew what had happened and would say so frankly.

"During our work on *Norma*, I felt her great beauty constantly. I tried to feed this beauty back to her in every way I could. I admired her, contemplated her. Everything I did was to make her look better, to reflect to the public what I saw in her, what she was for me. I love that woman so much. Deeply, deeply. She means so much. She made work so rewarding.

"I had known her Norma from her early days—at La Scala and Rome. But in Paris she was immensely more refined and subtle, infinitely more mature, more real, more human, more profound. Everything was reduced to the essence. She had found what it takes to hit the heart of an audience in a way she had never before achieved. If the voice was not all it had been, what did it matter in light of what she expressed in every other respect?"

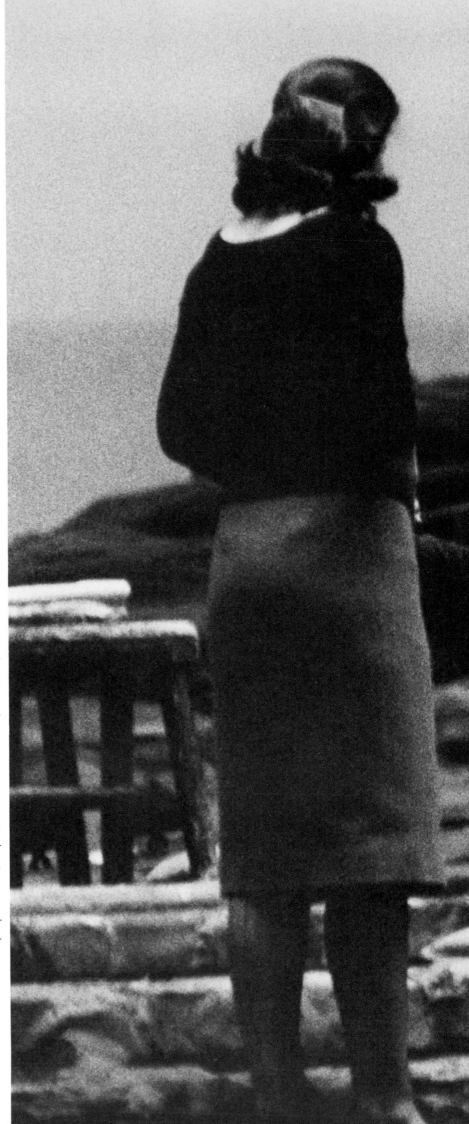

Zeffirelli's memories of the Paris *Norma* [right, a rehearsal for act two] stirred other observations drawn from their long friendship: "For all her fame, Maria has genuine humility and respects people of talent. I've heard her joke about every famous singer who ever lived, but I know she'd fall on her knees before Rosa Ponselle. She adores her. Years ago at Visconti's house, we played some records, voices from the Golden Age. Maria was amused and pointed out many wrong notes and examples of bad taste. These were great artists—Tetrazzini, Galli-Curci, Melba, Muzio. Then a voice started 'Ernani, involami.' Maria stopped laughing and told us to be silent. As she listened she began to sing with the record. She wanted to know who it was. It was Ponselle.

"Maria never erred artistically. Her mistakes were all offstage. Like Duse, a great artist and a woman who made dreadful blunders in her private life. This thing about becoming an important society lady. Such a stupid thing, café society! But if you remember the childhood Maria had—always dreaming to attain a certain position. Artistically she had traveled the full road, so, at a certain point, she tried to do the same in her personal life. She was simply reaching up. But at what a cost!

"Maria always chooses the wrong man. Again, one must remember that as a Greek girl she grew up being taught the ideal that a man must be the sultan, the god. Never the friend. It's sad. The person you love must be a friend before all else. Maria looks for the wrong qualities in the wrong places. What if she had married another artist—perhaps some great conductor—who could have comprehended her gifts, shared them, encouraged them? The whole Onassis episode took her mind away from the theater, shortened her career. And now what has she left? I think Maria is a very lonely girl.

"In her work, she never spared herself. Maria gave 100 percent, trying to do everything at once with all her grit and stamina. That's not the best way to conserve your resources. Look at Joan Sutherland. Year after year she keeps up the highest vocal standard by never leaving the *soprano leggiero* repertory. Her husband looks after her. She does not jump from *Medea* to *Lucia* or from *Chénier* to *Sonnambula*. Maria sang the most moving Gluck I ever heard, Alceste and Ifigenia. Magnificent! And fantastic Wagner! Everything a voice can do she did. This placed an awful strain on her. Even at the very end—Tosca, then Norma. Like all great artists she swept aside all that stood in her way to grasp a higher dimension and hold it. She was merciless with herself."

At work on *Norma* with Zeffirelli

When Zeffirelli's new production of *Norma* was unveiled in 1964, the Paris Opéra was not the splendidly revitalized theater it has recently become. However, to obtain the services of Callas, Prêtre, and Zeffirelli, the bureaucrats–who for decades had mishandled the venerable old theater–bent over backward to enable them to achieve an event of artistic merit. Zeffirelli remembers: "The Opéra was mad to have Maria, and the public was equally excited to see and hear her. In all my life I have never felt such electricity as on the opening night when Oroveso [Ivo Vinco, right] announced the arrival of Norma.

"My production was completely traditional–a very romantic approach to an old classic. *Norma* is not like a play by Shakespeare, where you can do literally anything: contrive and be intellectual, or different and interesting, or invent things just to please the critics, the actors, or your own whims. In *Norma* the designer and director must not parade themselves. All must be kept romantically beautiful, nothing more and nothing less. My visual concept was of a great forest which in each act changed with the seasons of the year: spring, summer, fall, then, in act four, late autumn–early winter, when russet leaves linger on the trees.

"During Maria's first scene, a moon shone through the foliage to evoke a buried world, that lost paradise of bel canto Maria had revealed to us [Zeffirelli sketch, below right]. For me, especially in *Norma*, Maria was a bridge, an absolute bridge of 150 years. She was the miraculous bearer of scents and values that were long lost and forgotten. She made them live again, repolished them and re-created them for us. I am sure she sang Norma as no one has ever sung the role, including its creator, Giuditta Pasta. I don't think even Pasta could have brought the justice to the piece that Maria did.

"For her entrance, I prepared a great spiral set, coming from below the stage, which permitted the audience to see her entire arrival during the long march. The set was big, but very intimate for the audience. Because Maria sees only vaguely onstage, I planned for her–covered in heavy veils, very mysterious–to be carried in on a portable altar by ten or twelve Druid priests. Then she was to sing her long recitative under the veils. But it didn't work out because we couldn't get everything balanced. Carrying the altar was uneven, untidy. Maria finally suggested that she simply walk in, which she did, veils and all. Just before she started her recitative, high on a rock, she threw back the veils to uncover her face. I'll never forget that moment. It really gave me a shiver.

"Vocally, 'Casta diva' had always been a trial for Maria, even in the early days of her career. Her approach to the music was dramatic, never detached. She was not like Sutherland or Caballé, who sing divinely but don't act a bit with their voices. There is no character when they do Norma. With all due respect, they are like singing armchairs.

"For Maria's first costume, Marcel Escoffier designed a very simple, immaculate white silk chiffon tunic, with a magnificent blue velvet cloak embroidered in gold [left]. A golden laurel wreath crowned her head. And what she did with her cloak!"

Norma, act one: Vinco as Oroveso,
Zeffirelli first-act sketch;
[next pages] Corelli as Pollione
and Cossotto as Adalgisa

"Romani's libretto for *Norma* was a very daring subject for Bellini to have chosen," points out Zeffirelli. "At the world premiere, at La Scala, the public was shocked to witness as the heroine a sacred priestess with the courage to be a sinner and clandestinely bear children out of wedlock. In 1831, such stories were not yet accepted in the theater. *Norma* was booed. A fiasco! Not for the music, which in itself could have made it the success of all time, but because of the hypocritical standards of the audience. This happened even though Bellini had put 'Casta diva' into the score to give some measure of purity to the character of Norma, this whorish liar whose life is a conflict between her religious vows and her feelings as a woman. That's why the opera is so important historically. It broke into the Romantic Era, away from the stateliness of baroque, classical heroines. This also keeps *Norma* extremely modern to this day.

"For the second act, I designed a forest pavilion that had the intimate feeling of a home standing in the shadows of thick foliage, protected from the summer sun. It looked like an old print, very warm and pastel [below]. The Druids, not having marble or metal, copied in wood the furnishings of their conquerors, the Romans. So Norma had a magnificent couch carved of wood. Escoffier made Maria the most beautiful costume ever–a flowing tunic of a thousand shades of cream, pink, apricot, and lilac [left and right]. In this she greeted Adalgisa [Fiorenza Cossotto, with Callas, at right], the novice priestess of Norma's temple who comes to confess that she is falling in love. During their long duet, Norma recalls her own first moments of romantic ecstasy [next pages]."

The Roman general Pollione, father of Norma's children, unexpectedly enters the pavilion where Norma is consoling the love-struck Adalgisa. The younger woman, surprised, innocently indicates that he is the very man who has sought to win her heart. In an instant Norma realizes the perfidy of her consort [above]. In perhaps the most difficult vocal passage in operatic literature, a brilliant cascade of dramatic coloratura declamation, Norma berates the unfaithful Pollione [right, top to bottom, Franco Corelli]. She asks why he trembles. It need not be for the safety of Adalgisa, who is blameless. But he must fear for himself, for his sons, and for Norma herself. Bursting with rage, Norma orders Pollione from her sight [opposite page].

With Corelli

Franco Zeffirelli describes the decor he created for the third act of Bellini's *Norma*, when the heroine, having discovered that she has been betrayed by Pollione, resolves to take revenge on him by murdering their two sons. "To my eye it was the best of the four sets, with the foliage autumnal in color. I made a corner in the forest, a kind of grotto closed off by a great burlap tapestry [above]. Here, the children slept on fur skins by a little lantern. Maria, dressed by Escoffier in a dark purple gown of Egyptian silk decorated with bronze objects and covered by a rust-colored cloak, opened the tapestry. Silhouetted by the moon, her shadow reaching to the children, she drew a dagger and, after a long moment of agony, moved to strike the helpless babes. Suddenly, she is overcome with maternal love and cannot bring herself to kill them. Norma awakens her sons to embrace and caress them [left].

"During rehearsals, Maria did not fuss too much with the children. She said it would be better not to get too familiar, for they might grow stale in their acting. She wanted to surprise the children by her affection, hit them fresh with her feelings so they would not be prepared. She understood that stage children are easily conditioned. When they know what will happen, they anticipate, or react in an affected way, or don't react at all. How many times did Maria sing Norma and Medea? She knew how to handle children in the theater, not to spoil them. She established a good relationship so that they would not be frightened of her, and after a few days they came to respect her very much. And this is important, for it prevented the danger of the children laughing during actual performance.

"But when the premiere came, Maria was so tender with them. Immensely tender. Like a real mother. My God, what a pity this woman never had a child. Really, she would have been...well, perhaps her child was her work.

"After all, artists of her stature cannot have complete fulfillment in their private lives. Otherwise they would never attain the kind of desperate extra dimension that sets them apart. Think of the great geniuses of history. They were never fully satisfied. Never. Leonardo, Michelangelo, who? Think how tormented Puccini was, Beethoven, Berlioz—Bellini, for that matter—though on a whole composers are a better balanced lot. But Duse, Nijinsky, Nureyev, Brando—all very sad people underneath. And Magnani, with the tragedy of her child. But somehow, this unhappiness helps them find that extra something that makes an artist really great. A fully contented human being never reaches that kind of peak.

"Olivier, for instance, was a far more compelling actor when he was at odds with his life. Now he is so happy with his wife and children. And I'm glad he is, because he suffered enough. But I believe there are two things that never go too well together. Full achievement as a human being—in private life, love, emotions—and that diabolical power in art that springs from total despair and anguish. Maria felt this conflict and gave it voice through music."

Act three of *Norma*,
Zeffirelli sketch [above]

Norma realizes she must find some solution to her dilemma. Calling her confidante Clotilde [right, Marie-Luce Bellary], she orders her to find Adalgisa and bring her to the grotto. Clotilde replies that the girl is nearby, alone, praying and weeping.

Soon Adalgisa enters, asking why Norma's entire being seems consumed with grief. The high priestess, replying it is a veil of death, unbears her shame as a woman and bids Adalgisa comply with a single request: take her two children to the Roman encampment and live with Pollione in happiness. As for herself, Norma says, she will perish. Adalgisa protests and falls on her knees by Norma [below], begging her in the duet, "Mira, o Norma," to pity her sons even if she has no pity for herself, for they need the love of a real mother. Any passion she had felt for Pollione, adds Adalgisa, died when she learned the truth. Now, all must be restored to Norma that is hers by the rights of man and heaven. At length Norma is persuaded to live, and, in a joyful cabaletta, the two women swear eternal friendship [opposite page, below].

Zeffirelli speaks of Callas at this moment in her career. "All of us concerned with this *Norma* felt such an honor to be working with Maria. As things turned out, it was the last new production she ever did. A year later, she gave her final performance in opera, a *Tosca* at Covent Garden in July of 1965. In Paris, Maria and Corelli looked so stunning together. What a shame he couldn't do all the *Norma*s, for when a substitute came in, all the weight fell on Maria's shoulders. Franco was so nice to Maria, helped her, understood the privilege of still having her on the stage. Unfortunately, this did not apply to Madame Cossotto. In the duets, Norma and Adalgisa must sing in close harmony, holding hands. When Maria would signal to end a phrase, Cossotto would ignore her sign and hold on to the final note a few extra seconds. So ungenerous! Maria was hurt by this. I went backstage and swore to her I'd never work with Cossotto again. And I never have.

"I'm glad Maria has finally begun to sing in public again. There is still so much she can do, but I mean in the theater. I once suggested she sing Poppea in Monteverdi's *L'Incoronazione di Poppea.* No one can deliver recitar cantando as Maria can. It would be a revelation! Everything was organized for a production by me: The city of Rome offered the Campidoglio, giving me permission to move four pillars of Michelangelo to add some ramps and stairs. But Maria decided Ottavia was the better part: 'She gets the most dramatic scenes and arias, and I must do a title role!' Infuriating!

"I wish Maria would record some Monteverdi–Ottavia's 'Addio Roma,' the 'Lamento d'Arianna,' and the 'Lettera amorosa.' It would be perfection. There are many roles she could do superbly onstage–the greatest Carmen. I'd stage it to prove it to her. Why should she deprive herself or the new generation? Who cares if she is no longer thirty and can't hit an E-flat. Callas means much more than high notes."

"Mira, o Norma," with Cossotto

At the beginning of act four, Norma calmly enters a forest clearing certain that all will soon change. She trusts Adalgisa: In time, a penitent Pollione will return to her. But this blissful dream of love renewed is abruptly cut short when Clotilde breathlessly rushes in with news: Pollione has sworn to abduct Adalgisa, even if this means tearing her from the altar of the Druid temple. Revenge once more brims over in Norma's heart as she cries out for Roman blood; taking up a huge sword, she strikes a sacred shield to summon her people. They have wanted war with their conquerors, now Norma will permit war. After the populace shouts for carnage and destruction, a group of soldiers leads in Pollione, whom they have captured while he was seeking Adalgisa in the cloister of the novice priestesses. In a frenzy of anger, Norma draws her dagger to kill the villain, but she cannot bring herself to do it, for she still loves Pollione deeply. On

the pretext of questioning the prisoner, she sends everyone away. Pollione is defiant [above] as Norma seeks to reconcile their differences, reminding him of all they have shared and of their children [right and next pages]. When the man remains unmoved, Norma threatens the life of Adalgisa and summons back her people [following pages].

Act four of *Norma*, with Corelli
[also on following pages]

Franco Zeffirelli speaks of the final scene of Bellini's *Norma* as he staged it for Callas in 1964. "The clearing in the forest was the place where the Druids had erected their temple, a temple very much like Stonehenge, that huge oval of megalithic posts and lintels. The center platform—like a big stone drum—was encircled by larger rocks and immense stone pillars. I had time to design only half the set, but since it was absolutely symmetrical, the scenery shop had only to duplicate the side I had done.

"Now the colors were those of late autumn, almost winter, when the thick foliage which completely covered the sky had turned deep red. For Maria's final costume, Escoffier created a tunic of warm, cream-colored hue, with a red cloak embossed with the warmest tones of gold.

"As a character, Norma is a woman of great ideals and prestige, a high priestess, the head of her tribe. She must give her people morality. From her first speech in act one, you understand the vision and power she possesses. She must not only be a religious leader, she must be a diplomat and a politician. But under it all, she is human, a woman.

"This conflict was the kind that became so fashionable during the Romantic Era, a trend *Norma* started. How many heroines are there like this in the operas of the nineteenth century—queens, princesses, priestesses—who have this battle between responsibility to their people and their own private feelings? Perhaps 90 percent of the great tragic operas revolve on the theme of women in such a dilemma. From Norma to Aida. And even up into the twentieth century—Puccini's Turandot, for one.

"Norma is fascinating because she is a split personality. She was so daring for her time—the time of the Druids—and also for the time of Bellini. A woman of enormous position and authority who maintains a secret, scandalous life. But what Norma does is done for love, and because of this she must be forgiven all her sins.

"During the course of the action Norma switches character constantly, from priestess to woman to priestess again. She is a Jekyll and Hyde, a complex of warring feelings. If the strongest of her people, she is also the weakest of all women on earth. Not until the very end does she resolve her struggle. With humility she steps before the Druids to say, 'Yes, I am your chief, but I am also the most miserable among you. The most condemnable of all.' Pollione has thought up to this point she is going to accuse Adalgisa of sacrilege. Instead, Norma has the courage to confess, 'Son io!'—I am the guilty one. It is I. I am a woman [top left]. Then, in a touching farewell to her father, Oroveso, Norma kneels at his feet, begging him to take care of her two children after she kills herself [right]. As a funeral pyre is lit for her immolation, Pollione is overcome with remorse. Recognizing the sublime sacrifice Norma has made, he joins her as she walks into the flames [next pages].

"Maria was at her greatest in these final moments. So intensely moving. I think she identified with Norma greatly. In a way it was her own story. Maria, after all, is a high priestess—the high priestess of her art. Yet, at the same time, she is the most fallible of women. Very human. As Norma, Maria created the maximum of what opera can be. In a lifetime, one can see many great things in the theater. But to see Maria Callas in *Norma*, what is there to compare to it?"

In *Norma* finale, with Vinco as Oroveso [also next pages]

After her final appearances as Tosca and Norma, at the Paris Opéra in 1965, Maria Callas's next performance in the theater would not take place until February 10, 1970. But she would not appear as a singer. Instead, she would star in the world premiere of *Medea*, a color film conceived and directed by the Italian poet Pier Paolo Pasolini. In his adaptation of the ancient Greek legend, Pasolini was not concerned to follow the tragedies of Euripides, Seneca, or Corneille. Rather, he distilled his subject from every available source, giving his imagination full rein. In so doing, his screen images often displayed the timeless quality associated with Japanese films.

"Most emphatically, I did not want to film Cherubini's opera," the director says. "The problem was to avoid banality while clearly interpreting classical mythology for modern sensibilities." Outside Italy, where Pasolini is widely esteemed for his poetry, he is chiefly known for his motion picture work–*Oedipus Rex, Teorema, The Gospel According to St. Matthew.* His verse, with its use of onomato-poeia and rugged dialects, all but defies translation. *Medea*, however, a film virtually without dialogue, often captured the values of Pasolini's poems through visual means.

"In my films, I do not use representation," adds Pasolini. "If I want to show a tree, I show a real tree. The actor is no different. He is himself. With Maria Callas, her personal qualities fascinated me. I see Callas as a modern woman in whom dwells an ancient woman–strange, magical, with terrible inner conflicts. These I tried to capture in *Medea.*" To do so, the director worked with only a few notes as a scenario, improvising each scene to see what Callas and her fellow actors could bring forth in any given dramatic situation. Often there was no rehearsal, just preliminary discussion before actual filming. And often the first shooting was the finished take.

Medea emerged a series of stylized tableaux summoning up a primitive, ritualistic culture in which cannibalism, carnage, and the supernatural were part of daily existence. Below, Callas's Medea escapes Colchis; left, she rages at her betrayal by Jason.

Prior to taking a frame of film, Pasolini carefully selected a striking series of locations in which to unfold the action of *Medea*. Subsequently he and his cast traveled to Goreme in Turkey; Aleppo in Syria; Pisa; the lagoons and islands of Grado, not far from Venice; Tor Caldara and Tor Calbona, beaches near Rome; and Cinecitta's studios. Pasolini found monolithic hills of rock and clay, dazzling blanched dunes and deserts resembling moonscapes, infinite mud flats baked by the sun. Each he used to astonishing effect, creating a lost, unknown, mystical world.

Piero Tosi, who designed *La sonnambula* for Maria Callas at La Scala, in 1955, also created her costumes for Pasolini's *Medea*, garbing her in fierce, heavy gowns encrusted with huge ropes of pagan jewels. "Every day," Tosi recounts, "Maria would arrive very early to be made up and dressed. She always carried a portable radio, usually tuned to some soap opera. She'd follow every word with incredible concentration, participating in the action, muttering, 'What's that? What did you say! Go! Go!' All in Veronese dialect. She gets so involved with whatever she is doing, even if it's only some trivial broadcast.

"Maria trusted Pasolini, but felt uneasy during close-ups, which he loved since he was entranced by her face, so like a Greek mask. She liked long shots, especially those with action. I'm sure she then imagined herself onstage in a theater, free to move. She'd beg Pasolini, 'Shoot from far away, for me!' In the end, Maria was right. The close-ups are beautiful but static. Her best moments are distant action shots."

For the episode shown here, Callas had to run around frantically in a mud flat. Finally, she fainted from the 100-degree heat and sun exposure. As she regained consciousness, she stammered, "Please forgive me! I'm so stupid. I shouldn't have done that. It's cost everyone so much time and money."

Filming Pasolini's *Medea*

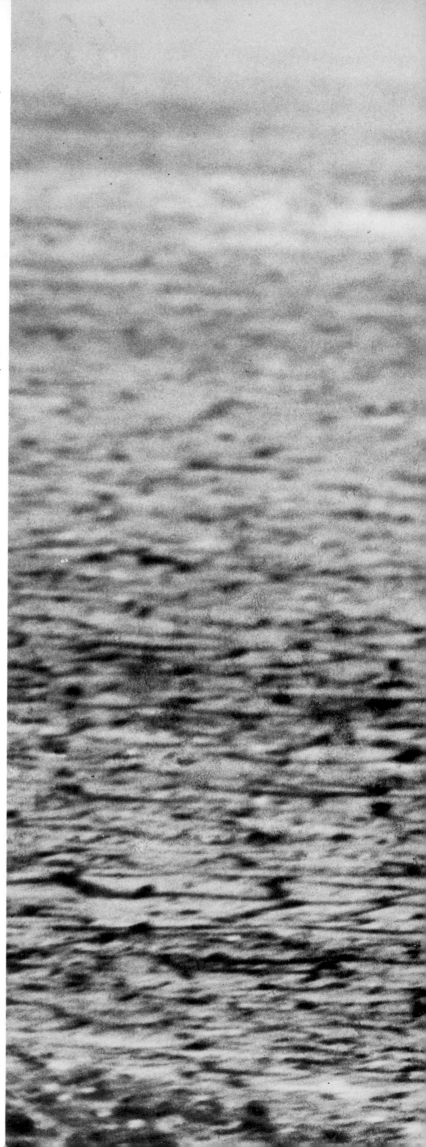

Medea's brutality is not shown when she kills her children. Earlier, however, it is graphically depicted. First she butchers her young brother with an ax, dropping his limbs from a cart to detain her father as she and Jason flee with the Golden Fleece. Later, she kills Jason's bride, burning her with a magic robe sent as a wedding gift. Creon also perishes in the conflagration.

In contrast, Medea is gentle and loving with her sons. As one lies dead, she calmly bathes the other, then puts him to sleep. Pasolini's scenario poetically describes the action: "But the boy is not very sleepy; his somber eyes remain open, the mother rocks him tenderly, and finally, to make him sleep, she begins to sing an old lullaby. At first this has the opposite effect, for he is curious to hear the song, lifts his head from his mother's shoulder, where he has laid it, and looks at her with amusement and curiosity, gazing into her eyes, but she never stops singing and remains expressionless, lost in the melody. The boy puts his head down again and at last closes his eyes. Medea takes the knife that glitters behind the chair and sinks it into the boy's spine. He makes a little start, stretched out as he is in her arms; his eyes roll up, and he falls back against her shoulder, as before when he was sleeping."

Pasolini's film of *Medea* was not the first nor the last offer Maria Callas had to make a motion picture. Franco Zeffirelli discussed doing *La traviata* and *Tosca* with her, and at another time there was talk of her filming Cherubini's *Medea* onstage at La Scala. Luchino Visconti once proposed the biblical Sarah as a theme—a project he himself eventually abandoned. And after *Medea*, there were rumors of *Mother Courage*. Callas pondered each offer. "I always knew my cinema debut would be no easy matter. It had to be something special, a character with which I felt totally involved. Pasolini's approach to Medea gave me no doubts. And during our work, I discovered my choice was right." As in the opera house, Callas candidly questioned her acting with colleagues: "Tell me, is this gesture too grand? Too operatic? I know my rhythms, but not those of the camera. They are something else."

In Pasolini's concept, "What makes Medea kill is not born from a spasm of vengeance or hate or passion. Rather, her crazed and criminal actions assume the significance of a flight from a world that is not hers and in which she can no longer live. For Medea and her race, death is not an end, but only a prelude to rebirth in another world. So her faith spurs her on to killing her children so that they all may return in regeneration. Jason, striving for all that is rich and powerful, is left with the values of a world in chaos."

Critical reception to the overall quality of Pasolini's film was divided, but Callas was invariably singled out for her searing portrayal of the title role. Janet Flanner in *The New Yorker* stated, "*Medea* turned out to contain the greatest acting performance of her career—being, moreover, immovably set in its perfection by the camera, so that the grandeur of her accomplishment cannot alter or diminish from one showing to another, as did her singing performances, until they at last became only tragic infidelities of what one's memory retained."

Piero Tosi was on the set when the final moments of the film were shot. "Medea must build a great fire, and holding the bodies of her dead sons, perish in the flames while defying their faithless father. Here Maria reached the apex of her performance. It was very dangerous, because she had to stand on a high wooden platform with flames roaring before her. A stand-in was available, but Maria insisted on doing everything herself. It was a sacred ritual and Maria, blind as she was, had to hurl herself into the holocaust, or at least seem to do so for the camera's eye. Three times she acted out the scene, and during the last take she nearly fell right into the arms of the inferno. For Maria, it could have been done no other way. After all, she was Callas."

Holding her sons' lifeless bodies,
Medea is consumed by flames

CHRONOLOGY

This chronology has been assembled from, and checked with, many sources—Callas; books by George Jellinek, Evangelia Callas, and Stelios Galatopoulos; *Discoteca* and *Opera* magazines; annals of the Metropolitan, La Scala, and Covent Garden, plus those of the companies of Venice, Turin, Verona, Trieste, Florence, Paris, Buenos Aires, Chicago, and Dallas; and correspondence with individuals and opera companies. Yet, there are facts relative to Callas's career which will remain confused and uncertain. This is particularly true of a number of recording dates, cast changes within a series of performances, the number of repetitions of a work in a single series, and even the identity of key cast members and conductors.

The date given with each entry in the case of operatic performances is that of the first in a series; the number which follows is the total of performances in a series, if known. This means, of course, that the totals at the end must be considered approximate. Callas's role is given after the title of the work when her character's name is not the title of the opera. Last names of other principal cast members, when known, follow (full names can be found in the index). In this chronology, they are listed in order by the voice range of their roles: soprano, mezzo-soprano, contralto, tenor, baritone, bass. A slash between names indicates that two or more artists alternated in the same role. The conductor's name follows the semicolon. In the case of recordings, only published commercial material is included.

1938

CAVALLERIA RUSTICANA:
 Santuzza
Olympia Theater, Athens
November

1940

SUOR ANGELICA
Mandikian
Conservatory, Athens
May

UN BALLO IN MASCHERA
 (act three): Amelia
 (with *Aida* excerpt?)
Olympia Theater, Athens
May

BOCCACCIO: Beatrice
Royal Theater, Athens
November 27

1942

TOSCA
Thellentas, Ksirelis
Athens
July 4 (approximately 20)

CONCERT: Opera scenes and arias
Thellentas and others
White Tower Theater, Salonika
August (2)

1943

HO PROTOMASTORAS: Smaragda
Arena Herodes Atticus, Athens
March

CONCERT: Songs and arias
White Tower Theater, Salonika
August (2)

1944

TIEFLAND: Marta
Thellentas, Mangliveras
Royal Theater, Athens
April

CAVALLERIA RUSTICANA:
 Santuzza
Royal Theater, Athens
May or June

FIDELIO: Leonore
Thellentas
Arena Herodes Atticus, Athens
September

TIEFLAND: Marta
Royal Theater, Athens
October or November

1945

CONCERT: Songs and arias
Rex Theater, Athens
July

DER BETTELSTUDENT: Laura
Royal Theater, Athens
September (?)

1947

LA GIOCONDA
Nicolai, Canali, Tucker, Tagliabue,
 Rossi-Lemeni; Serafin
Arena, Verona
August 3 (5)

TRISTAN UND ISOLDE: Isolde
Barbieri, Tasso, Torres, Christoff;
 Serafin
Teatro la Fenice, Venice
December 30 (4)

1948

TURANDOT
Rizzieri, Soler, Carmassi; Sanzogno
Teatro la Fenice, Venice
January 28 (5)

TURANDOT
Ottani, Soler, Maionica; de Fabritiis
Teatro Puccini, Udine
March 30

LA FORZA DEL DESTINO:
 Leonora
Canali, Vertechi, Franci, Siepi;
 Parenti
Politeama Rossetti, Trieste
April 17 (4)

TRISTAN UND ISOLDE: Isolde
Nicolai, Lorenz, Torres, Rossi-Lemeni;
 Serafin
Teatro Grattacielo, Genoa
May 13 (3)

TURANDOT
Montanari, Masini, Flamini;
 de Fabritiis
Terme di Caracalla, Rome
July 4 (3)

TURANDOT
Rizzieri/Tognoli/de Cecco,
 Salvarezza, Rossi-Lemeni; Votto
Arena, Verona
July 27 (4)

TURANDOT
Montanari, del Monaco, Maionica;
 Questa
Teatro Carlo Felice, Genoa
August 12 (2)

AIDA
Nicolai/Colasanti, Turrini, de Falchi;
 Serafin
Teatro Lirico, Turin
September 18 (4)

AIDA
Pirazzini, Turrini, Viaro; Berrettoni
Teatro Sociale, Rovigo
October 20

NORMA
Barbieri, Picchi, Siepi; Serafin
Teatro Comunale, Florence
November 30 (2)

1949

DIE WALKÜRE: Brünnhilde
Magnoni, Pini, Voyer, Torres,
 Dominici; Serafin
Teatro la Fenice, Venice
January 8 (4)

I PURITANI: Elvira
Pirino, Savarese, Christoff; Serafin
Teatro la Fenice, Venice
January 19 (3)

DIE WALKÜRE: Brünnhilde
Magnoni, Sani, Voyer, Neri,
 Carmassi; Molinari-Pradelli
Teatro Massimo, Palermo
January 28 (2)

TURANDOT
Montanari, Salvarezza, Petri; Perlea
Teatro San Carlo, Naples
February 12 (4)

PARSIFAL: Kundry
Beirer, Cortis, Siepi; Serafin
Teatro dell'Opera, Rome
February 27 (4)

CONCERT: *Tristan und Isolde:*
 "Liebestod";
 Norma: "Casta diva";
 I Puritani: "Qui la voce";
 Aida: "O patria mia"
Molinari-Pradelli
RAI, Turin
March 7

RECORDING SESSION:
Tristan und Isolde: "Liebestod";
Norma: "Casta diva";
I Puritani: "Qui la voce"
Basile
Cetra Records, Turin
March

TURANDOT
Arizmendi, del Monaco,
  Zanin/Rossi-Lemeni; Serafin
Teatro Colón, Buenos Aires
May 20 (4)

NORMA
Barbieri, Vela, Rossi-Lemeni; Serafin
Teatro Colón, Buenos Aires
June 17 (4)

AIDA
Barbieri, Vela, Damiani; Serafin
Teatro Colón, Buenos Aires
July 2

CONCERT: *Norma:* "Casta diva";
  Turandot: act three
Arizmendi, del Monaco,
  Rossi-Lemeni; Serafin
Teatro Colón, Buenos Aires
July 9

CONCERT: *San Giovanni Battista*
Corsi, Pirazzini, Berdini, Siepi;
  Santini
Chiesa di San Pietro, Perugia
September 18

NABUCCO: Abigaille
Pini, Sinimberghi, Bechi, Neroni;
  Gui
Teatro San Carlo, Naples
December 20 (3)

1950

NORMA
Nicolai, Penno, Pasero; Votto
Teatro la Fenice, Venice
January 11 (3)

AIDA
Pini, del Monaco, Protti; Erede
Teatro Grande, Brescia
February 2 (4)

TRISTAN UND ISOLDE: Isolde
Nicolai, Seider, Franci, Neri/Neroni;
  Serafin
Teatro dell'Opera, Rome
February 6 (5)

NORMA
Stignani, Masini, Neri/Cassinelli;
  Serafin
Teatro dell'Opera, Rome
February 23 (5)

NORMA
Gardino, Picchi, Stefanoni;
  Berrettoni
Teatro Massimo Bellini, Catania
March 16

AIDA
Barbieri, del Monaco,
  de Falchi/Protti; Capuana
Teatro alla Scala, Milan
April 12 (2)

AIDA
Stignani, Picchi, Savarese;
  Serafin
Teatro San Carlo, Naples
April 27 (3)

NORMA
Simionato, Baum, Moscona; Picco
Palacio de las Bellas Artes,
  Mexico City
May 23 (2)

AIDA
Simionato, Baum/Filippeschi,
  Weede; Picco
Palacio de las Bellas Artes,
  Mexico City
May 30 (3)

TOSCA
Filippeschi, Weede; Mugnai
Palacio de las Bellas Artes,
  Mexico City
June 8 (2)

IL TROVATORE: Leonora
Simionato, Baum, Warren/Petroff,
  Moscona; Picco
Palacio de las Bellas Artes,
  Mexico City
June 20 (3)

TOSCA
Turrini, Azzolini; Questa
Teatro Duse, Bologna
September 24

AIDA
Stignani, Picchi, de Falchi; Bellezza
Teatro dell'Opera, Rome
October 2

TOSCA
Masini, Poli; Santarelli
Teatro Verdi, Pisa
October 8

IL TURCO IN ITALIA: Fiorilla
Canali, Valletti, Stabile,
  Bruscantini, Calabrese; Gavazzeni
Teatro Eliseo, Rome
October 19 (4)

PARSIFAL: Kundry
Baldelli, Panerai, Christoff; Gui
RAI, Rome
November 20–21

1951

LA TRAVIATA: Violetta
Albanese, Mascherini; Serafin
Teatro Comunale, Florence
January 14 (3)

IL TROVATORE: Leonora
Elmo, Lauri-Volpi/Vertechi, Silveri,
  Tajo; Serafin
Teatro San Carlo, Naples
January 27 (3)

NORMA
Nicolai, Gavarini, Neri; Ghione
Teatro Massimo, Palermo
February 9 (2)

AIDA
Pirazzini, Soler, Manca-Serra;
  del Cupolo
Teatro Comunale, Reggio Calabria
February 28

CONCERT: *Un ballo in maschera:*
  "Ma dall'arido";
  Mignon: "Je suis Titania";
  Variations on "Deh torna, mio ben";
  Oberon: "Ocean, thou mighty monster"
Wolf-Ferrari
RAI, Turin
March 12

LA TRAVIATA: Violetta
Campora, Poli; Molinari-Pradelli
Teatro Massimo, Cagliari
March 15 (2)

CONCERT: *Norma:* "Casta diva";
  I Puritani: "Qui la voce";
  Aida: "O patria mia";
  La traviata: "Ah! fors'è lui"
La Rosa Parodi
Teatro Giuseppe Verdi, Trieste
April 21

I VESPRI SICILIANI: Elena
Kokolios-Bardi, Mascherini,
  Christoff; Kleiber
Teatro Comunale, Florence
May 26 (4)

ORFEO ED EURIDICE: Euridice
Tygesen, Christoff; Kleiber
Teatro della Pergola, Florence
June 9 (2)

AIDA
Domínguez, del Monaco, Taddei;
   de Fabritiis
Palacio de las Bellas Artes,
   Mexico City
July 3 (3)

CONCERT: *La forza del destino:*
   "Pace, pace";
   Un ballo in maschera:
   "Morrò, ma prima in grazia"
Radio, Mexico City
July 15

LA TRAVIATA: Violetta
Valletti, Taddei/Morelli; de Fabritiis
Palacio de las Bellas Artes,
   Mexico City
July 17 (4)

NORMA
Barbieri, Picchi, Rossi-Lemeni; Votto
Teatro Municipal, São Paulo
September 7

LA TRAVIATA: Violetta
di Stefano, Gobbi; Serafin
Teatro Municipal, São Paulo
September 9

NORMA
Nicolai, Picchi, Christoff; Votto
Teatro Municipal, Rio de Janeiro
September 12 (2)

CONCERT: *La traviata:* "Ah! fors'è lui";
   Aida: "O patria mia"
Teatro Municipal, Rio de Janeiro
September 14

TOSCA
Poggi, Silveri; Votto
Teatro Municipal, Rio de Janeiro
September 24

LA TRAVIATA: Violetta
Poggi, Salsedo; Gaioni
Teatro Municipal, Rio de Janeiro
September 28 (2)

LA TRAVIATA: Violetta
Giulini
Teatro Donizetti, Bergamo
October

NORMA
Simionato, Penno, Christoff; Ghione
Teatro Massimo Bellini, Catania
November 3

I PURITANI: Elvira
Wenkow, Tagliabue, Christoff;
   Wolf-Ferrari
Teatro Massimo Bellini, Catania
November 8

I VESPRI SICILIANI: Elena
Conley, Mascherini, Christoff/Modesti;
   de Sabata/Quadri
Teatro alla Scala, Milan
December 7 (7)

LA TRAVIATA: Violetta
Pola, Savarese; de Fabritiis
Teatro Regio, Parma
December 29

1952

I PURITANI: Elvira
Conley, Tagliabue, Rossi-Lemeni;
   Serafin
Teatro Comunale, Florence
January 9 (2)

NORMA
Stignani, Penno, Rossi-Lemeni;
   Ghione
Teatro alla Scala, Milan
January 16 (9)

CONCERT: *Macbeth:*
   "Vieni! t'affretta!";
   Lucia di Lammermoor:
   "Ardon gli incensi";
   Nabucco: "Anch'io dischiuso";
   Lakmé: "Où va la jeune Indoue"
de Fabritiis
RAI, Rome
February 18

LA TRAVIATA: Violetta
Filacuridi, Mascherini;
   Molinari-Pradelli
Teatro Massimo Bellini, Catania
March 8

DIE ENTFÜHRUNG AUS
   DEM SERAIL: Constanze
Menotti/Duval, Munteanu, Prandelli,
   Baccaloni; Perlea
Teatro alla Scala, Milan
April 2 (4)

ARMIDA
Albanese, Ziliani, Salvarezza,
   Filippeschi, Raimondi; Serafin
Teatro Comunale, Florence
April 26 (3)

I PURITANI: Elvira
Lauri-Volpi/Pirino, Silveri, Neri;
   Santini
Teatro dell'Opera, Rome
May 2 (3)

I PURITANI: Elvira
di Stefano, Campolonghi, Silva;
   Picco
Palacio de las Bellas Artes,
   Mexico City
May 29 (2)

LA TRAVIATA: Violetta
di Stefano, Campolonghi; Mugnai
Palacio de las Bellas Artes,
   Mexico City
June 3 (2)

LUCIA DI LAMMERMOOR
di Stefano, Campolonghi, Silva;
   Picco
Palacio de las Bellas Artes,
   Mexico City
June 10 (3)

RIGOLETTO: Gilda
Garcia, di Stefano, Campolonghi,
   Ruffino; Mugnai
Palacio de las Bellas Artes,
   Mexico City
June 17 (2)

TOSCA
di Stefano, Campolonghi; Picco
Palacio de las Bellas Artes,
   Mexico City
June 28 (2)

LA GIOCONDA
Nicolai, Canali, Poggi, Inghilleri,
   Tajo; Votto
Arena, Verona
July 19 (2)

LA TRAVIATA: Violetta
Campora, Mascherini;
   Molinari-Pradelli
Arena, Verona
August 2 (4)

RECORDING SESSION:
   La Gioconda
Barbieri, Amadini, Poggi, Silveri,
   Neri; Votto
Cetra Records, Turin
September

NORMA
Stignani, Picchi, Vaghi;
   Gui/Pritchard
Royal Opera House, London
November 8 (5)

MACBETH: Lady Macbeth
Penno, Mascherini, Tajo/Modesti;
    de Sabata
Teatro alla Scala, Milan
December 7 (5)

LA GIOCONDA
Stignani, Danieli, di Stefano,
    Tagliabue, Tajo/Modesti; Votto
Teatro alla Scala, Milan
December 26 (5)

1953

LA TRAVIATA: Violetta
Albanese, Mascherini/Tagliabue;
    Questa
Teatro la Fenice, Venice
January 8 (2)

LA TRAVIATA: Violetta
Albanese, Savarese; Santini
Teatro dell'Opera, Rome
January 15 (3)

LUCIA DI LAMMERMOOR
Lauri-Volpi/di Stefano, Bastianini,
    Arie; Ghione
Teatro Comunale, Florence
January 25 (4)

RECORDING SESSION:
    Lucia di Lammermoor
di Stefano, Gobbi, Arie; Serafin
E.M.I.–Angel Records, Florence
February

IL TROVATORE: Leonora
Stignani, Penno, Tagliabue, Modesti;
    Votto
Teatro alla Scala, Milan
February 23 (5)

LUCIA DI LAMMERMOOR
di Stefano, Mascherini, Algorta;
    Ghione
Teatro Carlo Felice, Genoa
March 14 (2)

RECORDING SESSION:
    I Puritani: Elvira
di Stefano, Panerai, Rossi-Lemeni;
    Serafin
E.M.I.–Angel Records, Milan
March 24–30

NORMA
Barbieri, Corelli, Neri; Santini
Teatro dell'Opera, Rome
April 9 (4)

LUCIA DI LAMMERMOOR
Raimondi, Taddei, Arie; de Fabritiis
Teatro Massimo Bellini, Catania
April 23

MEDEA
Tucci, Barbieri, Guichandut,
    Petri; Gui
Teatro Comunale, Florence
May 7 (3)

LUCIA DI LAMMERMOOR
Poggi, Guelfi, Cassinelli; Gavazzeni
Teatro dell'Opera, Rome
May 19 (3)

AIDA
Simionato, Baum, Walters;
    Barbirolli
Royal Opera House, London
June 4 (3)

NORMA
Simionato, Picchi, Neri; Pritchard
Royal Opera House, London
June 15 (4)

IL TROVATORE: Leonora
Simionato, Johnston, Walters,
    Langdon; Erede
Royal Opera House, London
June 26 (3)

RECORDING SESSION:
    Cavalleria rusticana: Santuzza
di Stefano, Panerai; Serafin
E.M.I.–Angel Records, Milan
July, August

AIDA
Nicolai/Pirazzini, del Monaco/
    Filippeschi/Zambruno, Protti/
    Malaspina; Serafin/Ghione
Arena, Verona
July 23 (5)

RECORDING SESSION:
    Tosca
di Stefano, Gobbi; de Sabata
E.M.I.–Angel Records, Milan
August 10–21

IL TROVATORE: Leonora
Danieli, Zambruno, Protti, Maionica;
    Molinari-Pradelli
Arena, Verona
August 15

RECORDING SESSION:
    La traviata: Violetta
Albanese, Savarese; Santini
Cetra Records, Turin
September

NORMA
Nicolai, Corelli, Christoff; Votto
Teatro Giuseppe Verdi, Trieste
November 18 (4)

MEDEA
Nache, Barbieri, Penno, Modesti;
    Bernstein
Teatro alla Scala, Milan
December 10 (5)

IL TROVATORE: Leonora
Barbieri/Pirazzini, Lauri-Volpi,
    Silveri, Neri; Santini
Teatro dell'Opera, Rome
December 16 (3)

1954

LUCIA DI LAMMERMOOR
di Stefano/Poggi, Panerai, Modesti;
    Karajan
Teatro alla Scala, Milan
January 18 (7)

LUCIA DI LAMMERMOOR
Infantino, Bastianini, Tozzi; Questa
Teatro la Fenice, Venice
February 13 (3)

MEDEA
Tucci, Pirazzini, Gavarini, Tozzi; Gui
Teatro la Fenice, Venice
March 2 (3)

TOSCA
Ortica, Guelfi; Ghione
Teatro Carlo Felice, Genoa
March 10 (4)

ALCESTE
Gavarini, Silveri, Panerai; Giulini
Teatro alla Scala, Milan
April 4 (4)

DON CARLO: Elisabetta
Stignani, Ortica, Mascherini,
    Rossi-Lemeni; Votto
Teatro alla Scala, Milan
April 12 (5)

RECORDING SESSION:
    Norma
Stignani, Filippeschi, Rossi-Lemeni;
    Serafin
E.M.I.–Angel Records, Milan
April 23–May 3

LA FORZA DEL DESTINO: Leonora
Gardino, del Monaco, Protti, Modesti;
    Ghione
Teatro Alighieri, Ravenna
May 23

RECORDING SESSION:
Pagliacci: Nedda
di Stefano, Monti, Gobbi, Panerai;
   Serafin
E.M.I.–Angel Records, Milan
May 25–June 17

MEFISTOFELE: Margherita
de Cecco/de Cavalieri, Tagliavini/
   di Stefano, Rossi-Lemeni; Votto
Arena, Verona
July 15 (3)

RECORDING SESSION:
La forza del destino: Leonora
Nicolai, Tucker, Tagliabue,
   Rossi-Lemeni; Serafin
E.M.I.–Angel Records, Milan
August 17–27

RECORDING SESSION:
Il Turco in Italia: Fiorilla
Gardino, Gedda, Stabile, Rossi-Lemeni,
   Calabrese; Gavazzeni
E.M.I.–Angel Records, Milan
August 31–September 8

RECORDING SESSION:
Manon Lescaut: "In quelle trine
   morbide," "Sola, perduta";
La Bohème: "Sì. Mi chiamano Mimì,"
   "Donde lieta";
Madama Butterfly: "Un bel dì,"
   "Tu! Tu! piccolo iddio";
Suor Angelica: "Senza mamma";
Gianni Schicchi: "O mio babbino";
Turandot: "In questa reggia,"
   "Signore, ascolta," "Tu che di gel";
Adriana Lecouvreur: "Io son l'umile
   ancella," "Poveri fiori";
La Wally: "Ebben? Ne'andrò";
Andrea Chénier: "La mamma morta";
Mefistofele: "L'altra notte";
Il barbiere di Siviglia:
   "Una voce poco fa";
Dinorah: "Ombre légère";
Lakmé: "Où va la jeune Indoue";
I vespri siciliani: "Mercè, dilette
   amiche"
Serafin
E.M.I.–Angel Records, London
September 15–21

LUCIA DI LAMMERMOOR
Tagliavini, Savarese, Maionica;
   Molinari-Pradelli
Teatro Donizetti, Bergamo
October 6

NORMA
Simionato, Picchi, Rossi-Lemeni;
   Rescigno
Lyric Theatre
Civic Opera House, Chicago
November 1 (2)

LA TRAVIATA: Violetta
Simoneau, Gobbi; Rescigno
Lyric Theatre
Civic Opera House, Chicago
November 8 (2)

LUCIA DI LAMMERMOOR
di Stefano, Guelfi, Stewart; Rescigno
Lyric Theatre
Civic Opera House, Chicago
November 15 (2)

LA VESTALE: Giulia
Stignani, Corelli, Sordello,
   Rossi-Lemeni; Votto
Teatro alla Scala, Milan
December 7 (5)

CONCERT: *Die Entführung aus
   dem Serail:* "Marten aller Arten";
   Dinorah: "Ombre légère";
   Louise: "Depuis le jour";
   Armida: "D'amore al dolce impero"
Simonetto
RAI, San Remo
December 27

1955

ANDREA CHENIER: Maddalena
del Monaco/Ortica, Protti/Taddei; Votto
Teatro alla Scala, Milan
January 8 (6)

MEDEA
Tucci, Barbieri, Albanese, Christoff;
   Santini
Teatro dell'Opera, Rome
January 22 (4)

LA SONNAMBULA: Amina
Ratti, Valletti, Modesti/Zaccaria;
   Bernstein
Teatro alla Scala, Milan
March 5 (9)

IL TURCO IN ITALIA: Fiorilla
Gardino, Valletti, Stabile, Rossi-Lemeni,
   Calabrese; Gavazzeni
Teatro alla Scala, Milan
April 15 (5)

LA TRAVIATA: Violetta
di Stefano/Prandelli, Bastianini;
   Giulini
Teatro alla Scala, Milan
May 28 (4)

RECORDING SESSION:
Medea: "Dei tuoi figli";
La vestale: "Tu che invoco,"
   "O nume tutelar," "Caro oggetto"
Serafin
E.M.I.–Angel Records, Milan
June 9–12

NORMA
Stignani, del Monaco, Modesti;
   Serafin
RAI, Rome
June 29

RECORDING SESSION:
Madama Butterfly: Cio-Cio-San
Danieli, Gedda, Borriello; Karajan
E.M.I.–Angel Records, Milan
August 1–6

RECORDING SESSION:
Aida
Barbieri, Tucker, Gobbi; Serafin
E.M.I.–Angel Records, Milan
August 10–24

RECORDING SESSION:
Rigoletto: Gilda
Lazzarini, di Stefano, Gobbi,
   Zaccaria; Serafin
E.M.I.–Angel Records, Milan
September 3–16

LUCIA DI LAMMERMOOR
di Stefano/Zampieri, Panerai,
   Zaccaria; Karajan
Teatro alla Scala
Stadtische Oper, Berlin
September 29 (2)

I PURITANI: Elvira
di Stefano, Bastianini, Rossi-Lemeni;
   Rescigno
Lyric Theatre
Civic Opera House, Chicago
October 31 (2)

IL TROVATORE: Leonora
Stignani/Turner, Bjoerling,
   Bastianini/Weede, Wildermann;
   Rescigno
Lyric Theatre
Civic Opera House, Chicago
November 5 (2)

MADAMA BUTTERFLY: Cio-Cio-San
Alberts, di Stefano, Weede; Rescigno
Lyric Theatre
Civic Opera House, Chicago
November 11 (3)

NORMA
Simionato/Nicolai, del Monaco,
    Zaccaria; Votto
Teatro alla Scala, Milan
December 7 (9)

1956

LA TRAVIATA: Violetta
Raimondi, Bastianini/Protti/
    Tagliabue/Colzani; Giulini/Tonini
Teatro alla Scala, Milan
January 19 (17)

IL BARBIERE DI SIVIGLIA: Rosina
Alva/Monti, Gobbi, Rossi-Lemeni,
    Luise/Badioli; Giulini
Teatro alla Scala, Milan
February 16 (5)

LUCIA DI LAMMERMOOR
Raimondi, Panerai, Zerbini;
    Molinari-Pradelli
Teatro San Carlo, Naples
March 22 (3)

FEDORA
Zanolli, Corelli, Colzani; Gavazzeni
Teatro alla Scala, Milan
May 21 (6)

LUCIA DI LAMMERMOOR
di Stefano, Panerai, Zaccaria;
    Karajan
Teatro alla Scala
Staatsoper, Vienna
June 12 (2)

RECORDING SESSION:
    Il trovatore: Leonora
Barbieri, di Stefano, Panerai,
    Zaccaria; Karajan
E.M.I.–Angel Records, Milan
August 3–9

RECORDING SESSION:
    La Bohème: Mimì
Moffo, di Stefano, Panerai,
    Zaccaria; Votto
E.M.I.–Angel Records, Milan
August 20–25, September 3–4

RECORDING SESSION:
    Un ballo in maschera: Amelia
Ratti, Barbieri, di Stefano, Gobbi;
    Votto
E.M.I.–Angel Records, Milan
September 5–12

CONCERT: La vestale: "Tu che invoco";
    Semiramide: "Bel raggio";
    Hamlet: "A vos jeux, mes amis";
    I Puritani: "Vieni al tempio"
Simonetto
RAI, Milan
September 27

NORMA
Barbieri, del Monaco/Baum,
    Siepi/Moscona; Cleva
Metropolitan Opera, New York
October 29 (5)

TOSCA
Campora, London; Mitropoulos
Metropolitan Opera, New York
November 15 (2)

TELEVISION:
    Tosca (excerpts, act two)
London; Mitropoulos
CBS, New York
November 25

NORMA
Barbieri, Baum, Moscona; Cleva
Metropolitan Opera
Academy of Music, Philadelphia
November 27

LUCIA DI LAMMERMOOR
Campora/Tucker, Sordello/
    Valentino, Moscona; Cleva
Metropolitan Opera, New York
December 3 (4)

CONCERT: Il trovatore:
    "D'amor sull'ali rosee";
    Norma: "Casta diva";
    La traviata: "Ah! fors' è lui"
Schaefer, pianist
Italian Embassy, Washington, D.C.
December 17

1957

CONCERT: La sonnambula:
    "Ah! non credea";
    Dinorah: "Ombre légère";
    Turandot: "In questa reggia";
    Norma: "Casta diva";
    Il trovatore: "D'amor sull'ali rosee";
    Lucia di Lammermoor:
    "Ardon gli incensi"
Cleva
Civic Opera House, Chicago
January 15

NORMA
Stignani, Vertechi, Zaccaria; Pritchard
Royal Opera House, London
February 2 (2)

RECORDING SESSION:
    Il barbiere di Siviglia: Rosina
Alva, Gobbi, Ollendorff, Zaccaria;
    Galliera
E.M.I.–Angel Records, London
February 7–14

LA SONNAMBULA: Amina
Ratti, Monti/Spina, Zaccaria; Votto
Teatro alla Scala, Milan
March 2 (6)

RECORDING SESSION:
    La sonnambula: Amina
Ratti, Monti, Zaccaria; Votto
E.M.I.–Angel Records, Milan
March 3–9

ANNA BOLENA
Simionato, Carturan, Raimondi,
    Rossi-Lemeni; Gavazzeni
Teatro alla Scala, Milan
April 14 (7)

IPHIGENIE EN TAURIDE
Albanese, Colzani, Dondi; Sanzogno
Teatro alla Scala, Milan
June 1 (4)

CONCERT: La traviata: "Ah! fors' è lui";
    Lucia di Lammermoor:
    "Ardon gli incensi"
Moralt
Tonhalle, Zurich
June 19

LUCIA DI LAMMERMOOR
Fernandi, Panerai, Modesti;
    Serafin
RAI, Rome
June 26

LA SONNAMBULA: Amina
Angioletti, Monti, Zaccaria; Votto
Teatro alla Scala
Grosseshaus, Cologne
July 4 (2)

RECORDING SESSION:
    Turandot
Schwarzkopf, Fernandi, Zaccaria;
    Serafin
E.M.I.–Angel Records, Milan
July 9–15

RECORDING SESSION:
    Manon Lescaut
di Stefano, Fioravanti, Calabrese;
    Serafin
E.M.I.–Angel Records, Milan
July 18–27

CONCERT: *Il trovatore:*
  "D'amor sull'ali rosee";
  La forza del destino: "Pace, pace";
  Hamlet: "A vos jeux, mes amis";
  Tristan und Isolde: "Liebestod";
  Lucia di Lammermoor:
  "Regnava nel silenzio"
Votto
Arena Herodes Atticus, Athens
August 5

LA SONNAMBULA: Amina
Martelli, Monti, Zaccaria; Votto
La Piccola Scala
King's Theatre, Edinburgh
August 19 (4)

RECORDING SESSION:
  Medea
Scotto, Pirazzini, Picchi, Modesti;
  Serafin
Ricordi Records, Milan
September 12–19

CONCERT: *Die Entführung aus
  dem Serail:* "Marten aller Arten";
  I Puritani: "Qui la voce";
  Macbeth: "Vieni! t'affretta!";
  La traviata: "Ah! fors'è lui";
  Anna Bolena: "Al dolce guidami"
Rescigno
Civic Opera
State Fair Music Hall, Dallas
November 21

UN BALLO IN MASCHERA: Amelia
Ratti, Simionato, di Stefano,
  Bastianini/Roma; Gavazzeni
Teatro alla Scala, Milan
December 7 (5)

TELEVISION:
  Norma: "Casta diva"
RAI, Rome
December 31

1958

NORMA (act one)
Pirazzini, Corelli, Neri; Santini
Teatro dell'Opera, Rome
January 2

CONCERT: *Don Giovanni:*
  "Non mi dir";
  Macbeth: "Vieni! t'affretta!";
  Il barbiere di Siviglia:
  "Una voce poco fa";
  Mefistofele: "L'altra notte";
  Hamlet: "A vos jeux, mes amis";
  Nabucco: "Anch'io dischiuso"
Rescigno
Civic Opera House, Chicago
January 22

LA TRAVIATA: Violetta
Barioni/Campora, Zanasi; Cleva
Metropolitan Opera, New York
February 6 (2)

LUCIA DI LAMMERMOOR
Bergonzi/Fernandi, Sereni,
  Moscona/Scott/Tozzi; Cleva
Metropolitan Opera, New York
February 13 (3)

TOSCA
Tucker, Cassel/London; Mitropoulos
Metropolitan Opera, New York
February 28 (2)

CONCERT: *Norma:* "Casta diva";
  Il trovatore: "D'amor sull'ali rosee";
  Mefistofele: "L'altra notte";
  Hamlet: "A vos jeux, mes amis"
Morelli
Cinema Monumental, Madrid
March 24

LA TRAVIATA: Violetta
Kraus, Sereni; Ghione
Teatro Nacional de São Carlos, Lisbon
March 27 (2)

ANNA BOLENA
Simionato, Carturan, Raimondi,
  Siepi; Gavazzeni
Teatro alla Scala, Milan
April 9 (5)

IL PIRATA: Imogene
Corelli, Bastianini; Votto
Teatro alla Scala, Milan
May 19 (5)

CONCERT: *I Puritani:* "Qui la voce"
Pritchard
Royal Opera House, London
June 10

TELEVISION:
  Tosca: "Vissi d'arte";
  Il barbiere di Siviglia:
  "Una voce poco fa"
BBC, London
June 17

LA TRAVIATA: Violetta
Valletti, Zanasi; Rescigno
Royal Opera House, London
June 20 (5)

TELEVISION:
  Madama Butterfly: "Un bel dì";
  Norma: "Casta diva"
BBC, London
September 14 (?)

RECORDING SESSION:
  Macbeth: "Vieni! t'affretta!"
  "La luce langue," "Una macchia";
  Nabucco: "Anch'io dischiuso";
  Ernani: "Ernani, involami";
  Don Carlo: "Tu che le vanità";
  Anna Bolena: "Al dolce guidami";
  Hamlet: "A vos jeux, mes amis";
  Il pirata: "Col sorriso"
Sinclair, Lanigan; Rescigno
E.M.I.–Angel Records, London
September 19–25

CONCERTS: *La vestale:*
  "Tu che invoco";
  Macbeth: "Vieni! t'affretta!";
  Il barbiere di Siviglia:
  "Una voce poco fa";
  Mefistofele: "L'altra notte";
  La Bohème: "Quando me'n vo'";
  Hamlet: "A vos jeux, mes amis"
Rescigno
Municipal Auditorium, Birmingham;
  Municipal Auditorium, Atlanta;
  Forum, Montreal;
  Maple Leaf Gardens, Toronto;
  Public Music House, Cleveland;
  Masonic Auditorium, Detroit;
  Constitution Hall, Washington, D.C.;
  War Memorial, San Francisco;
  Shrine Auditorium, Los Angeles;
  Kiel Auditorium, St. Louis
October 11, 14, 17, 21; November 15,
  18, 22, 26, 29; January 11, 1959

LA TRAVIATA: Violetta
Filacuridi, Taddei; Rescigno
Civic Opera
State Fair Music Hall, Dallas
October 31 (2)

MEDEA
Carron, Berganza, Vickers, Zaccaria;
  Rescigno
Civic Opera
State Fair Music Hall, Dallas
November 6 (2)

CONCERT: *Norma:* "Casta diva";
    Il trovatore: "D'amor sull'ali rosee,"
    "Miserere";
    Il barbiere di Siviglia:
    "Una voce poco fa";
    Tosca: act two
Lance, Gobbi, Mars; Sebastian
Théâtre National de l'Opéra, Paris
December 19

1959

CONCERT: *Mefistofele:* "L'altra notte";
    Il barbiere di Siviglia:
    "Una voce poco fa";
    Hamlet: "A vos jeux, mes amis"
Ormandy
Academy of Music, Philadelphia
January 24

IL PIRATA: Imogene
Ferraro, Ego; Rescigno
American Opera Society
Carnegie Hall, New York;
    Constitution Hall, Washington, D.C.
January 27, 29

RECORDING SESSION:
    Lucia di Lammermoor
Tagliavini, Cappuccilli, Ladysz;
    Serafin
E.M.I.–Angel Records, London
March 16–21

CONCERT: *Don Giovanni:*
    "Non mi dir";
    Macbeth: "Vieni! t'affretta!";
    Semiramide: "Bel raggio";
    La Gioconda: "Suicidio";
    Il pirata: "Col sorriso"
Rescigno
Teatro del Zarzuela, Madrid
May 2

CONCERT: *Don Carlo:*
    "Tu che le vanità";
    Mefistofele: "L'altra notte";
    Il barbiere di Siviglia:
    "Una voce poco fa";
    Tosca: "Vissi d'arte";
    La Bohème: "Quando me'n vo'";
    Il pirata: "Col sorriso"
Rescigno
Gran Teatro del Liceo, Barcelona
May 5

CONCERTS: *La vestale:*
    "Tu che invoco";
    Macbeth: "Vieni! t'affretta!";
    Il barbiere di Siviglia:
    "Una voce poco fa";
    Don Carlo: "Tu che le vanità";
    Il pirata: "Col sorriso"
Rescigno
Musikhalle, Hamburg;
    Liederhalle, Stuttgart;
    Deutsches Museum, Munich;
    Kursaal, Wiesbaden
May 15, 19, 21, 24

MEDEA
Carlyle, Cossotto, Vickers, Zaccaria;
    Rescigno
Royal Opera House, London
June 17 (5)

CONCERTS: *La vestale:*
    "Tu che invoco";
    Ernani: "Ernani, involami";
    Don Carlo: "Tu che le vanità";
    Il pirata: "Col sorriso"
Rescigno
Concertgebouw, Amsterdam;
    Théâtre de la Monnaie, Brussels
July 11, 14

RECORDING SESSION:
    La Gioconda
Cossotto, Companeez, Ferraro,
    Cappuccilli, Vinco; Votto
E.M.I.–Angel Records, Milan
September 5–10

CONCERT: *Don Carlo:*
    "Tu che le vanità";
    Hamlet: "A vos jeux, mes amis";
    Ernani: "Ernani, involami";
    Il pirata: "Col sorriso"
Rescigno
Coliseo Albia, Bilbao
September 17

CONCERT: *Don Carlo:*
    "Tu che le vanità";
    Il pirata: "Col sorriso";
    Hamlet: "A vos jeux, mes amis";
    Macbeth: "Una macchia"
Rescigno
Royal Festival Hall, London
September 23

TELEVISION:
    La Bohème: "Sì. Mi chiamano Mimì";
    Mefistofele: "L'altra notte"
Sargent
BBC, London
October 3

CONCERT: *Don Giovanni:*
    "Non mi dir";
    Ernani: "Ernani, involami";
    Don Carlo: "Tu che le vanità";
    Hamlet: "A vos jeux, mes amis"
Rescigno
Titania Palast, Berlin
October 23

CONCERT: *Don Giovanni:*
    "Non mi dir";
    Lucia di Lammermoor:
    "Regnava nel silenzio";
    Ernani: "Ernani, involami";
    Il pirata: "Col sorriso"
Rescigno
Loew's Midland Theater, Kansas City
October 28

LUCIA DI LAMMERMOOR
Raimondi, Bastianini, Zaccaria;
    Rescigno
Civic Opera
State Fair Music Hall, Dallas
November 6 (2)

MEDEA
Williams, Merriman, Vickers,
    Zaccaria; Rescigno
Civic Opera
State Fair Music Hall, Dallas
November 19 (2)

1960

NORMA
Morfoniou, Picchi, Mazzoli; Serafin
Greek National Opera
Arena, Epidaurus
August 24 (2)

RECORDING SESSION:
    Norma
Ludwig, Corelli, Zaccaria; Serafin
E.M.I.–Angel Records, Milan
September 5–12

POLIUTO: Paolina
Corelli, Bastianini, Zaccaria;
    Votto/Tonini
Teatro alla Scala, Milan
December 7 (5)

1961

RECORDING SESSION:
   Orphée et Eurydice:
     "J'ai perdu mon Eurydice";
   Alceste: "Divinités du Styx";
   Carmen: Habanera, Séguedille;
   Samson et Dalila: "Printemps qui
     commence," "Amour! viens aider";
   Roméo et Juliette: "Je veux vivre";
   Mignon: "Je suis Titania";
   Le Cid: "Pleurez, mes yeux";
   Louise: "Depuis le jour"
Prêtre
E.M.I.–Angel Records, Paris
March 28–31, April 4–5

CONCERT: *Norma:* "Casta diva";
   Le Cid: "Pleurez, mes yeux";
   Don Carlo: "Tu che le vanità";
   Mefistofele: "L'altra notte"
Sargent, pianist
St. James's Palace, London
May 30

MEDEA
Glantzi, Morfonioù, Vickers,
   Modesti; Rescigno
Greek National Opera
Arena, Epidaurus
August 6 (2)

RECORDING SESSION:
   Il pirata: "Sorgete, è in me dover"
Young; Tonini
E.M.I.–Angel Records, London
November 15

MEDEA
Tosini/Rizzoli/Nardi, Simionato, Vickers,
   Ghiaurov; Schippers
Teatro alla Scala, Milan
December 11 (5)

1962

CONCERT: *Don Carlo:* "O don fatale";
   Le Cid: "Pleurez, mes yeux";
   La cenerentola: "Nacqui all'affanno";
   Anna Bolena: "Al dolce guidami";
   Macbeth: "La luce langue";
   Oberon: "Ocean, thou mighty monster"
Prêtre
Royal Festival Hall, London
February 27

CONCERT: *Don Carlo:* "O don fatale";
   Le Cid: "Pleurez, mes yeux";
   La cenerentola: "Nacqui all'affanno";
   Carmen: Habanera, Séguedille;
   Ernani: "Ernani, involami"
Prêtre
Deutsches Museum, Munich;
   Musikhalle, Hamburg;
   Städischer Saalbau, Essen;
   Beethovenhalle, Bonn
March 12, 16, 19, 23

CONCERT: *Carmen:* Habanera,
   Séguedille
Wilson, pianist
Madison Square Garden, New York
May 19

TELEVISION:
   Don Carlo: "Tu che le vanità";
   Carmen: Habanera, Séguedille
Prêtre
BBC, London
November 4

1963

RECORDING SESSION:
   Iphigénie en Tauride:
     "O malheureuse Iphigénie";
   La damnation de Faust:
     "D'amour l'ardente flamme";
   Les pêcheurs de perles:
     "Comme autrefois";
   Manon: "Adieu, notre petite table,"
     "Je marche sur tous les chemins";
   Werther: Air des lettres;
   Faust: "Il était un roi," "Ah! je ris"
Prêtre
E.M.I–Angel Records, Paris
May 3–8

CONCERTS: *Semiramide:* "Bel raggio";
   Norma: "Casta diva";
   Nabucco: "Anch'io dischiuso";
   La Bohème: "Quando me'n vo'";
   Madama Butterfly: "Tu! tu! piccolo
     iddio";
   Gianni Schicchi: "O mio babbino"
Prêtre
Deutsche Oper, Berlin;
   Rheinhalle, Düsseldorf;
   Liederhalle, Stuttgart;
   Royal Festival Hall, London;
   Falkoner Centret, Copenhagen
May 17, 20, 23, 31, June 9

CONCERT: *Semiramide:* "Bel raggio";
   La cenerentola: "Nacqui all'affanno";
   Werther: Air des lettres;
   Manon: "Adieu, notre petite table";
   Nabucco: "Anch'io dischiuso";
   La Bohème: "Quando me'm vo'";
   Madama Butterfly: "Tu! tu! piccolo iddio";
   Gianni Schicchi: "O mio babbino"
Prêtre
Théâtre des Champs-Elysées, Paris
June 5

RECORDING SESSION:
   "Ah, perfido";
   Don Giovanni: "Or sai chi l'onore,"
     "Non mi dir," "Mi tradì";
   Le nozze di Figaro: "Porgi amor";
   Oberon: "Ocean, thou mighty monster";
   Otello: "Salce, salce," "Ave Maria";
   Aroldo: "Ah! dagli scanni",
     "Salvami, salvami";
   Don Carlo: "O don fatale,"
     "Non pianger, mia compagna";
   La cenerentola: "Nacqui all'affanno";
   Guglielmo Tell: "Selva opaca";
   Semiramide: "Bel raggio"
Rescigno
E.M.I.–Angel Records, Paris
December 6–January 8

1964

TOSCA
Cioni, Gobbi; Cillario
Royal Opera House, London
January 21 (6);
   February 9 (act two only, BBC-TV)

RECORDING SESSION:
   La figlia del reggimento:
     "Convien partir";
   Lucrezia Borgia: "Com'è bello";
   L'elisir d'amore: "Prendi, per me";
   Attila: "Liberamente or piangi";
   I vespri siciliani: "Arrigo! ah parli";
   I Lombardi: "O madre, dal cielo";
   Un ballo in maschera: "Ma dall'arido";
   Aida: "Ritorna vincitor"
Rescigno
E.M.I.–Angel Records, Paris
February 20–April 24

NORMA
Cossotto, Craig/Corelli, Vinco;
   Prêtre
Théâtre National de l'Opéra, Paris
May 22 (8)

RECORDING SESSION:
Carmen
Guiot, Gedda, Massard; Prêtre
E.M.I.–Angel Records, Paris
July 6–20

RECORDING SESSION:
Tosca
Bergonzi, Gobbi; Prêtre
E.M.I.–Angel Records, Paris
December 3–14

1965

TOSCA
Cioni, Gobbi; Prêtre/Rescigno
Théâtre National de l'Opéra, Paris
February 19 (9)

TOSCA
Corelli/Tucker, Gobbi; Cleva
Metropolitan Opera, New York
March 19 (2)

NORMA
Simionato/Cossotto, Cecchele,
    Vinco; Prêtre
Théâtre National de l'Opéra, Paris
May 14 (5–last scene canceled final
    performance)

TELEVISION:
Manon: "Adieu, notre petite table";
La sonnambula: "Ah! non credea";
Gianni Schicchi: "O mio babbino"
Prêtre
RTF, Paris
May 18

TOSCA
Cioni, Gobbi; Prêtre
Royal Opera House, London
July 5

1973-1974

Callas's return to professional life in 1973 was an extended concert tour with tenor Giuseppe di Stefano which began October 25 in Hamburg, Germany. The program there, and in successive cities, listed eleven arias for Callas, eight arias plus four songs for di Stefano, and seven duets. From this printed list was selected the material for each concert; this varied from city to city. Callas's repertory consisted of "Pleurez, pleurez mes yeux" from *Le Cid*, Habanera from *Carmen*, "Suicidio" from *La Gioconda*, "L'altra notte" from *Mefistofele*, "Non pianger, mia compagna" and "Tu che le vanità" from *Don Carlo*, "Mercè, dilette amiche" from *I vespri siciliani*, "O mio babbino" from *Gianni Schicchi*, "Quando m'en vo'" from *La Bohème*, and "In quelle trine morbide" and "Sola, perduta" from *Manon Lescaut*. Of these, she performed principally the arias from *Gioconda* and *Gianni Schicchi*, later adding "Voi lo sapete" from *Cavalleria rusticana*, "Vissi d'arte" from *Tosca*, Air des lettres from *Werther*, and "Adieu, notre petite table" from *Manon* to her tour repertory. The duets, all sung in one city or another, were "Laisse-moi" from *Faust*, the "C'est toi, c'est moi" from *Carmen*, "Una parola, o Adina" from *L'elisir d'amore*, "Ah! per sempre" from *La forza del destino*, "Io vengo a domandar" from *Don Carlo*, "Tu qui, Santuzza?" from *Cavalleria rusticana*, and "Quale, o prode" from *I vespri siciliani*. Her European appearances following Hamburg included Berlin, Frankfurt, Düsseldorf, Mannheim, Madrid, London, Paris, Amsterdam, Monte Carlo, and Stuttgart. The American segment of the tour opened in Philadelphia on February 11, 1974, and included Toronto, Washington, D.C., Boston, Chicago, New York, Detroit, Dallas, Miami Beach, Montreal, Columbus, Cincinnati, Seattle, Portland, Vancouver, Los Angeles, and San Francisco. The tour was performed with pianists Ivor Newton, in Europe, and Robert Sutherland, in the United States and Canada.

Total operatic performances in chronology, excluding recorded performances and single acts:

AIDA (31)
ALCESTE (4)
ANDREA CHENIER (6)
ANNA BOLENA (12)
ARMIDA (3)
BALLO IN MASCHERA (5)
BARBIERE DI SIVIGLIA (5)
BETTELSTUDENT (1)
BOCCACCIO (1)
CAVALLERIA RUSTICANA (2)
DON CARLO (5)
ENTFÜHRUNG AUS DEM SERAIL (4)
FEDORA (6)
FIDELIO (1)
FORZA DEL DESTINO (5)
GIOCONDA (12)
IPHIGENIE EN TAURIDE (4)
LUCIA DI LAMMERMOOR (43)
MACBETH (5)
MADAMA BUTTERFLY (3)
MEDEA (31)
MEFISTOFELE (3)
NABUCCO (3)
NORMA (84)
ORFEO ED EURIDICE (2)
PARSIFAL (5)
PIRATA (7)
POLIUTO (5)
PROTOMASTORAS (1)
PURITANI (13)
RIGOLETTO (2)
SONNAMBULA (21)
SUOR ANGELICA (1)
TIEFLAND (2)
TOSCA (53)
TRAVIATA (58)
TRISTAN UND ISOLDE (12)
TROVATORE (20)
TURANDOT (23)
TURCO IN ITALIA (9)
VESPRI SICILIANI (11)
VESTALE (5)
WALKÜRE (6)

Callas performed forty-three roles approximately 535 times. Eighteen of these were recorded commercially, and an additional ten, from live sources, have been issued on private discs. Four roles (Nedda in *Pagliacci*, Mimì in *La Bohème*, Manon Lescaut, and Carmen) were performed for records only, bringing her total repertory to forty-seven roles. Her concert appearances numbered almost one hundred.

INDEX

Operas are listed under their composers, opera houses under the city in which they are located. Photo references are in brackets.

PICTURE CREDITS

Courtesy of Angel Records, 3, 9 left

Beth Bergman (New York), 41

Bernand (Paris), 238, 250

Bibliothèque Nationale (Paris), 228 bottom

Anthony Crickmay (London), 206 bottom, 208 bottom, 209, 210, 221 bottom, 222, 222-223 bottom, 226

Dalmas (Paris), 39

Zoë Dominic (London), 199 bottom, 204 top, 208 top, 212 top left, 218 top, 224 bottom

Courtesy of the Friends of Covent Garden (London), 199 top

Henry Grossman (New York), Endpapers

Louis Mélançon (New York), 217, 224 top

Courtesy of Frances Moore, 14, 20 right, 25, 27, 28 right, 30, 37 center, 39

Il Museo Teatrale alla Scala (Milan), 5, 6

Opera News (New York), 16 left, 28 left, 159

Paris Match/Le Tellier, 41

Roger Pic (Paris), 10, 205, 211, 212 top center and bottom, 213, 216 bottom, 218 bottom, 220, 221 top, 222-223 top and center, 224 center, 225, 232, 233 top and center, 234, 236 top, 237, 240-242, 244-249, 252 top, 254

Erio Piccagliani (Milan), 13, 24, 31, 32, 37 right, 48-157, 160-174 left, 175-179, 182 bottom, 184-197

Pix Incorporated (New York), 39

Alda Radaelli (Milan), 174 right, 180-181

Houston Rogers (London), 182 top, 183, 198, 202, 216 top, 219, 227

Bill Sauro, 37 center

Arthur Siegel, 37 left

Courtesy of Mr. and Mrs. Dario Soria, 37 left

Donald Southern (London), 206 top, 214

Christian Steiner (New York), 3

Time/Life Picture Agency, 46

The Times (London), 46

Mario Tursi (Rome), Jacket, 40, 256-263

Wide World Photos (New York), 35

Reg Wilson (London), 201, 204 bottom, 207, 215, 223 right

Courtesy of Franco Zeffirelli, 16 right, 228 top, 229-231, 233 bottom, 235 bottom, 243, 253